Which one is you?
Which one is me?.

THE

❧ CASTLES OF ENGLAND ☙

THE
CASTLES
OF
ENGLAND

Frederick Wilkinson

Letts**Guides**

Frontispiece: Corfe Castle. *This and all other*
photographs appearing in this book are reproduced by
courtesy of the British Tourist Authority

This book was designed and produced by
Alban Book Services Limited,
147 London Road, St. Albans, Herts, England

ISBN 0 85097 183 7

First published in Great Britain by
GEORGE PHILIP & SON LIMITED
12–14 Long Acre, London WC2E 9LP
Paperback edition by
CHARLES LETTS & COMPANY LIMITED
Diary House, Borough Road, London SE1 1DW

Cover: Mathew Hypolite
Filmset in 9/10pt. Times New Roman 327
Printed in Great Britain by
WILLIAM CLOWES & SONS LIMITED
London, Beccles and Colchester

CASTLE BUILDING IN BRITAIN.

T HE dictionary defines a castle as any stronghold or fortified group of buildings; however, many purists, for example D. O'Neil who wrote the introductory guide to *"Castles of England and Wales"* published in 1954 by H.M.S.O., limit their definition to those strongholds erected since the Norman Conquest. The word itself is derived from *castella* which is the diminutive form of *castrum*, Latin for a fort, so that there is no etymological reason for such a limiting definition.

The legions of Rome never camped at night without erecting some form of defensive works, and in the barrack towns these were made elaborate and permanent. When the Romans left these shores in the 5th Century A.D. the Saxon *burgh* or *tun* became the conventional form of defence, whereby the town or village was surrounded by some fortification such as a ditch or a wall of timber. The difference between these burghs and the castles of the Middle Ages was that the first were essentially public defences while those constructed from the Conquest on were designed as the private residence of a man of authority or wealth.

When the invaders landed in 1066 approximately half of the total force was composed of Normans and the rest were a mixture of French, Bretons and other nationals. Naturally these men expected some reward for their support of William, and the most usual arrangement was that land was distributed more or less in accordance with the man's importance or the size of his contribution to the invasion. The larger landowners, the tenants-in-chief, were given a number of holdings or manors, which might be scattered over the country or grouped together to form a *"castellaria"* within the proximity of the headquarters or main castle. In return for the land the lord was expected to support the king with his troops; this system of exchanging land for protection was the basis of the feudal system in this country, although the continental systems varied in detail. The tenant was expected to serve with the king's army for a period, normally forty days, should he be called upon by the king or his tenant-in-chief. He could also be called on to serve as castle guard. This system worked very well to start with, but as time passed problems arose. It was feasible for a minor or a woman to inherit the estate, in which case they were obviously useless as far as discharging their obligations in war or guard duties were concerned. To overcome this situation there arose the system of "scutage", whereby a sum of money was paid which

A: *Plan of earthworks of a typical early Norman castle, with a motte, two baileys and a wet ditch or moat*

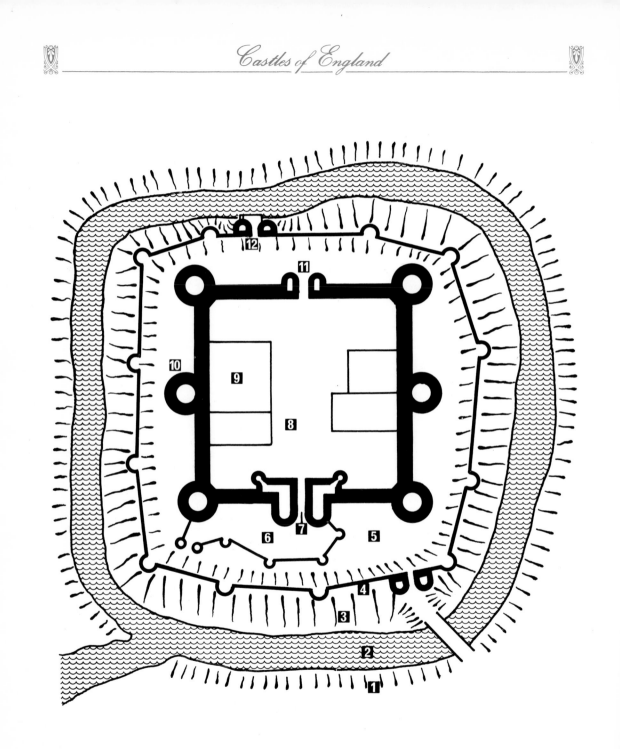

then relieved the tenant of the duty to serve. Scutage was collected and used to hire mercenaries to serve with the army or to act as castle guards.

In the years immediately following the Conquest it was essential that the castle should be erected quickly; the situation was potentially very hazardous since the Normans were in a rebellious countryside which might rise against them at any time. The castle had to be simple and capable of being erected very quickly and, almost invariably, the earliest Norman castles were of the motte and bailey type. They were scattered over the countryside at strategic points, and at least one hundred were erected in the first half century. With the aid of pressed peasantry a deep circular ditch was dug and the excavated earth thrown into the centre to form a mound, the "motte"; the top of this was flattened and on it was erected a simple wooden palisade. At first the main defence was simply a wooden fence but, no doubt, a wooden lookout tower and some form of dwelling were soon added. At the base of the motte was another open space also encircled by some form of ditch, and this area was known as the "bailey". There might be one, two or even three, and each might be encircled with a ditch. The earth excavated was used to erect a small defensive wall or rampart around the edge of the bailey. Not every castle had an artificial motte, for if some natural feature, a crag, a mound or a hill could be used then time and labour were saved by building the palisade at the top of such a feature. The most immediate and greatest potential danger to such castles was, of course, fire. In order to overcome this hazard the wooden defences were replaced as soon as possible with masonry; indeed, in one or two cases of important castles such as the Tower of London, the castle was actually built with masonry *ab initio*.

Despite popular belief, castle building was rigidly controlled and it was normal for application to be made to the king for permission to build a castle, in which case a "licence to crenellate" was granted. This procedure was normally followed although during periods of stress—such as the civil war of Stephen's reign (1135–1154), numbers of so-called "adulterine" castles were erected without permission. When Henry II came to the throne in 1154 he destroyed large numbers of these castles.

Apart from the introduction of masonry walls another very important feature of early 12th Century castles was the adoption of the great stone tower. These were not exclusive to the 12th Century, and there are instances of some earlier than this, but the majority are of this period. The towers vary greatly in detail but they conform to a broad pattern; they are square or rectangular, tall, and the walls are frequently reinforced with small buttresses or pilasters. At the corners were small towers, normally rectangular in shape on the early ones. Such strongholds were known as the "great tower", the "keep" or the "donjon", the latter a term whose meaning has become confused and is now most often used in the sense of a prison. Some cells were often to be found in the keep, but contrary to popular belief they were not in the basement; in practice the majority of castles at which it is known that prisoners were kept have the cells or places of confinement on the upper floors. The base of most keeps are splayed slightly to give greater stability, and also to provide a convenient point of ricochet for any stones dropped from above. To reduce the possibility of men and missiles entering, the lower part of the keep was usually devoid of openings, or else any which existed were very narrow. The main entrance to the keep was normally, but not invariably, on the first floor and approached by a flight of steps set at right angles to the entrance, that is running up the side of the wall. This made it extremely difficult for attackers to build up momentum when using anything like a battering ram to break down the door. It also reduced the

B: Simplified plan of a typical concentric castle built on a natural hillock, with outer earthwork defences:
1. *counterscarp*   2. *moat or wet ditch*
3. *scarp and berm*
4. *outer curtain, with open-backed towers*
5. *outer bailey*
6. *barbican*   7. *gatehouse*
8. *inner bailey*
9. *great hall*
10. *towers on inner curtain, linked by wall walks and passages*
11. *rear gatehouse*
12. *postern*

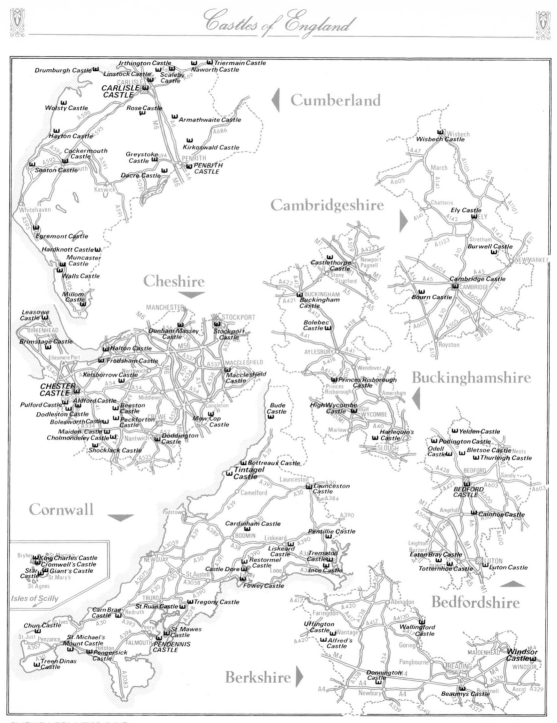

Drumburgh Castle
Irthington Castle
Linstock Castle
Scaleby Castle
Triermain Castle
Naworth Castle
CARLISLE
CARLISLE CASTLE
Wolsty Castle
Rose Castle
Armathwaite Castle
Hayton Castle
Cockermouth Castle
Greystoke Castle
Kirkoswald Castle
PENRITH
PENRITH CASTLE
Seaton Castle
Dacre Castle
Keswick
Whitehaven

Cumberland

Egremont Castle
Hardknott Castle
Muncaster Castle
Walls Castle
Millom Castle

Wisbech
Wisbech Castle
March

Cambridgeshire

Chatteris
Ely Castle
ELY
Stretham
Burwell Castle
NEWMARKET
Cambridge Castle
CAMBRIDGE
Bourn Castle
Royston

Leasowe Castle
BIRKENHEAD
Brimstage Castle
Ellesmere Port

Cheshire

MANCHESTER
STOCKPORT
Dunham Massey Castle
Stockport Castle
Halton Castle
Frodsham Castle
MACCLESFIELD
Kelsborrow Castle
Northwich
Macclesfield Castle
CHESTER CASTLE
Middlewich
Congleton
Pulford Castle
Aldford Castle
Beeston Castle
Dodleston Castle
Peckforton Castle
Bolesworth Castle
Mow Cop Castle
Maiden Castle
Cholmondeley Castle
Nantwich
Doddington Castle
Shocklack Castle

Castlethorpe Castle
Newport Pagnell
Stony Stratford
BUCKINGHAM
Buckingham Castle
Bolebec Castle
AYLESBURY
Wendover
Princes Risborough Castle
Princes Risborough
Amersham

Buckinghamshire

High Wycombe Castle
HIGH WYCOMBE
Marlow
Harlequin's Castle
SLOUGH

Yelden Castle
Podington Castle
Odell Castle
Bletsoe Castle
Thurleigh Castle
BEDFORD
BEDFORD CASTLE
Sandy
Cainhoe Castle
Ampthill
Leighton Buzzard
Eaton Bray Castle
Totternhoe Castle
DUNSTABLE
Luton Castle
LUTON

Bude Castle
Bottreaux Castle
Tintagel Castle
Launceston Castle
Camelford

Cornwall

Bryher
King Charles's Castle
Cromwell's Castle
Star Castle
Giant's Castle
St. Mary's
St. Agnes
Isles of Scilly

Padstow
NEWQUAY
Cardinham Castle
BODMIN
Liskeard
Liskeard Castle
Restormel Castle
Trematon Castle
Ince Castle
Castle Dore
Looe
Fowey Castle
Pentillie Castle

Carn Brae Castle
Redruth
St. Ruan Castle
Tregony Castle
Chun Castle
St. Ives
St. Just Penzance
St. Michael's Mount Castle
Helston
St. Mawes Castle
FALMOUTH
PENDENNIS CASTLE
Pengersick Castle
Treen Dinas Castle

Abingdon
Faringdon
Uffington Castle
Wantage
Alfred's Castle
Goring

Bedfordshire

Berkshire

Pangbourne
READING
MAIDENHEAD
Windsor Castle
WINDSOR
Ascot
Donnington Castle
Newbury
Beaumys Castle

number of attackers able to assault the door at any one time simply by the physical limitations of space. Sometimes the motte was of insufficient strength to support these heavy masses of masonry and extra foundations were put in; in other cases the keep was erected on a different site. The internal arrangements of the keep varied but, in general, the large chambers were divided by cross walls and access to the various floors was obtained by stairs set within the thickness of the wall or spiral staircases fitted into the corner turrets. The entrance was often given extra protection by the construction of a forebuilding which might include other means of defence such as a drawbridge or a portcullis.

A variation on the large, rectangular keep was known as a "shell keep". These are more often found on the top of the original motte and consist of a large, circular wall which replaced the original wooden palisade. On the inside of the wall were built the kitchens, the buttery, the larder, the store houses, the smithy, a chapel and a hall. Frequently these inside buildings were of wood and in many cases no trace of them has survived; in others the buildings were of stone, and many of these have survived in various degrees.

The baileys, too, were surrounded by masonry walls, and a lesson which the military architect soon learnt was that the wall had to be covered by some form of flanking fire. To this end small projecting towers were spaced along the wall so that archers might loose arrows at any attackers who had managed to reach the foot of the wall. Entrances to the bailey, which were potentially a point of weakness, were normally given extra protection in the form of a strong gatehouse, often with forward works, known as the "barbican". These usually had one or more portcullises, double doors and long passageways through which any attacker had to pass, during which time he was subject to attack from above by means of openings in the roof known as "murder holes". The vast majority of castles were very well equipped to resist attack and very few of them were carried by storm; the majority of victories came as a result of starvation or treachery.

Against the castle every means of attack could be and was employed. Basically the attacker had four possibilities: through, over or under the wall, or starvation brought on by a long siege. To get over the wall there was the scaling ladder, difficult to use since the wall might be twenty to thirty feet high and to get to the foot of the wall a moat, either wet or dry, had to be crossed. It was also essential to use large numbers of ladders to enable a maximum number of men to attack at once. The moat had to be filled with debris or bridged, during which time the attackers were at the mercy of the defenders. The siege tower could be used; this timber, wheeled staging was erected on the site and pushed into position against the wall. When a drawbridge was lowered from the top of the tower to the top of the wall, the attackers could rush over. Breaking through the wall was normally attempted by means of artillery in the form of catapults of various kinds. There were the trebuchet and the mangonel, both of which could be used to hurl heavy stones against the points of weakness, usually the corner of a tower or the junction of walls. Slower and more hazardous was the pick, which was a battering ram with a sharpened end, the object being to break away stones and achieve some form of breach. The battering ram might be used against doorways but against masonry walls it was relatively useless. Possibly the most effective means of direct attack was under the wall by means of a mine; in this process a tunnel was dug until the foundations of the tower—normally the corner, the weakest point—were reached. These were chipped away or burrowed under and the masonry supported on wooden props. The space was then filled with all manner of inflammable material—straw, pitch, bacon fat, carcasses, etc.—and, at an arranged time, the debris was ignited. As the flames burnt through the wooden props support for the entire weight of masonry was suddenly removed and the corner of the tower would drag itself down. This method was employed very successfully at Rochester, and later repairs are indicated by the fact that the original square tower was replaced by a round one.

One of the features of Edwardian castles was the adoption of this rounded tower, which had several military advantages; it reduced the number of blind points, it removed the dangerous corners which were always points of weakness, and also it was geometrically better able to deflect boulders and other projectiles. The first rounded towers were probably made very late in the 12th Century or very early in the 13th; the first ones were solid and possibly could be described better as bastions. A "D"-shaped tower had many of the same advantages, and was cheaper than a round one.

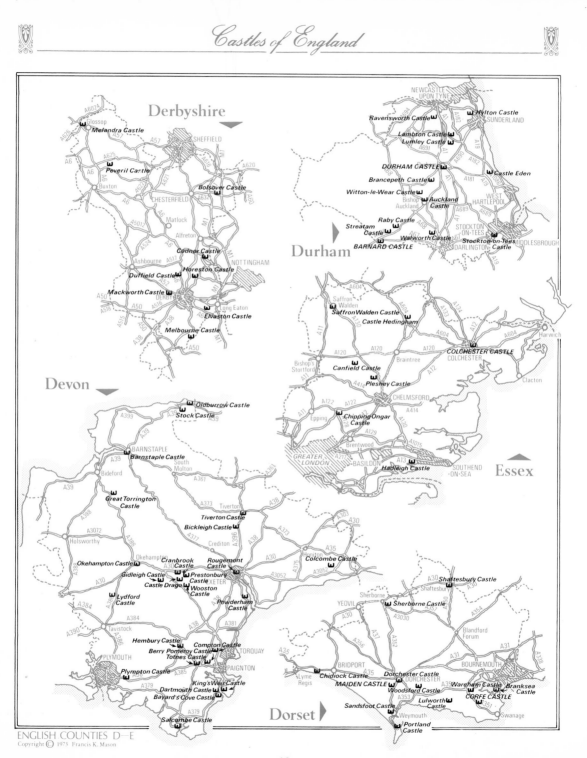

Derbyshire

A6024
Glossop
A57
A6
A625
Melandra Castle
A57
SHEFFIELD
A6
A6
A621
A616
M1
A620
Peveril Castle
A623
Buxton
A6
Bolsover Castle
A632
CHESTERFIELD
A6
A619
A617
Matlock
A5012
M1
Alfreton
A6
A574
Ashbourne
A517
Codnor Castle
NOTTINGHAM
A52
Horeston Castle
A38
DERBY
Duffield Castle
A52
A50
Mackworth Castle
A5111
A578
A515
A516
A50
A6
Long Eaton
Elvaston Castle
A50
A453
Melbourne Castle
A514
A50
M1

Durham

NEWCASTLE UPON TYNE
A1
A182
Hylton Castle
Ravensworth Castle
SUNDERLAND
A691
A19
Lambton Castle
A182
Lumley Castle
DURHAM CASTLE
A690
A181
Castle Eden
Brancepeth Castle
A181
Witton-le-Wear Castle
WEST HARTLEPOOL
Bishop Auckland
Auckland Castle
A689
A689
Raby Castle
Streatam Castle
A1
STOCKTON-ON-TEES
Walworth Castle
Stockton-on-Tees Castle
MIDDLESBROUGH
BARNARD CASTLE
A67
DARLINGTON
A19

Essex

A604
Saffron Walden
A133
A13
Saffron Walden Castle
A604
A12
Castle Hedingham
A604
Harwich
A120
A120
A120
Braintree
A12
COLCHESTER CASTLE
COLCHESTER
Bishop's Stortford
A11
Canfield Castle
Clacton
A414
Pleshey Castle
CHELMSFORD
A414
A122
A122
A1
Epping
Chipping Ongar Castle
A129
Brentwood
A12
A1015
GREATER LONDON
A21
BASILDON
A13
Hadleigh Castle
SOUTHEND-ON-SEA

Devon

A399
Oldburrow Castle
A39
Stock Castle
A39
BARNSTAPLE
Barnstaple Castle
A39
South Molton
Bideford
A361
A39
A377
A386
Great Torrington Castle
A373
Tiverton
A38
Tiverton Castle
Bickleigh Castle
A373
Holsworthy
A3072
A386
Crediton
A396
A30
A35
Okehampton
Honiton
Okehampton Castle
Cranbrook Castle
Rougemont Castle
Colcombe Castle
A3052
Gidleigh Castle
EXETER
A30
Prestonbury Castle
Castle Drago
Wooston Castle
A386
Lydford Castle
Powderham Castle
A384
A381
Tavistock
A386
A38
Hembury Castle
Compton Castle
PLYMOUTH
Berry Pomeroy Castle
TORQUAY
Totnes Castle
Plympton Castle
PAIGNTON
A385
A379
King's Weir Castle
Dartmouth Castle
Bayard's Cove Castle
A379
Salcombe Castle

Dorset

A30
Shaftesbury Castle
Shaftesbury
A354
Sherborne
A30
Sherborne Castle
YEOVIL
A3030
Blandford Forum
A357
A352
A31
A31
A35
A356
BRIDPORT
BOURNEMOUTH
A35
Dorchester Castle
A338
Lyme Regis
Chidiock Castle
DORCHESTER
Wareham Castle
Branksea Castle
MAIDEN CASTLE
A353
Woodsford Castle
CORFE CASTLE
A351
Sandsfoot Castle
Lulworth Castle
Weymouth
Swanage
Portland Castle

ENGLISH COUNTIES D—E
Copyright © 1973 Francis K. Mason

In addition to the main entrance to the castle there were often a number of postern gates, which were small and so placed that a raiding party from inside might slip out but the gate itself was not vulnerable to an outside attack. A feature which was probably borrowed from France was the machicolation; these were parapets, often quite narrow, built projecting above an entrance, with holes let into the floor. These looked down directly on the wall beneath so that the defender could pour boiling water, burning tar or any other objectionable material directly down on the heads of the attackers. Sometimes in place of the more elaborate machicolations a simple enclosed wooden platform, known as a brattice, was fitted into place on a series of wooden beams let into holes in the wall. The simplest defence for the wall walks of a castle were crenellations—popularly, battlements—the pierced stone parapets which allowed defenders to avoid undue exposure. Often these were fitted with heavy wooden shutters which could be closed over the gaps or embrasures to present an unbroken wall to the attackers.

During the 13th and 14th Centuries the emphasis began to shift away from the massive keep. While it could be made almost impregnable it had certain disadvantages from a military point of view; it forced the defenders to adopt a relatively passive approach, gave the attackers the initiative, and by its very lack of easy entrances and exits was comparatively simple to blockade. Many castles built in the late 13th and early 14th Centuries featured greatly strengthened outer defences. Several main towers, linked by strong walls guarded by projecting towers at regular intervals, offered a more flexible defence. The keep could remain as the last citadel, but the greater area defended could be used to accommodate both men and livestock. In practice the attacker still had to concentrate on one or two major points of assault, so the defender was not forced to spread his garrison thinly—while the greater length of defended wall presented problems for the besieger attempting to establish a tight blockade. The number of smaller towers spaced along the walls proliferated, allowing enfilading fire to be brought down on attackers at any point. The individual strength of these towers increased, until many were small self-contained fortresses which might hold out even when the curtain wall on either side had fallen to the attacker, representing a continuing threat to his flanks and rear.

The ingenuity displayed by the castle-builders of Britain in the early 14th Century, as each new technique of defensive design learned from the Continent, the Middle East, or local conflicts was incorporated, reached its peak in the great concentric castles which sprang up in the wake of Edward I's campaigns. An outer curtain of massive walls with strong towers and a complex barbican encircled an inner ring of defences as strong as the first, with the gatehouse off-set some distance from the outer barbican. The two rings of defence were often quite close, with the inner ring at the top of a slope. Thus attackers were faced initially by two banks of defenders; and even if the outer curtain was penetrated and all its towers subdued—no easy task—the space between the curtains became little more than a killing-ground. The castle itself was as strong as ever, with huge round or polygonal towers to defy the most energetic mining, and the layout of the defences often rendered mining of the inner ring or the keep impossibly difficult. With such sophisticated fortifications, castles were often defended successfully by surprisingly small garrisons.

In the early 14th Century the appearance of a weapon new to the West forced a great deal of re-thinking on the matter of castle design. Firearms made their appearance in Europe at about this time and it is known for certain that they were here by 1326. Their possession gave the king a considerable advantage for, as a rule, he alone possessed the facilities to produce gunpowder in bulk; but the advent of cannon meant that even the most powerful defences could be breached. When the handgun developed this too had a minor effect on design, since the arrow slits which had been cut into the wall for the archer were normally vertical and, although narrow, enabled the archer to cover a wide arc of fire. In order to give the gunner the same ability to traverse his weapon cross-slits had to be added to produce the cruciform slits. Embrasures "splayed" on the outside, to allow traversing, also appeared.

As military necessity declined in England there was less emphasis placed on defence and more on comfort. By the 15th Century the majority of new buildings, while having some defensive features, were primarily designed for comfortable living conditions, and castles such as Tattershall were the latest style. Earlier strongholds were gradually modified, or abandoned outright and replaced by great houses of a richer and more relaxed style nearby. The construction of fortified houses steadily declined during

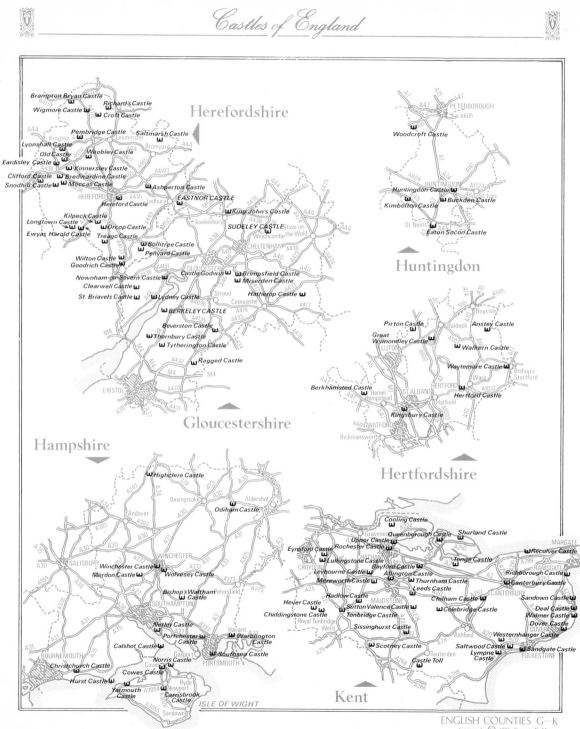

Herefordshire

Brampton Bryan Castle
Richard's Castle
Wigmore Castle
Croft Castle

Pembridge Castle
Saltmarsh Castle
Lyonshall Castle
Old Castle
Weobley Castle
Eardisley Castle
Kinnersley Castle
Clifford Castle
Bredwardine Castle
Snodhill Castle
Moccas Castle
Ashperton Castle
Hereford Castle
EASTNOR CASTLE
King John's Castle
Kilpeck Castle
SUDELEY CASTLE
Longtown Castle
Orcop Castle
Ewyas Harold Castle
Treago Castle
Bollitree Castle
Penyard Castle
Wilton Castle
Goodrich Castle
Newnham-on-Severn Castle
Castle Godwin
Brimpsfield Castle
Clearwell Castle
Miserden Castle
St. Briavels Castle
Lydney Castle
Hatherop Castle
BERKELEY CASTLE

Beverston Castle
Thornbury Castle
Tytherington Castle
Ragged Castle

Gloucestershire

Hampshire

Highclere Castle

Odiham Castle

Winchester Castle
Merdon Castle
Wolvesey Castle
Bishop's Waltham Castle
Netley Castle
Portchester Castle
Warblington Castle
Calshot Castle
Southsea Castle
Christchurch Castle
Norris Castle
Hurst Castle
Cowes Castle
Yarmouth Castle
Carisbrook Castle
ISLE OF WIGHT

PETERBOROUGH

Woodcroft Castle

HUNTINGDON
Huntingdon Castle
Buckden Castle
Kimbolton Castle
St. Neots
Eaton Socon Castle

Huntingdon

Pirton Castle
Anstey Castle
Great Wymondley Castle
Walkern Castle
Waytemore Castle
Berkhamsted Castle
Kingsbury Castle
Hertford Castle

Hertfordshire

Cooling Castle
Queenborough Castle
Shurland Castle
Uphor Castle
Eynsford Castle
Rochester Castle
Reculver Castle
Lullingstone Castle
Tonge Castle
Richborough Castle
Leybourne Castle
Bayford Castle
Allington Castle
Canterbury Castle
Mereworth Castle
Thurnham Castle
Leeds Castle
Hadlow Castle
Chilham Castle
Sandown Castle
Hever Castle
Sutton Valence Castle
Colebridge Castle
Deal Castle
Chiddingstone Castle
Tonbridge Castle
Walmer Castle
Dover Castle
Sissinghurst Castle
Westenhanger Castle
Scotney Castle
Saltwood Castle
Sandgate Castle
Castle Toll
Lympne Castle
FOLKESTONE

Kent

ENGLISH COUNTIES G–K
Copyright © 1973   Francis K. Mason

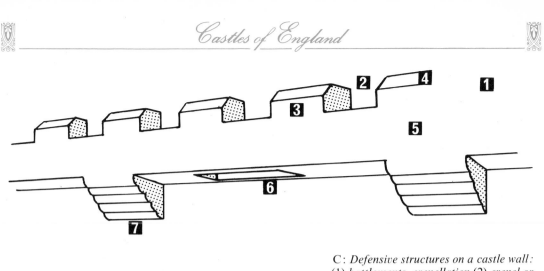

C: *Defensive structures on a castle wall:*
(1) battlements, crenellation (2) crenel or
embrasure (3) merlon (4) chamfer on
merlon (5) parapet (6) machicolation
(7) corbel

the 15th Century; and in the 16th Century, in general, the only form of castles built or developed were those intended for coastal defence, specifically designed to mount artillery. Henry VIII built large numbers of these along the south coast to ward off attack from France, and Elizabeth I maintained them against the Spaniards. Castles briefly regained some of their importance during the Civil Wars of the 17th Century. Many were held as important strongholds of Parliamentary or Royalist forces, and suffered repeated attacks. Despite isolated epics of endurance, their ancient fabric and design had now been outstripped by the developing technology of firearms; even those which survived Cromwell's cannon did not long survive his engineers, for it became established policy for the victorious troops of the Lord Protector to "slight" captured castles—that is, to destroy their defensive value by partial demolition. It is surprising how soon many castles decayed, considering the massive solidity of their structure, but the records of repairs and reconstructions show clearly that in a comparatively short period a castle could fall into a very considerable state of disrepair. When abandoned they could quickly be reduced to rubble by local people using them as convenient sources of dressed stone and other building materials.

Despite their decline, the castles of Britain had established themselves firmly in national folklore, and many wealthy gentlemen of the 18th and 19th Centuries fed their pretensions by christening their newly-built houses "the Castle" or "the Towers". (This practice had its valuable side—for it was this tide of rather ill-informed romanticism which eventually led to the first serious efforts to preserve and restore many ruined castles for the interest of posterity.) Some even paid for the erection of "sham" castles, stark ruins in a "ready aged" condition, with no other function than to lend glamour to an imposing landscape—or to the estates of some *nouveau riche* magnate.

In the rugged North and West fortified residences were a practical necessity long after the southern and central areas of Britain had lapsed into comparative peace. In Scotland clan warfare persisted, and apart from the great Norman castles of the Middle Ages and the splendid baronial piles of the 16th to 19th Centuries, a more modest type of castle was still to be found in great numbers. These stark tower-houses were the strongholds of chieftains and landowners of every degree, their sophistication or lack of it reflecting the different levels of wealth and power of their lords. At their greatest, they were rebuilt or enlarged over the centuries to bring them closer into line with the mainstream of castle design, but often retained signs of their earlier simplicity. At their most modest, they were simply plain stone towers with attached halls and projecting turrets, which could be defended against feuding clansmen or border reivers by a relatively small number of bowmen or musketeers. Most of them ran little risk of

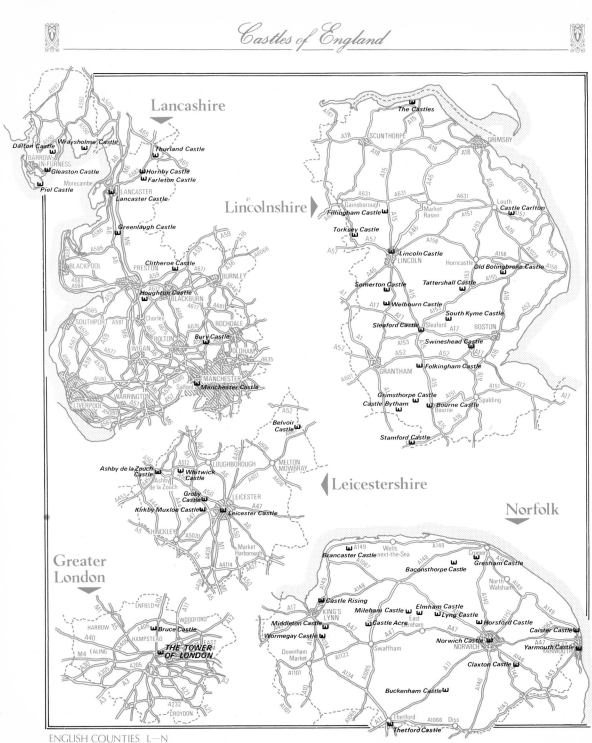

Lancashire

Lincolnshire

Leicestershire

Norfolk

Greater London

The Castles

GRIMSBY

SCUNTHORPE

Dalton Castle
Wraysholme Castle
BARROW-IN-FURNESS
Thurland Castle
Gleaston Castle
Hornby Castle
Farleton Castle
Piel Castle
Morecambe
LANCASTER
Lancaster Castle

Greenlaugh Castle

Clitheroe Castle
PRESTON
BLACKPOOL
BURNLEY
Houghton Castle
BLACKBURN
ROCHDALE
SOUTHPORT
Chorley
BOLTON
WIGAN
Bury Castle
OLDHAM
MANCHESTER
Salford
Manchester Castle
WARRINGTON
LIVERPOOL

Gainsborough
Fillingham Castle
Market Rasen
Louth
Castle Carlton
Torksey Castle
Lincoln Castle
LINCOLN
Horncastle
Old Bolingbroke Castle
Somerton Castle
Tattershall Castle
Welbourn Castle
South Kyme Castle
Sleaford Castle
Sleaford
BOSTON
Swineshead Castle
Folkingham Castle
GRANTHAM
Grimsthorpe Castle
Castle Bytham
Bourne Castle
Bourne
Spalding
Stamford Castle

Belvoir Castle

Ashby de la Zouch Castle
LOUGHBOROUGH
MELTON MOWBRAY
Whitwick Castle
Ashby de la Zouch
Groby Castle
LEICESTER
Kirkby Muxloe Castle
Leicester Castle
HINCKLEY
Market Harborough

Brancaster Castle
Wells next-the-Sea
Cromer
Gresham Castle
Baconsthorpe Castle
North Walsham
Castle Rising
KING'S LYNN
Mileham Castle
Elmham Castle
Lyng Castle
Horsford Castle
Middleton Castle
Castle Acre
East Dereham
Wormegay Castle
Norwich Castle
NORWICH
Caister Castle
Yarmouth Castle
Downham Market
Swaffham
Claxton Castle
Buckenham Castle
Thetford
Diss
Thetford Castle

Bruce Castle
ENFIELD
WOODFORD
HARROW
HAMPSTEAD
EALING
THE TOWER OF LONDON
CROYDON

attack with heavy artillery; their structure was adequate to hold off the comparatively small and lightly armed war parties of the day, and they were threatened by starvation, surprise assaults and treachery more than by advanced engineering techniques. The same conditions governed the emergence of many of the smaller strongholds in Wales. The Norman penetrations brought some of the greatest castles in Britain to the western mountains and estuaries, but there were also many simpler fortresses which had features in common with the Scots pattern. The holds of Welsh chiefs and obscure Norman frontier lords rose according to wealth or manpower, often on sites of great natural strength and sometimes utilizing the foundations of earthworks of earlier Roman and Celtic settlements.

GLOSSARY OF TERMS

THE following is a glossary of some of the most common terms connected with the structure of castles and siege warfare which occur in the body of the text:

bailey: defended courtyard or ward of a castle

ballista: early missile weapon resembling large crossbow on portable carriage, firing metal bolts, arrows or stone slugs

balustrade: ornamental parapet of posts and railing

barbican: fortified outwork defending gate of a castle or town

barmkin: Scottish term for defended courtyard of a castle, often rather smaller than conventional ward or bailey; possibly a corruption of "barbican". Also, the wall enclosing such an area

bartizan: overhanging corner turret

belfry: siege tower; wooden tower mounted on wheels or rollers, often covered with wet hides as protection against fire, which could be pushed against the wall of a besieged castle. Many had drop-bridges at the top, so that attackers could fight their way across on to the towers or wall walks

berm: flat area between base of wall and edge of ditch or moat

bratticing: wooden housing erected on top of walls, sometimes with machicolations (*qv*). When erected on top of towers, sometimes also known as "war-head"

bore: iron-tipped battering ram for attacking masonry, also known as pick

castellation: battlements, implying use as decorative feature

chamfer: bevelled face formed by cutting off corner of stone or timber structure

constable: title of governor of castle: also warden, captain, castellan

corbel: projecting stone (or timber) feature on a wall to support an overhanging parapet, platform, turret, etc.

crenellation: fortification—a "licence to crenallate" was official permission to raise a fortified building or fortify an existing structure. The "crenel" was the gap or embrasure in the battlements along a wall

curtain: wall enclosing a bailey, courtyard, or ward

donjon: keep or great tower, the main citadel of a castle of the 11th and 12th Centuries. The corruption "dungeon", in the sense of a prison cell, has little basis in fact

embrasure: see *crenellation*

enciente: enclosure or courtyard

forebuilding: projecting defensive work screening entrance of keep or other structure from direct attack

garderobe: latrine

hoarding: wooden shuttering fitted to parapet of wall as extra protection for defenders

keep: see *donjon*

machicolation: openings in floor of projecting parapet or platform along wall or above archway, through which defenders could drop or shoot missiles vertically on attackers below

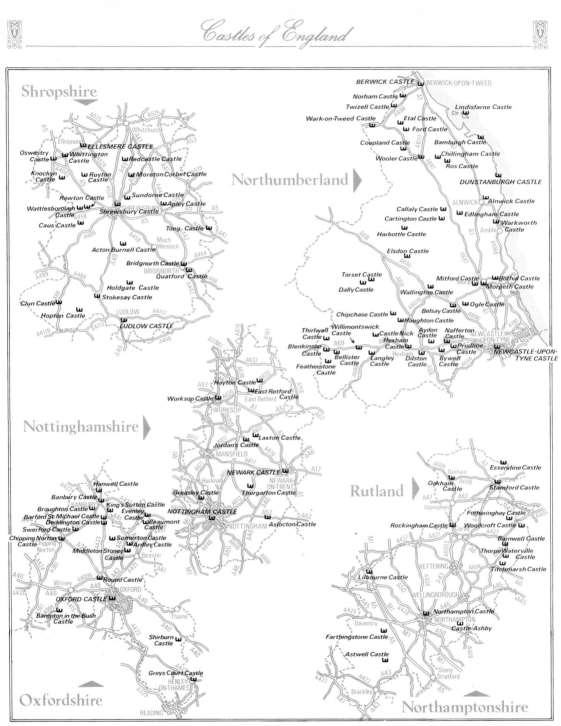

Shropshire

Northumberland

Nottinghamshire

Rutland

Oxfordshire

Northamptonshire

BERWICK CASTLE · BERWICK-UPON-TWEED
Norham Castle
Twizell Castle
Wark-on-Tweed Castle · Etal Castle · Ford Castle · Lindisfarne Castle
Coupland Castle · Bamburgh Castle
Wooler Castle · Chillingham Castle · Ros Castle
DUNSTANBURGH CASTLE
ALNWICK · Alnwick Castle
Callaly Castle · Edlingham Castle
Cartington Castle · Warkworth Castle
Harbottle Castle · Amble
Elsdon Castle
Tarset Castle · Mitford Castle · Bothal Castle
Dally Castle · Morpeth Castle
Wallington Castle · Ogle Castle
Chipchase Castle · Belsay Castle
Thirlwall Castle · Willimontswick Castle · Haughton Castle
Blenkinsop Castle · Castle Nick · Aydon Castle · Nafferton Castle · NEWCASTLE-UPON-TYNE
Bellister Castle · Hexham · Prudhoe Castle
Featherstone Castle · Langley Castle · Dilston Castle · Bywell Castle · NEWCASTLE-UPON-TYNE CASTLE

ELLESMERE CASTLE
Whitchurch
Oswestry Castle · Whittington Castle · Redcastle Castle
Knockyn Castle · Ruyton Castle · Moreton Corbet Castle
Rowton Castle · Sundorne Castle
Wattlesborough Castle · Apley Castle
Shrewsbury Castle
Caus Castle · Tong Castle
Acton Burnell Castle · Much Wenlock
Bridgnorth Castle
Holdgate Castle · Quatford Castle
Stokesay Castle
Clun Castle · LUDLOW
Hopton Castle · LUDLOW CASTLE

Hayton Castle
Worksop Castle · East Retford Castle
WORKSOP
MANSFIELD
Jordan's Castle · Laxton Castle
Hucknall
NEWARK CASTLE
NEWARK-ON-TRENT
Hanwell Castle · Greasley Castle · Thurgarton Castle
Banbury Castle
Broughton Castle · King's Sutton Castle
Barford St Michael Castle · Evenley Castle · NOTTINGHAM CASTLE
Deddington Castle · Beaumont Castle · NOTTINGHAM
Swerford Castle · Aslocton Castle
Chipping Norton Castle · Somerton Castle
Middleton Stoney Castle · Ardley Castle · Bicester
Round Castle · Witney · OXFORD
OXFORD CASTLE · Thame
Bampton in the Bush Castle
Shirburn Castle
Greys Court Castle · HENLEY-ON-THAMES
READING

Essendine Castle
Oakham Castle · Stamford Castle
Uppingham
Fotheringhay Castle
Rockingham Castle · Woodcroft Castle
Corby · Barnwell Castle
KETTERING · Thorpe Waterville Castle
Titchmarsh Castle
Lilbourne Castle · WELLINGBOROUGH
Northampton Castle · NORTHAMPTON
Daventry · Castle Ashby
Farthingstone Castle
Astwell Castle · Stony Stratford
Brackley

ENGLISH COUNTIES N—S
Copyright © 1973 Francis K. Mason

mangonel: siege engine for hurling heavy stones

merlon: the "teeth" of battlements, between the crenels or embrasures

motte: artificial (or improved natural) mound on which castle was built. "Motte and bailey" implies crude 11th Century defence comprising simple timber palisade on top of earth mound, with or without buildings inside

murder holes: openings in the roofs of passageways, especially entrances, through which attackers could be ambushed

parapet: protective wall on outer side of wall walk

pit prison: underground cell, with access through hatch in ceiling only. Also known sometimes as "bottle dungeons", from their shape in section

portcullis: heavy wooden, iron, or combination grille protecting an entrance, either in isolation

or combined with a conventional door; raised and lowered by winches in gatehouse

postern: small door or gate, usually some distance from main entrance of castle or ward. Often obscure or actually hidden, they enabled defenders to slip in and out of a castle, without being vulnerable to major attacks. If specifically designed to enable surprise flank attacks on besiegers, known as "sallyports"

solar: private living quarters of lord, usually adjacent to great hall

turning bridge: early variation on drawbridge, operating on "see-saw" principle

yett: Scottish variation on portcullis—gate made of intersecting iron bars penetrating each other vertically and horizontally. This formidable defence was ultimately banned

THE CASTLES OF ENGLAND: A NOTE ON SELECTION

BECAUSE of the very long, complex, and in many cases obscure history of military activity in England, it would be foolish to claim that the selection of castles described in this book is comprehensive. In many hundreds of cases the only trace of ancient fortifications which survives today is an overgrown mound or a series of banks in some isolated spot. A mound may be evidence that at some time during the period following the Norman Conquest some nameless knight threw up some sort of simple defended hold of earth and timber. It may, equally, be the trace of some pre-Roman or pre-Conquest site, or a Roman marching camp. If it is a Norman site, then all documentary evidence may be lacking; this may well be true even of those sites which were strengthened at a later date and which still show fragmentary traces of masonry. Many sites and buildings have been so altered and modified over the intervening centuries that their only survival is in the form of materials incorporated in structures of much later periods. The surprising thing is that so many castles of the medieval period *have* survived to a degree which allows reasonably accurate description of their original form, and that evidence on the ground can be tied in with contemporary records with some success.

The author and publisher have adopted the following conventions in compiling this book. Firstly, they have not attempted to define the term "castle" according to any pedantic technical criteria. Entries are limited to those buildings and sites known in written records or by common usage as "——— Castle" or "Castle ———". With the single exception of the Tower of London, all others have been excluded. Secondly, only those sites of which real evidence survives on the ground have been included in the main part of the text. A selection of castles which are described in surviving documents but which have entirely disappeared are listed at the end of the main text. Thirdly, while it is necessarily accepted that the means of selection requires mention of sites which are not true medieval castles—if only for the purposes of elimination—the descriptions of these have been limited to the barest essentials. In this category are included pre-Roman, Roman and pre-Conquest sites; and "stately homes" dignified with the names of castles but erected long after the age of true castles had passed.

The castles are listed alphabetically, under their most common names. Where they are in a town or

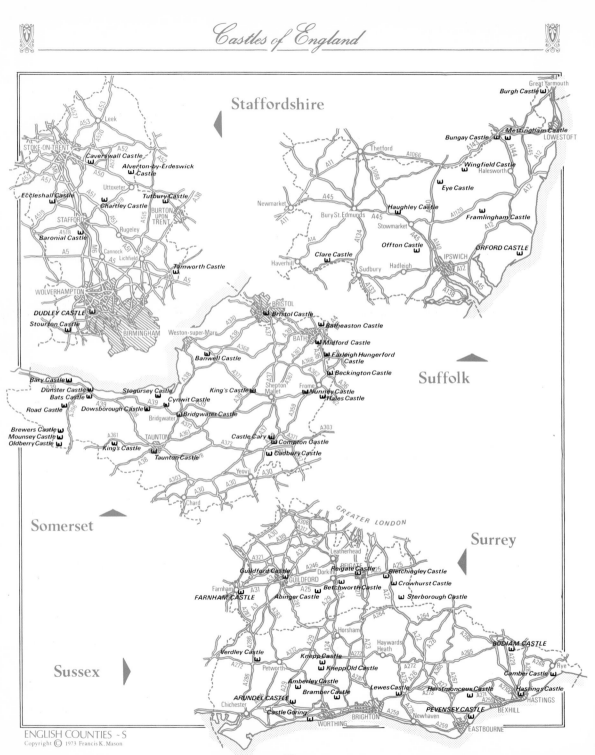

Staffordshire

Great Yarmouth
Burgh Castle
Metingham Castle
Bungay Castle · LOWESTOFT
Wingfield Castle
Halesworth
Leek
Caverswall Castle
Alverton-by-Erdeswick Castle
Thetford
Eye Castle
STOKE-ON-TRENT
Uttoxeter
Newmarket
Haughley Castle
Eccleshall Castle
Tutbury Castle
Chartley Castle
BURTON UPON TRENT
Framlingham Castle
STAFFORD
Bury St.Edmunds
Stowmarket
Rugeley
Offton Castle
Baronial Castle
Cannock
Lichfield
Clare Castle
ORFORD CASTLE
Haverhill
IPSWICH
Tamworth Castle
Sudbury
Hadleigh
WOLVERHAMPTON

DUDLEY CASTLE
Stourton Castle
BIRMINGHAM
Weston-super-Mare
BRISTOL
Bristol Castle
Batheaston Castle
BATH
Midford Castle
Farleigh Hungerford Castle
Banwell Castle
Beckington Castle

Suffolk

Bary Castle
Dunster Castle
Bats Castle
Stogursey Castle
Cynwit Castle
King's Castle
Shepton Mallet
Frome
Munney Castle
Hales Castle
Road Castle
Dowsborough Castle
Bridgwater
Bridgwater Castle
Brewers Castle
Mounsey Castle
Oldberry Castle
King's Castle
TAUNTON
Castle Cary
Compton Castle
Cadbury Castle
Taunton Castle
Yeovil
Chard

Somerset

GREATER LONDON
Leatherhead

Surrey

Guildford Castle
GUILDFORD
Reigate Castle
Bletchingley Castle
Crowhurst Castle
Farnham
Betchworth Castle
Sterborough Castle
FARNHAM CASTLE
Abinger Castle
Horsham
Haywards Heath
BODIAM CASTLE
Verdley Castle
Knepp Castle
Rye
Petworth
Knepp Old Castle
Camber Castle
Sussex
Amberley Castle
Lewes Castle
Hastings Castle
ARUNDEL CASTLE
Bramber Castle
Herstmonceux Castle
HASTINGS
Chichester
Castle Goring
PEVENSEY CASTLE
BEXHILL
BRIGHTON
EASTBOURNE

18

village, or very close to one, they are located simply by the name of the town and the county. Where important or interesting sites are rather more isolated, brief directions are also given. The *major* sites are shown on the county maps which accompany the introduction, in approximate relation to the nearest major roads. While these directions will be found sufficient in many cases, they are not claimed to be so in every instance. It is recommended that potential visitors correlate the directions with the relevant Ordnance Survey sheet or a good local road map, especially in the case of very isolated and fragmentary remains.

In the entries will be found descriptions of the known history, original form, and surviving traces of the most important castles. The length of each entry is to some extent governed by the accident of surviving records, but in general the historical importance or physical interest of the site has been the governing factor. In many cases all one can reliably say is that "there is evidence of a motte". In these instances the author has not robbed more interesting castles of space by indulging in speculation, and the publisher has not crammed the county maps with these obscure sites.

Where castles or sites are advertised as being open to the public, the conditions of access are generally quoted. In many cases admission fees are also quoted, but this detail is complicated by the current reappraisal of many charges in view of taxation reforms. Where a site is stated to be open to the public but no charge is quoted, it may be assumed that the entrance fee will fall in the area of 10p to 30p. Many sites are located on private land, and where known these are annotated in the text. The absence of a note to this effect *should in no case be taken as implying public right of way; in all cases of doubt careful local enquiries should be made*. In many cases the owners of private property will be willing to grant access to sites on their land *if prior written permission is obtained*.

MINOR SITES

THE castles in the following list—almost invariably the sites of 11th and 12th Century Norman motte-and-bailey castles—have been excluded from the main list as being both physically unimpressive and historically obscure. All masonry, where it was ever present, has now disappeared, and the sites may be traced by banks and/or ditches only; at the same time, all reliable historical information as to their origins is lacking. For clarity, earthworks "proper" of earlier periods have been included among the main entries.

Abbey Town Castle, Abbey Town, Cumberland
Alderbury Castle, Alderbury, Wiltshire
Almeley Castle, Almeley, Herefordshire
Alnham Castle, Alnham, Northumberland
Aure Castle, Aure, Gloucestershire
Barby Castle, Barby, Northamptonshire
Bardsey Castle, Bardsey, West Riding, Yorkshire
Barwick Castle, Barwick-in-Elmet, West Riding, Yorkshire
Bellingham Castle, Bellingham, Northumberland
Benefield Castle, Benefield, Northamptonshire
Benington Castle, Benington, Hertfordshire
Bessingham Castle, Bessingham, Norfolk
Bonbury Castle, Bonbury, Kent

Bothamsall Castle, Bothamsall, Nottinghamshire
Bradwell Castle, Bradwell, Buckinghamshire
Bulland's Castle, Penselwood, Somerset
Bury Castle, Bury Hall, Somerset
Caernarvon Castle, Beckermet St. John, Cumberland
Castle Bromwich Castle, Castle Bromwich, Warwickshire
Castle Donnington, Castle Donnington, Leicestershire
Castle Howe, Tebay, Westmorland
Castle Kirkby, Moorside, North Riding, Yorkshire
Castle Pulverbatch, Church Pulverbatch, Shropshire

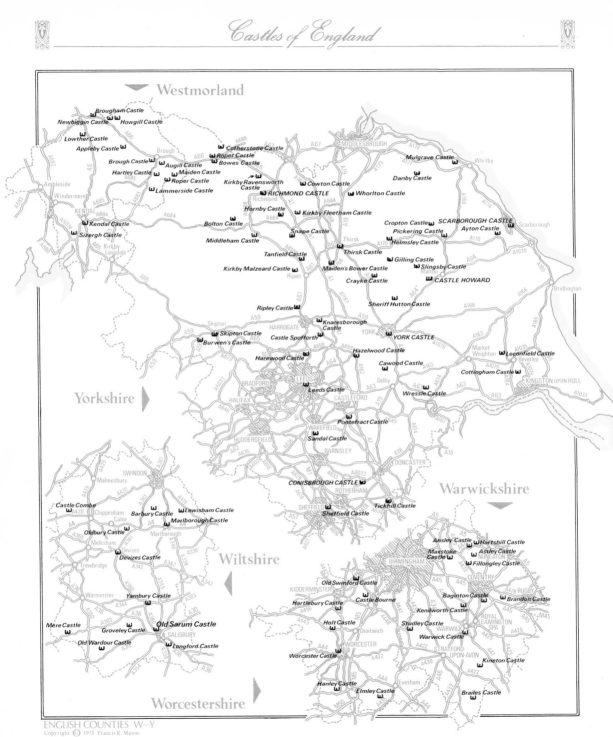

Westmorland

Brougham Castle
Newbiggin Castle   Howgill Castle

Lowther Castle
Appleby Castle   Brough

Cotherstone Castle
Brough Castle   Roper Castle
Augill Castle   Bowes Castle   Mulgrave Castle
Hartley Castle   Maiden Castle   Danby Castle
Roper Castle
Lammerside Castle   Kirkby Ravensworth Castle   Cowton Castle
RICHMOND CASTLE   Whorlton Castle
Hornby Castle   Kirkby Fleetham Castle
Bolton Castle   Cropton Castle   SCARBOROUGH CASTLE
Snape Castle   Pickering Castle   Ayton Castle
Middleham Castle   Helmsley Castle
Kendal Castle   Thirsk Castle
Sizergh Castle   Tanfield Castle   Gilling Castle
Kirkby Malzeard Castle   Maiden's Bower Castle   Slingsby Castle
Crayke Castle   CASTLE HOWARD

Ripley Castle   Sheriff Hutton Castle

Knaresborough Castle
Skipton Castle   Castle Spofforth   YORK CASTLE
Burwen's Castle   Hazelwood Castle   Leconfield Castle
Harewood Castle   Cawood Castle
Cottingham Castle

Yorkshire ▶   Leeds Castle   Wressle Castle

Pontefract Castle
Sandal Castle

CONISBROUGH CASTLE

Warwickshire ▼

Tickhill Castle
Sheffield Castle

Castle Combe
Barbury Castle   Lewisham Castle
Marlborough Castle
Oldbury Castle   Ansley Castle   Hartshill Castle
Maxstoke Castle   Astley Castle
Devizes Castle   Fillongley Castle

Wiltshire ◀   Old Swinford Castle
Yarnbury Castle   Hartlebury Castle   Castle Bourne   Baginton Castle   Brandon Castle
Kenilworth Castle
Mere Castle   Studley Castle
Groveley Castle   Old Sarum Castle   Holt Castle   Warwick Castle
Old Wardour Castle   Longford Castle   Worcester Castle   Kineton Castle

Hanley Castle   Elmley Castle   Braile's Castle

Worcestershire ▶

Castle Tump, Dymoch, Gloucestershire

Catterick Castle, Catterick, North Riding, Yorkshire

Chalgrove Castle, Chalgrove, Bedfordshire

Chichester Castle, Chichester, Sussex

Clavering Castle, Clavering, Essex

Corby Castle, Corby, Lincolnshire

Cornhill Castle, Cornhill, Northumberland

Croglan Castle, Croglan, Westmorland

Cublington Castle, Cublington, Buckinghamshire

Culworth Castle, Culworth, Oxfordshire

Cusop Castle, Cusop, Herefordshire

Dingerein Castle, Garrans, Cornwall

Durpley Castle, Newton St. Petrock, Devonshire

Earl Shilton Castle, Earl Shilton, Leicestershire

Egmarton Castle, Egmarton, Nottinghamshire

Felixkirk Castle, Felixkirk, North Riding, Yorkshire

Fenham Castle, Fenham, Northumberland

Fleet Castle, Fleet, Lincolnshire

Flitwick Castle, Flitwick, Bedfordshire

Fowberry Castle, Wooler, Northumberland

Fulbroke Castle, Warwick, Warwickshire

Fulking Castle, Poynings, Sussex

Gannock's Castle, Tempsford, Bedfordshire

Grantham Castle, Grantham, Lincolnshire

Great Somerford Castle, Great Somerford, Wiltshire

Great Staughton Castle, Great Staughton, Huntingdonshire

Grove Mill Castle, Grove Mill, Oxfordshire

Guisborough Castle, Guisborough, North Riding, Yorkshire

Hallaton Castle, Hallaton, Leicestershire

Hartfield Castle, Hartfield, Sussex

Hartham Park Castle, Hartham Park, Wiltshire

Haverhill Castle, Haverhill, Suffolk

Hodnet Castle, Hodnet, Shropshire

Hough-on-the-Hill Castle, Hough-on-the-Hill, Lincolnshire

Ilderton Castle, Ilderton, Northumberland

Kimberworth Castle, Kimberworth, West Riding, Yorkshire

Lavendon Castle, Lavendon, Buckinghamshire

Legsby Castle, Legsby, Lincolnshire

Little Dean Castle, Little Dean, Gloucestershire

Lockington Castle, Lockington, North Riding, Yorkshire

Long Buckby Castle, Long Buckby, Northamptonshire

Meppershall Castle, Meppershall, Bedfordshire

Milden Castle, Milden, Suffolk

Moulton Castle, Moulton, Lincolnshire

Mount Bures Castle, Mount Bures, Essex

Mouse Castle, Cusop, Herefordshire

Newington Bagpath Castle, Newington Bagpath, Gloucestershire

Northwich Castle, Northwich, Cheshire

Norwood Castle, Oaksey, Wiltshire

Old Charlton Castle, Charlton Hill, Shropshire

Otley Castle, Otley, Suffolk

Pelton Castle, Pelton, Shropshire

Pickhill Castle, Pickhill, North Riding, Yorkshire

Preston Capes Castle, Preston Capes, Northamptonshire

Ramsey Castle, Ramsey, Huntingdonshire

Roborough Castle, Lynton, Devonshire

Rayleigh Castle, Rayleigh, Essex

St. Devereux Castle, St. Devereux, Herefordshire

Salgrave Castle, Salgrave, Oxfordshire

Sharwardine Castle, Sharwardine, Shropshire

Sibbertoft Castle, Sibbertoft, Northamptonshire

Sigston Castle, Sigston, North Riding, Yorkshire

Sopley Castle, Sopley, Huntingdonshire

Stainby Castle, Stainby, Lincolnshire

Stanstead Mountfichet Castle, Stanstead Mountfichet, Essex

Stockbury Castle, Stockbury, Kent

Stody Castle, Stody, Norfolk

Sulgrave Castle, Sulgrave, Northamptonshire

Tilsworth Castle, Tilsworth, Bedfordshire

Toddington Castle, Toddington, Bedfordshire

Tothill Castle, Tothill, Lincolnshire

Tregate Castle, Llanrothal, Herefordshire

Turret Castle, Huntingdon, Herefordshire

Upper Slaughter Castle, Upper Slaughter, Gloucestershire

Wark Castle, Simonburn, Northumberland

Watlington Castle, Watlington, Oxfordshire

West Felton Castle, West Felton, Shropshire

Weston Turville Castle, Weston Turville, Buckinghamshire

Wing Castle, Wing, Buckinghamshire

Wolverton Castle, Wolverton, Buckinghamshire

Wood Walton Castle, Wood Walton, Huntingdonshire

Wybert Castle, Wyberton, Lincolnshire

Yafforth Castle, Yafforth, North Riding, Yorkshire

A

Aberbury Castle, *Aberbury, Shropshire. South of the church.*

This Welsh Marches castle has part of a tower and some bits of wall still standing.

Abinger Castle, *Abinger, Surrey.*

There are traces of a Norman castle to the north-west of the church and excavations revealed the remains of wooden post holes.

Acton Burnell Castle, *Acton Burnell, Shropshire.*

Like Spofforth (qv) this is essentially a fortified manor house rather than a true castle; it takes its name from the place—Acton—and the very powerful Burnell family who lived there. Acton was part of a small manor, originally belonging to Roger FitzCorbet, but in the 12th Century owned by William Burnell. The man responsible for the fame and power of the family was Roger Burnell, who began his career as a clerk to Prince Edward, the eldest son of Henry III (1216–1272). In 1270 he was appointed, with two others, to serve as the Prince's representative during his absence on a Crusade. When the prince succeeded to the throne as Edward I, Robert became Chancellor, and was elected Bishop of Bath and Wells in 1274. In 1278 the king tried very hard to arrange his election as Archbishop of Canterbury but with no success. In 1284 the king granted him licence to construct his manor at Acton Burnell, as well as permission to cut timber from the Royal Shropshire forest. His possessions and influence increased until his death at Berwick in 1292, whilst still serving the king. The castle passed out of the Burnell family during the Wars of the Roses and then through a number of hands, until in 1934 the then-owner

Sir Edward Smythe placed the castle under the guardianship of the Commissioners of Works.

The original Acton Burnell Castle was undoubtedly little more than a timbered manor house and no trace of it remains. The present manor house had a central block with rectangular towers at the four corners and on the western end a projecting structure set between the towers. The buildings seem to have been all of one date and there are very few signs of any later alterations. By about 1420 the castle had been abandoned, although throughout the 13th and early 14th Centuries it provided accommodation for the Chancellor and his household. Most of the upper floor in the central block was taken up by the great hall, while at the west end was the great chamber and in the north-east tower was the chapel. Robert's private apartments were probably at the west end on the top floor, and were approached by a stair leading up from the great chamber through the south-west tower. The ground floor is divided into four rooms by cross walls, of which only the base survives. Three of the four sections on the upper floor were taken up by the great hall. The northern side has survived largely complete but the southern end survives only to sill level. The great chamber comprised the western bay on the first floor and was a low room with a flat ceiling with the entrance in the north-west corner. Between the north-west and south-west towers is a block which is divided into two small chambers.
Open to the public at any time: admission free.

Afton or Aston Castle, *West Warlington, Devon.*

This was a stronghold of the Stucleys; it was later restored by Sir George Stukeley and converted to a farm house. There are, however, a few remains of an early castellated building.
On private land.

Aldford Castle, *Aldford, Cheshire. On high ground above the crossing of the river Dee, three miles south of Chester and north of the Church.*

Only the earthworks have survived, shaped rather like a harp. An outer ward, roughly triangular, measures 130 by 120 by 55 yards, and in the north-west corner is the motte. This is about 120 feet in

diameter and was known locally as Bloob Hill, whilst the lower, outer court was called Hall Croft. The castle was probably built during the reign of Henry II (1154–89) when the land belonged to the Aldford family. It later passed through many hands, including the Crown, but little is known for certain of its history.

Alfred's Castle, *Swinley Down, Ashdown Park, Berks.*

This is a prehistoric site, some two and a half acres of a roughly circular hill fort with rampart faced with boulders, with a single rampart and ditch. There are gaps on the north-east, north-west and south-east. Little is known of it.
On private land.

Allington Castle, *Allington, Kent. Two miles north of Maidstone, off the A20.*

Following the Norman conquest the land in this area, as was so much of Kent, was given to the Conqueror's brother Bishop Odo, but when he fell from favour the land was transferred to other owners. The original wooden fortifications were

Acton Burnell Castle, taking its name from a powerful 13th Century bishop and state official

replaced by stone at an early date and there are grounds for believing that it may have been the work of Gundulf, who was employed by the Conqueror to build the Tower of London. In 1224 the land was in the possession of Sir Stephen de Porchester who, in 1281, obtained a licence to crenellate. The castle later passed to the Wyatt family, who enjoyed a somewhat chequered career during the reign of Henry VIII, swinging in and out of favour like a pendulum. Sir Thomas Wyatt the younger was very deeply involved in a plot against Catholic Queen Mary's marriage to Philip of Spain and it was at this castle that the first meeting of the plotters was held. On the 25th January 1554 the start of the rebellion was signalled by the ringing of church bells. Sir Thomas left Allington and made his way towards London, but the rebellion failed and Sir Thomas Wyatt paid for this with his life. By the 16th Century the castle seems to have been largely in ruins and remained so until this century, when it was restored by Lord Conway. In 1951 the Carmelite Order of monks founded a house of retreat here which is still in use.

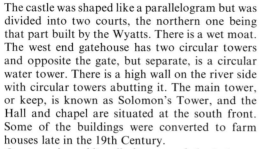

The castle was shaped like a parallelogram but was divided into two courts, the northern one being that part built by the Wyatts. There is a wet moat. The west end gatehouse has two circular towers and opposite the gate, but separate, is a circular water tower. There is a high wall on the river side with circular towers abutting it. The main tower, or keep, is known as Solomon's Tower, and the Hall and chapel are situated at the south front. Some of the buildings were converted to farm houses late in the 19th Century.

Open to the public all the year, daily 2–4 p.m. (guided tours of castle) and at other times by appointment. Admission 15p, Children 5p.

Alnwick Castle, *Alnwick, Northumberland. Thirty miles north of Newcastle, off the A1.*

Ivo de Vescy was the Norman who was granted the land on which Alnwick stood, and it soon became obvious that there was an urgent need for a castle here to restrain the Scots. In about 1140 the then-owner, Eustace Fitzjohn, began this present castle. It saw action against the Scots on several occasions; it then consisted of a shell keep with a motte and bailey, protected on the north by the river Alne and on the south and east by a deep ravine. In 1309 the castle was purchased by Henry de Percy, and he and his son carried out a great deal of re-construction and repairs. Semi-circular towers were added on the town side, and a fine gate and barbican were built with two octagonal towers known as Abbot's or Postern Tower and the Constable Tower. The surviving Great Hall cellars are also their work. In 1405 the castle was under siege, and was taken by Henry IV. In 1462 it was again besieged and, indeed, no less than nine of the Lords of Alnwick have died violent or mysterious deaths.

Alnwick was neglected and fell into ruins before the first Duke of Northumberland carried out repairs and rebuilding in about 1764; Robert Adam supervised much of the decoration. There was further extensive modernisation and rebuilding in the mid-19th Century.

Open to the public May 5th to September 30th daily except Fridays 1 p.m.–5 p.m. No admission after 4.30 p.m. Admission 25p, Children 10p (1973).

Alverton by Erdeswick Castle, *Alton, Staffordshire. North of Uttoxeter.*

Fragmentary remains of a castle around a small courtyard, situated on a cliff opposite Alton Towers, a 19th Century mansion by the great Victorian architect Pugin.

Amberley Castle, *Amberley, Sussex. On B2139 between Storrington and Arundel, three miles north-west of Arundel.*

The gateway from the church leads to the castle, which belonged to the Bishops of Chichester. A licence to crenellate a manor house was granted in 1377 but today little survives beyond some remains of the hall, a semi-circular gatehouse on which the battlements were restored in 1908/13, and a bit of curtain wall dating from *circa* 1380. One of the rooms has an early 16th Century painting.

On private land.

Ansley Castle, *Ansley, Warwickshire. One-and-a-half miles from Arley Station.*

Licensed in 1300 by Johannes de Hastings, but deserted at an early period and now disappeared. There are a few traces of an earlier Norman castle built by Hugh Hadreshall.

Anstey Castle, *Anstey, Hertfordshire. North of the church.*

A fine motte 30 feet high and 220 feet in diameter with a wet ditch 30–50 feet wide and a narrow ditch which encircles the bailey on the north-east.

Apley Castle, *Apley, Shropshire. North of Wellington.*

A licence was given in 1308, but John de Charlton had already built an earlier castle on this site. In the 17th Century a manor house was built and this was altered in the 1780s and again in the 1850s.

On private land.

Appleby Castle, *Appleby, Westmorland.*

Standing above the county town, the castle was probably started by Randolph de Meschines, prior to 1088 when its existence is recorded. Owing to its exposed position it suffered grievously from Scottish attacks and the present fabric dates largely from the time of Thomas, Lord Clifford, who rebuilt it around 1450/54. Towering to 80 feet is the strong keep known as Caesar's Tower, which has spiral staircases in the south-east and south-west corners which connect with all floors, whereas in the other towers the staircases lead only to the top floors. Garderobes and other chambers are set into the wall. In the middle of the east wall is a sallyport with its portcullis grooves. The gatehouse bears the arms of John, Lord Clifford and his wife and dated from *circa* 1418. The castle was slighted during a rebellion of the Earls of Northumberland and Westmorland in 1569 but was restored and repaired by Anne, Countess of Pembroke in 1651. There were two moats which surrounded the castle except for the side which faces the river.
Open to the public by appointment only.

Ardley Castle, *Ardley, Oxfordshire. Three-and-a-half miles from Bicester, west of the church.*

Earthwork remains and some masonry of a Norman castle and an early British earthwork. Probably destroyed by Henry II.

Armathwaite Castle, *Armathwaite, Cumberland. By the side of the river Eden.*

A four-storeyed pele-tower to which has been added various extensions, mostly early 18th Century.

Arundel Castle, *Arundel, Sussex. In centre of town.*

The original castle dated from the late 11th Century and belonged to Roger Montgomery, Earl of Shrewsbury; it had a motte and two baileys. During the reign of Henry II, about 1170–90, a shell keep was erected as well as the curtain wall and the Bevis Tower. The Well Tower and Barbican outside the original gate were added at a later date. The castle was badly damaged during the English Civil War. During the 18th Century there was a great deal of rebuilding, with additions in the Gothic style during the period 1791–1815; and finally, between 1890–1903, it was largely rebuilt. Indeed the greater part of the front is reproduction, although the barbican dates from 1295 and has its original portcullis slot. The keep is approximately 60 feet across, has a number of flat buttresses and a wall walk and battlements. The entrance is on the ground floor although the original entrance on the east side was blocked about 1170. On the south is the Well Tower, whilst on the north the Bevis Tower is a mixture of late 13th Century and 1890 work. The curtain wall also dates from *circa* 1890.
Open to the public April 16th to May 11th, Mondays to Thursdays 1–4.30 p.m.; May 14th to June 15th, Mondays to Fridays 1–4.30 p.m.; June 18th to September 28th, Mondays to Fridays 12–4.30 p.m. (also August Sundays 5th, 12th, 19th, 26th); Easter Monday and Spring Bank Holiday Monday 12–4.30 p.m. Admission (1973) 40p, Children 20p, car park 15p.

Ashby de la Zouch Castle, *Ashby de la Zouch, Leicestershire.*

After the Conquest the Manor of Ashby was part of the property of the principal Norman landowner in Leicestershire, Hugh de Grentmeisnil. In the 12th Century it became the property of Robert de Beaumont, later Earl of Leicester, but the castle itself dates only from the mid-12th Century. In about 1160 the land went to Alan la Zouch, whose family came originally from Brittany, and here they built a stone hall and a solar. In 1314 the Shropshire family of Mortimers inherited the manor and took the name Zouch. The works were extended by Sir William Mortimer, who built a new solar, converting the old one into a buttery. During the Wars of the Roses Ashby flourished. When they broke out the castle belonged to the Earl of Ormonde but after the Battle of Towton in 1461 he was beheaded by the Yorkists and his lands were forfeited. They were given to Lord Hastings, Lord Chamberlain of Edward IV who obtained a licence to crenellate in April 1474. The earlier buildings were modified and encircled by a very large curtain wall and half-

Alnwick Castle watching over the border marches of Northumberland

way along this wall, on the south front, he built the tower-house which survives today and is known as the Hastings Tower. It measures some 48 feet by 41 feet, with walls over eight feet thick which rose to a height of 90 feet, and was built of sandstone ashlar. On the middle of the east side a square wing rises the full height of the main building. The main body of the tower contains four storeys and in the wing there are seven, the lowest one being vaulted. The lower floor in the basement of the main building is a vaulted store and on the first floor is the kitchen, while above are the hall and great chamber. In the north-west turret and connecting to the hall is a small oratory. An unusual feature in this castle is that the entrance is at ground level, but it is protected by a portcullis. All the floors are connected by a spiral staircase in the north-east tower which rises right up to the wall walk. Beneath the foot of the stair is a small pit, or prison. The top of the wall is fitted with a machicolated parapet and at each angle are tall, octagonal turrets. In 1483 Lord Hastings was accused by Richard III of treachery, found guilty and beheaded. In 1569 and again in 1586 Mary, Queen of Scots was brought to Ashby and in 1617 her son James I was entertained here by George Hastings, Earl of Huntingdon.

During the English Civil War Ashby was gar-

risoned for the king under the command of Colonel Henry Hastings. The Mount House in the Leicester Road was erected for his horsemen and he connected it to the castle by an underground passage. In 1644 Lord Gray led the Parliamentary forces which captured the town, although Hastings held out. After the Battle of Naseby in June 1645 Parliament was obviously winning, and hunger and privation led to the surrender of the castle in February 1646. In 1648 it was reported that the tower was so strong that Parliament feared it might be used again and issued orders that it was to be destroyed. The south wall was blown up with gunpowder, as was all the outer part of the building.

Open to the public:

	Weekdays	Sundays
March–April	*9.30 a.m.–5.30 p.m.*	*2–5.30 p.m.*
May–Sept.	*9.30 a.m.–7 p.m.*	*2–7 p.m.*
Oct.	*9.30 a.m.–5.30 p.m.*	*2–5.30 p.m.*
Nov.–Feb.	*9.30 a.m.–4 p.m.*	*2–4 p.m.*

Ashperton Castle, *Strellen Granshaw, Herefordshire. West of the church.*

A castle here was owned by the Grandison family, who had the land in the 13th Century, and a licence was granted in 1292. It stood on an island in a moat, connected by a causeway on the east, and there are indications of an outer enclosure also on the east.

Askerton Castle, *Askerton, Cumberland.*

Begun in the 15th Century, it had a tower added at each end by Thomas, Lord Dacre, early in the 16th Century. The tower in the east covered the original entrance; later in the 16th Century further building along the west and north was carried out, and further modifications included the insertion of windows. There is a fine timber roof to the hall which still bears the various markings to indicate assembly order, prior to erection.
On private land.

Aslackby Castle, *Aslackby, Lincolnshire.*

Near the church, but few traces remain.

Aslockton Castle, *Aslockton, Nottinghamshire.*

Motte and bailey castle of the 12th Century with two rectangular baileys and their ditches.

Astley Castle, *Astley, Warwickshire.*

Licence was given in 1266 but the present building is mostly of Tudor date, although still with battlements. It belonged for a period to the Grey family, made famous by "Queen" Jane Grey.
Not open to the public.

Astwell Castle, *Wappenham, Northamptonshire. Half-a-mile south-west of Wappenham.*

A crenellated manor house of the 15th Century with 17th Century additions.

Auckland Castle, *Bishops Auckland, County Durham. Ten miles south-west of Durham on a hill.*

A few remains exist, including a chapel in the north-east corner named after Bishop Bec. In the south-west corner is a tower. A building is recorded here in the late 13th Century, and the area was renowned for its good hunting. Various Bishops of Durham added to it and Charles I knew it both as a guest and a prisoner. In 1647 it passed to Sir Arthur Hastlerigg of Naseby, who set about converting it into a great mansion—blowing up the chapel in the process!

Augill Castle, *Brough, Westmorland. Three-quarters of a mile east of the village.*

Castellated, with round turrets and a gatehouse. It has the general appearance of an 18th Century house but was, in fact, built in 1842.

Avon Castle, *Ringwood, Hampshire. One-and-three-quarter miles south-west of the town.*

Built in 1874/5 for the Earl of Egmont.

Aydon Castle, *near Hexham, Northumberland.*

A licence to crenellate was granted in 1305 to Robert de Reymes, and the castle stands above Cor Burn which protects it on three sides. It is basically a fortified house; there is no keep and no separate Great Hall, this is on the first floor of the house. At the east end of the hall is the solar and below the hall is a large room with a fine fireplace. The hall is approached by an outside staircase; it had a dais at one end, and beneath the hall is another room with a large fireplace.
On private land.

Ayton Castle, *West Ayton, North Riding, Yorkshire.*

A pele-tower—quite plain and oblong, originally three storeys high with a basement of two small rooms.
The ruins are freely accessible.

Baconsthorpe Castle, *Baconsthorpe, Norfolk. Three miles east of Holt and three-quarters of a mile northwest of Baconsthorpe village.*

This castle, often known as Baconsthorpe Hall, is one of two manor houses in the village, both of which once belonged to the Bacon family and were acquired during the 15th Century by the Heydon family. The present castle was almost certainly started by John Heydon the first, who died in 1480. Heydon appears to have been a somewhat astute politician who survived many of the vicissitudes of the Wars of the Roses. The actual date of construction of the castle is unknown for Heydon apparently either did not apply for, or did not receive, a licence to crenellate, but it was probably started early in the 1450s. The ruins of the castle were acquired by the Ministry of Public Buildings and Works in 1940.

So much of the castle has collapsed and vanished that it is difficult to be precise about many of the details and the position is further complicated by the fact that the basic design of the castle does not conform to the traditional pattern. The first approach to the castle is by way of the outer gatehouse, but this was added at a later date and is not really part of the defensive works. There were probably other buildings between the outer and inner gatehouses but they have completely disappeared and the details are mostly unknown. The entrance to the inner court of the castle is by way of a double bridge crossing a moat, the first section of which was probably fixed and the second part originally a drawbridge. In about 1600 the moat here was made narrower and partly filled in, although this has now been restored to its original size. The inner gatehouse was very strong, standing three storeys high and faced on the outside with flint work. On the ground floor was a vaulted passageway and on either side of the gatehouse stood two self-contained dwellings with the usual offices. These are built in brick and were possibly used by the more important officials of the castle. Above these were a large set of chambers which were originally approached by means of a staircase housed within a tower on the western side. A section of the original wall extending west and north, together with one of the corner towers still survive and are faced with flint and fitted with several gun-ports. The hall, if such there were, probably lay at the northern end of the castle with the domestic offices on its right-hand side on the eastern side, for the well is in this position. Throughout the building of this castle great use was made of brick.

Open to the public:

	Weekdays	Sundays
March–April	9.30 a.m.–5.30 p.m.	2–5.30 p.m.
May–Sept.	9.30 a.m.–7 p.m.	2–7 p.m.
Oct.	9.30 a.m.–5.30 p.m.	2–5.30 p.m.
Nov.–Feb.	9.30 a.m.–4 p.m.	2–4 p.m.

Baginton Castle, *Baginton, Warwickshire. East of the church.*

Earthworks and some masonry of 14th Century date.

Bamburgh Castle, *Bamburgh, Northumberland. Sixteen miles north of Alnwick, six miles from Belford, three miles from Seahouses.*

The north of England, with its rugged terrain, has always been important for the English kings, since it stood between the riches of England and the avaricious, war-like Scots. Bamburgh stands near the coast of the North Sea and was of considerable strategic importance, since it helped bar the way to any invading Scottish army. Its outline juts into the sky and has every appearance of strength, solidity and compactness. The history of Bamburgh is long and can be traced with certainty back to the 6th Century, when the Angles first landed. Bamburgh was the centre of the Kingdom of Bernicia and takes its name from a Queen Bebba who was the queen of King Ethelfrith. When the area was fortified it was known as Bebbanburgh (Bebba's borough or strong point) from which comes the present name Bamburgh. By the 8th Century it was described as a very strongly fortified city "with an entrance cut from the very rock and raised in steps after a marvelous fashion", and it does indeed stand today on a large mass of basalt. Its importance grew when King Oswald united the two kingdoms of Bernicia and Deira but later its influence languished somewhat.

Bamburgh was lucky enough to escape the fate of so many towns and villages of the north during William the Conqueror's ruthless suppression of the northern rebellion. It was one of the few places apparently left untouched by the Conqueror's army. William recognised the strategic value of the fort, and indeed some of the local tenants were granted land in return for the rent service of bringing in fuel for the king's fire. During the troubles which followed the succession of William II Bamburgh was held by the rebels against the king. Robert de Mowbray, Earl of Northumberland defended the castle stoutly; but when he escaped from the castle—presumably to seek assistance—he was captured by William the Red. The king paraded him in front of the castle and sent a message to the Earl's wife, who was continuing the defence, saying that unless she surrendered her husband's eyes would be torn out.

Bamburgh was returned to the royal fold by Henry II in 1157. By 1164 it had been decided to build a new keep and this was erected between 1164 and 1170 at the cost, it is recorded, of £4, although later another £30 was spent. Henry III, after his visit in 1221, ordered the building of a large hall, one hundred and fifty feet by thirty feet, and this was completed the following year at a cost of nearly £47. There are reports of repairs to the tower of Elmund and the barbican in 1250

Bamburgh Castle: major fortifications
on this site date back to the 8th Century

and further repairs were carried out later to the castle and drawbridge in 1253. When Edward III came to the throne in 1327 a survey revealed that the buildings of Bamburgh had been allowed to fall into a very sad state but repairs were put in hand and six years later it was strong enough to resist attacks by an army of Scots. Bamburgh is closely associated with Scottish history; it was to this castle that King David II of Scotland was brought after being wounded at the Battle of Neville's Cross (1346) and it has been suggested that David's Tower, at present on the south-west wall, was probably that one in which the king was kept prisoner. For nearly one hundred years the castle was left in peace, until the Wars of the Roses, when it was twice besieged by Yorkists, in 1462 and in 1464. On both occasions it was forced to surrender and there is little doubt that the use of heavy artillery played a very large part in bringing about a successful conclusion to the sieges. In 1464 Edward IV declared that he regarded the castle with so much affection and respect that he regretted deeply having to attack it and warned the defenders that every cannon ball he was forced to fire into the castle would mean that one defender lost his head. The Lancastrians seemed not to have been unduly disturbed, for they fought on. From the 15th Century onwards the castle gradually mouldered into an honourable retirement. During the 18th and 19th Centuries some repairs and restorations were carried out, and the Archdeacon of Northumberland made a large number of alterations during the middle of the 18th Century. Indeed, so much was done that it is now difficult, if not impossible, to say with any degree of certainty what was the original arrangement of the rooms.

The actual site of the castle lies east to west forming a long, narrow area of some eight acres, and the rock on which it stands rises to a height of some 150 feet. The curtain wall of the castle incorporated some round and some square towers but the most obvious feature is the great keep. It stands only some 35 feet high, for the rock gives it all the height that is needed; it is nearly square, some 69 by 61 feet. As with the other Norman castles there are a number of pilasters strengthening the wall. At the corners of the keep are some square turrets, as at Rochester. Although basically conforming to standard Norman design Bamburgh differs in one important feature; the en-

trance, instead of being on the first floor, is on the ground floor. Technically this is a defensive weakness but, no doubt, the physical geography of the place decided the builders that they had little to fear on this account. The basement is vaulted and there is a straight staircase built into the wall, a somewhat unusual feature, although the more normal spiral staircase is to be found in the north-west turret. At the east end of the castle is a strong gatehouse and there are traces which seem to suggest that there was another one at the west end of the bailey. Another interesting feature is the fact that there are not two, as is normal, but three separate baileys.

Open to the public March 30th to September 30th daily including Sundays 2 p.m.–8 p.m. Admission 20p, Children 10p.

Bampton in the Bush Castle, *Bampton, Oxfordshire. Fourteen miles from Oxford. West of the church.*

A licence to crenellate is known to have been granted for a building on this site in 1315. The castle appears to have been quadrangular, with round towers at the four corners. There were gatehouses on both east and west sides, and traces of the western gatehouse are still visible. The physical remains are not extensive, however, and those which there are have largely been incorporated into buildings of later date.

Banbury Castle, *Banbury, Oxfordshire.*

This castle was built in 1125 as a stronghold of the Bishops of Lincoln. The moated area, including two baileys, covered a total in excess of three acres. Little of note is recorded about the castle's history over the next four hundred years, although it is known that in the 16th Century part of the building was pressed into service as a prison. Only a short section of the moat and a small stretch of the walls survive today, however, as the quiet life came to an abrupt end during the English Civil War. Early in the war the castle was captured without difficulty by Royalist forces. Later, in 1644, the new garrison was besieged by powerful elements of the Parliamentary army, who tried by every means to take it, without success. The siege was finally raised by a Royalist army. In January 1646 yet another siege was mounted with 3,000 men; the Royalist garrison of 400 still held out, but after the king's capture the commander agreed to surrender the castle. It was demolished, although the gatehouse stood at the north-east corner of the market place for some time.

Banwell Castle, *Banwell, Somerset. A quarter of a mile south-south-east of Banwell*

A castellated house built in the early 19th Century. It has a gatehouse, long wall and bastion, all with battlements.
On private land.

Barbury Castle, *Wroughton, Wiltshire. On Hackpen Hill, two miles from Wroughton.*

An Iron Age camp with double ramparts.

Barford St. Michael Castle, *Barford St. Michael, Oxfordshire. Two miles from Deddington.*

Close to the church, ruins of a small castle.

Barnard Castle, *Barnard Castle, County Durham.*

The castle was probably begun late in the 11th or early in the 12th Century by Barnard, the son of Guy de Baliol. In 1216, after a visit by King John, the castle was besieged by Alexander of Scotland but the attack was not pressed. In 1292 the owner of Barnard's Castle, who was then John Baliol, was crowned King of Scotland and forfeited the whole of his English estates to Edward I. The Bishop of Durham, Anthony Bek, claimed the castle from the Baliol family and indeed occupied it from 1296 to 1301 when the king took it back from the Bishop; but in 1305, in order to settle a continuing dispute, the castle was granted to Robert Clifford, who was a king's man. Later Edward I granted the castle to Guy Beauchamp, the Earl of Warwick. Throughout much of its life during the Middle Ages the castle was subject to dispute between various owners and the Bishops of Durham, who claimed always to have prior right. In 1569 the castle saw action again during a rebellion in the north by the Earls of Northumberland and Westmorland which led to the siege of the castle. It was successfully defended by Queen

Elizabeth's steward, Sir George Bowes, who held the castle for eleven days before the wall was breached. It was finally taken by the rebels only after being treacherously surrendered by the townspeople. The castle passed through a number of hands, but in 1952 Lord Barnard granted it to the Ministry of Works.

The castle itself is on the left bank of the Tees and uses the physical characteristics of the site as part of its defence. In the late 11th Century a ditch and rampart enclosed a roughly rectangular bailey of about six acres in size and it was not until the 17th or 18th Century that houses gradually spread into the wards. The original gateway leading into the outer ward was probably to the south but was demolished at some time to make room for new buildings. Most of the east wall has gone but to the north is a ditch which was part of the defence of the Town and Middle wards. To the north-west of the outer wards lies the Town ward which still retains much of its original wall. The north gate probably dates from the 14th Century; it is fitted with a round-headed arch and above this is a rectangular window. The gate was flanked on the west with a solid drum tower. There was a two-storey gatehouse with rooms on either side and a passage over the gate. The eastern doorway leads from the ward into a square room with a fireplace. Further to the south-west is a rectangular tower, while to the north-east is Brackenbury's tower which actually projects slightly beyond the line of the curtain and some 30 feet behind it. It is named after a lieutenant of the tower during the reign of Richard III. Tradition has it that it was used primarily as a prison. Between the Town ward and the outer ward is a small area which is known, rather grandly, as the Middle Ward. A modern bridge crosses the ditch but originally there was a drawbridge here. At the turn of the 16th Century there were many buildings within the wards, including—over the gate—a barn, with three stables and a smithy, but all the most important buildings were in the Inner Ward. The earliest castle was probably a ring work with a ditch and bank, and the wooden palisades were replaced by masonry in the late 11th or early 12th Century. Entrance to the Inner ward was via a gate in the southern wall which led in from the Middle ward, and part of the west wall still survives.

Nearly directly opposite the gate on the northern side is the main tower, usually known as the Baliol, or the Round Tower, half of which projects beyond the curtain wall. It is 36 feet in diameter and about 40 feet high. Entrance to the tower was through a building on the south to which it was connected by a round opening at first floor level, and by a passage which leads in to the large basement. The floor was lower than it is at present and there was a well, a fireplace and some long windows to light it. From this floor a stair, built into the wall, leads to the first floor, the Great Chamber. A similar mural staircase leads up to the second floor which in the 16th Century was known as My Lady's Chamber. To the south of the Round Tower were two more buildings, and in one of them there is carved over the window a wild boar, which probably dates from the occupation of the castle by Richard, Duke of Gloucester. The hall dates from the 14th Century and may even have been built by the Bishop of Durham early in the century. South of the hall is the Mortham tower, known, in the 16th Century, as the West Tower. It contained lodgings used, presumably, by officials and visitors. It was probably added to the early curtain wall in the 13th Century. There are the remains of several other towers dotted along the curtain wall.

Open to the public:

	Weekdays	Sundays
March–April	9.30 a.m.–5.30 p.m.	2–5.30 p.m.
May–Sept.	9.30 a.m.–7 p.m.	2–7 p.m.
Oct.	9.30 a.m.–5.30 p.m.	2–5.30 p.m.
Nov.–Feb.	9.30 a.m.–4 p.m.	2–4 p.m.

Barnstaple Castle, *Barnstaple, Devon.*

This castle belonged to Joel de Totnes at the time of the Conquest. At present only the mound and a few masonry fragments remain.

Barnwell Castle, *Barnwell, Northamptonshire. South of Oundle on A605.*

A castle was built here by Reginald de Moine in 1152, and there are remains of the motte and bailey to the north-west of the stone building, which was built by Berenger le Moyne in 1264 and later passed to the Montagu family. A curtain wall, some 30 feet high and twelve feet thick, forms a rectangle roughly 120 feet by 90 feet with typical circular corner towers of the period, each of which has a spiral staircase. On the south-east is a two-storeyed gatehouse beneath which is a vaulted basement. The entrance which opens into the central bailey is less than five feet wide, thus making it very easy to defend. However, the most distinctive features of this castle are the two northern towers, each of which consists of three circular towers uniting at the centre to form a clover-leaf structure. One contains the living quarters, one the spiral staircase and the third contains the garderobes, or privies. The castle is open once a year under the National Garden scheme.

Baronial Castle, *Stafford, Staffordshire. One-and-a-half miles north of the town on the Newport Road.*

Built probably in the 11th Century, the castle, like so many others, saw action during the Civil Wars, but little survives. On the motte are some masonry remains.

Bary Castle, *Selworthy, Somerset.*

On Selworthy Hill is an earthworks, square with rounded corners. It is approximately 200 feet by 150 feet with a deep ditch.

Bathealton Castle, *Bathealton, Somerset.*

An irregular earthwork fort of the Iron Age, about 700 feet by 400 feet with an entrance on the east side.
On private land.

Bats Castle, *Dunster, Somerset.*

Well hidden in a wood in the Deer Park behind Dunster Castle (qv) is this Iron Age Fort in very fine condition. It is about 400 feet in diameter with two entrances, one in the east and another in the west. There are two banks, the inside one being fifteen feet tall. There is a smaller earthworks not far away.
On private land.

Bawdrip Castle, *Bawdrip, Somerset.*

A sham castle built by Benjamin Greenhill in the middle of the 19th Century.
On private land.

Bayard's Cove Castle, *Dartmouth, Devonshire.*

This small fortification is really part of that described under Dartmouth Castle (qv). It was built to house artillery and can be dated to 1509/10, when there are extant records for its building. It is mentioned as a new castle in 1537. It is irregular in shape and has thick walls pierced by a line of eleven gun ports which are very similar to those found in Dartmouth Castle, in that they were designed for guns mounted on flat bases. The stairs lead up to a narrow wall walk; unfortunately, most of the parapet is now missing but it projected slightly outwards. In 1940 this fort was adapted to hold machine-guns, and was made over to the guardianship of the Ministry of Public Buildings and Works in 1954.
Open to the public at any time. Admission free.

Bayford Castle, *near Sittingbourne, Kent.*

Only traces of the moat and some fragments of stone mark the site of this fortified manor house, which probably occupied the same site as a fortified camp of the Danes and King Alfred.

Beaudesert Castle, *Beaudesert, Warwickshire. On a hill, south-east of the church.*

A castle of the de Montfort family dating, originally, from the 11th Century but with additions made in the 13th Century.

Beaufort Castle, *Corbridge, Northumberland. Two miles north-west of the village.*

A castellated house with a fine, tall tower near the entrance; the whole was built between 1837–41.

Beaumont Castle, *Mixbury, Oxfordshire.*

North of the church, some remains of a 12th Century castle.

Beaumys Castle, *Shinfield, Berkshire.*

A licence was granted to crenellate during the reign of Edward III but, apart from a slight mound and traces of the moat, little of the castle has survived.

Beckington Castle, *Beckington, Somerset. Junction of A361 and A36.*

Now transformed into a small mansion, it stands in the street with its battlements, its three steep gables and its two rounded towers.
On private land.

Bedford Castle, *Bedford, Bedfordshire.*

Started by Hugh de Beauchamp *circa* 1087, it was later besieged by Stephen and saw service during the English Civil War. The motte, about fifteen feet high and 160 feet in diameter, survives to the west of Newnham Road.

Beeston Castle, *Beeston, Cheshire. North of Beeston village off the A49, north of the junction of the A534.*

The castle was built by Ranulf, 7th Earl of Chester in about 1225, but in 1237 the family line died out and Henry III took over the title and Beeston became a Royal castle. Edward I carried out alterations and the towers were made higher and crenellated. A great wall, 34 feet high and 7 feet thick by 20 feet long, was also erected to take a new drawbridge. By the 16th Century the castle was already in ruins, but during the English Civil Wars the Royalists, led by Captain Sandford, captured the castle. They were promptly besieged by Parliament and finally surrendered in 1645, and in the following year the castle was slighted. It was taken over by the Ministry of Public Buildings and Works in 1959.
There was an inner and outer ward and at the north-west the inner ward was protected by a gatehouse with two towers, a curtain wall with three

towers and a ditch running from south to east. The sloping outer ward had its own gateway with two towers and seven other towers were placed along its two-thousand foot perimeter. On the north and west the five-hundred feet high cliff was considered sufficient protection. From the east a path leads to the gateway of the outer ward, but of the original tower only fragments survive. Around the ward there are the remains of five towers. On the top of the area is Peckforton Castle built by Salvin in 1850.

Open to the public:

	Weekdays	Sundays
March–April	9.30 a.m.–5.30 p.m.	2–5.30 p.m.
May–Sept.	9.30 a.m.–7 p.m.	2–7 p.m.
Oct.	9.30 a.m.–5.30 p.m.	2–5.30 p.m.
Nov.–Feb.	9.30 a.m.–4 p.m.	2–4 p.m.

Bellister Castle, *Bellister, Northumberland.*

A three-storeyed 18th Century house with a ruined square tower, of Thomas Blenkinsop, built during the 16th Century, standing on a mound and moated.

Belsay Castle, *Belsay, Northumberland. Fifteen miles north-west from Newcastle.*

The site was one of importance, protecting the main road between England and Scotland. In 1278 Edward I visited a manor house here which was owned by the Middleton family. The date of this castle is uncertain but it appears to be early 14th Century.

The castle consists of a rectangular tower on the west side, of which there are two wings guarding the entrance passage; the doorway is protected by a bratische which projects from the second floor. The main building has three large rooms situated one above the other. The lowest contains the castle well and is a store although, later, it was converted for use as a kitchen by the insertion of a large fireplace on the north wall. Above the store room is the hall, and then the upper hall or solar. The southern projection contains a spiral staircase which leads right up to the top of the tower and also to six small rooms; one on the hall level was the original kitchen. It has an opening leading through to the stair. The other projection carries various apartments one above the other. The main building is circled by a parapet fitted with machicolations and the turrets have parapets above them. In 1614 another house was attached to the tower.

On private land.

Belvoir Castle, *Belvoir, Leicestershire.*

Robert de Todeni built the first castle on this site in the late 11th Century, and in 1130 the name first appears as Belvedere. During the 13th Century the castle went to the de Ross family, who increased the defences. Edward IV hanged the last of the de Ross family, and it then passed to Lord Hastings. Much of the material was removed by him to help build Ashby de la Zouch Castle (qv) and soon the place was in ruins. In 1528 the first Earl of Rutland began to rebuild it, but it saw action during the Civil War and, as a result, was slighted. In 1654–68 the 8th Earl built himself a mansion with a very solid square appearance, but in 1800 the occupier, the Duke of Rutland, decided to convert it to a "medieval" castle. It was completed by 1816; almost immediately a fire destroyed most of the building, but repairs were undertaken and the work was finished by 1830. It is rectangular with an inner courtyard and various towers and turrets in a variety of styles. The interior is particularly elegant and handsome.

Open to the public: April 4th to September 30th Wednesdays, Thursdays, Saturdays 12 a.m.–6 p.m. Sundays 2–7 p.m. Good Friday and Bank Holiday Mondays and Tuesdays 11 a.m.–7 p.m. Also Sundays only during October 2–6 p.m. Admission 40p, Children 20p.

Berkeley Castle, *Berkeley, Gloucestershire. South of the town.*

The site is on rising ground, and there was a castle here during the reign of William I. Henry II granted the castle and Honour of Berkeley to Robert Fitzharding, whom he made Baron of Berkeley. The third Baron Berkeley was made custodian of the deposed Edward II but was forced to surrender the castle and prisoner to John, Lord Maltrevers and Thomas Gurney who, on the 22nd September 1327, murdered the king in an agonising, but allegedly undetectable fashion. During the Civil

War it was held by the king and withstood a siege by Parliament.

The shell keep, an irregular circle, is flanked by three semi-circular and one square towers, and is approached by an external staircase. Most of the domestic buildings are spaced around the inside wall of the inner ward and include a buttery, a very fine 14th Century hall, a hexagonal kitchen and two very fine chapels. The room in which the king was murdered is said to be above the external staircase and is known still as Edward II Tower.

Open to the public April 1st to September 30th daily (except Mondays) 2–5.30 p.m., also Bank Holiday Mondays 11 a.m.–5.30 p.m. Sundays only in October 2–4.30 p.m. Admission 30p, Children 15p.

Berkhampsted Castle, *Berkhampsted, Hertfordshire.*

It was at Berkhampsted that the defeated Saxon leaders made their submission to the victorious Duke William after the Battle of Hastings in 1066. The land was given to William's half-brother, Robert, Count of Mortain, and the earliest work on the castle was probably done during his ownership. In 1104 William the son of Robert, rebelled against Henry I, but when the rebellion was crushed he forfeited the castle which was made over to the king's Chancellor, Randulph. When he died in 1123 the land reverted to the crown, but was probably given to Reginald de Dunstanville, Earl of Cornwall, in 1140. From 1155–65 the castle was under the control of Thomas Becket, who was then Chancellor, and the oldest surviving masonry dates from this period. During the latter part of the 12th Century further building was carried out and by 1186 it would seem that the curtain walls and all main features had been finished. In 1216 Berkhampsted was one of the castles besieged by Prince Louis of France, and it held out for a fortnight before being captured. A three-storeyed tower was built in 1254 and in 1269 some repairs to the barbican, the keep and the turret were carried out. In 1336 the castle was granted to Edward, the Black Prince, when he was made Duke of Cornwall and since then it has always formed part of the lands belonging to the Duchy of Cornwall. A survey made at the time reported that the great tower was split in two places and needed a new roof, the curtain wall, turrets, outer walls and barbican were

all in a bad way. Presumably some repairs were undertaken for, in 1361, King John of France, who had been captured at the Battle of Poitiers in 1356, was imprisoned at Berkhampsted. When there was no Duke of Cornwall Berkhampsted was often given by the crown, and some of the notable owners of the castle have been Katherine of Aragon, Anne Boleyn, Jane Seymour and the future Queen Elizabeth. The castle was sold as part of the king's possession during the Civil War but became royal property again on the Restoration and has since remained part of the Duchy of Cornwall. In 1930 the site of the castle was placed under the guardianship of the Commissioners of Works.

Of the surviving features the earthwork is the most impressive, standing 45 feet high with a diameter at the top of 60 feet and at the base of 180 feet. It stands in the north-east corner of an oblong bailey which measures 450 feet by 300 feet. The bailey and the motte were surrounded by a wet ditch. The inner earthworks are also surrounded by a ditch and bank—both ditches are now dry. The outer defences have been much altered and levelled during the construction of a road and railway. Around the outside of the outer ditch, on the north and east side, is another earthwork which has several earth bastions set against the bank. It has been suggested that these were siege platforms for catapults set up in 1216, but this is open to doubt. Little or no masonry survives except the southern barbican, but on the motte are the remains of a circular keep 60 feet in diameter, together with a well. Little survives, although a staircase and fireplace can be identified and there are traces of a forebuilding. On the southern side of the motte there are two wing walls. The bailey was enclosed by a curtain wall with half-round towers and was divided by a wall which ran east to west across the northern end to form a forecourt at the foot of the motte. On the north side of the court was a small gate known as the dernegate (back gate) which led to a wooden bridge which crossed the moat. The buildings in the courtyard have not been identified, although it is likely that the remains of a rectangular building to the west are those of the chapel and it is also thought likely that the hall was on this side of the bailey. The main gateway was originally on the south with a wooden bridge over the moat leading to a stone barbican at the bridgehead. Much of the outer works of the castle were des-

troyed when the railway was made in 1838.
Open to the public:

	Weekdays	Sundays
March–April	9.30 a.m.–5.30 p.m.	2–5.30 p.m.
May–Sept.	9.30 a.m.–7 p.m.	2–7 p.m.
Oct.	9.30 a.m.–5.30 p.m.	2–5.30 p.m.
Nov.–Feb.	9.30 a.m.–4 p.m.	2–4 p.m.

Berry Castle, *Berry Castle Combe, Somerset.*

The very sparse remains of an Iron Age fort.
On private land.

Berry Pomeroy Castle, *Berry Pomeroy, Devonshire.*

At the time of the Conquest the land in this area was given to Ralph de Pomeroy, and it was he who built the original castle. Later the land passed into the possession of the Seymour family and Sir Edward Seymour, Duke of Somerset built a fine mansion here after the Pomeroys had lost their lands in 1549. The castle was damaged during the English Civil War and also suffered from a great fire in 1685. The 13th Century gatehouse survives in reasonably good condition and is three storeys high with two flanking towers. The portcullis grooves are still there and on the first floor is a guardroom loopholed for use with musket or bow. The stairs lead down to small vaulted rooms in the side towers. The walls are battlemented and there is a large turret known as Lady Margaret's Turret. The Tudor quarters are around the courtyard to the east.

Berwick Castle, *near Bath, Somerset.*

An Iron Age earthworks.

Berwick Castle, *Berwick, Northumberland.*

Like many others this castle was largely demolished to accommodate a railway station, and only part of the curtain wall, White Walls, and the Water Tower remain. It is mentioned in the mid-12th Century, when it was being rebuilt with stone, but by the 16th Century it was ruined. In its prime it was strong and impressive, with a drawbridge and many towers and a strong curtain wall.

Betchworth Castle, *Betchworth, Surrey.*

Two licences to crenellate were granted in 1379 and 1448 but the castle erected here was largely demolished in 1690. The last few fragments were totally removed in 1890, and only scattered pieces of masonry can be found in the park.
On private land.

Beverston Castle, *Beverston, Gloucestershire.*

The fragments would indicate a date of *circa* 1225, and the castle was quadrangular with large towers at the corners. In the 14th Century a gatehouse was put into the east wall and the angle towers modified, and part of this gatehouse still stands together with part of the western range of buildings. The 13th Century hall stood on the south and its site is occupied by the present house. In the south-west tower is a chapel on the first floor and above that the living quarters for the owner. In 1642 it stood for the king, but surrendered in 1644.
On private land.

Bewcastle Castle, *Bewcastle, Cumberland.*

A tall 90-foot-square tower, with a single tower on the west side, complete with walls 30 feet high to north and south.

Bewley Castle, *Bewley, Westmorland. One-and-a-quarter miles south, opposite Crackenthorpe.*

This was the residence of the Bishops of Carlisle but it was in ruins by the 18th Century. It was a rectangular building with a projecting tower at the south end.

Bickleigh Castle, *Bickleigh, Devonshire.*

The site belonged to the very rich and famous Courtenay family and some of the remains are of the Norman castle, but the majority date from the

Tudor period. The gatehouses are probably Norman and the Great Hall was opposite this building.
Open to the public April to September, Wednesdays and Bank Holiday Mondays 2–5 p.m. Admission 25p, Children 15p.

Bishop's Castle, *Bishop's Castle, Shropshire. Six miles north of Clun.*

The site now occupied by a bowling green and only a fragment of wall remains. It was built early in the 11th Century by a Bishop of Hereford, but by the 17th Century was neglected and ruinous.

Bishop's Waltham Castle, *Bishop's Waltham, Hampshire. South-west of the town.*

Founded by Bishop Henry de Blois, it was greatly expanded by William de Wykeham, Bishop of Winchester in the late 14th Century. A tower, seventeen feet square, and part of the walls remain as do other parts of the palace.

Bladon Castle, *Newton Solney, Derbyshire.*

An early 19th Century brick house which began as a sham castle but was later adapted as a dwelling house.
On private land.

Blenkinsop Castle, *Blenkinsop, Northumberland.*

Licensed in May 1349, this castle had a moat and a curtain wall, but now only part of the north-east tower remains.

Bletchingley Castle, *Bletchingley, Surrey.*

To the west of the town, in the grounds of Castle Hill south of the road, there survive one or two pieces of a 12th Century castle demolished in 1264. The moat and some remains of the keep may be found.
On private land.

Bletsoe Castle, *Bletsoe, Bedfordshire.*

Licence to crenellate was given to John de Patishull in 1327; and today there are still a few remains of the moat, over 50 feet wide and 15 feet deep, as well as some Elizabethan buildings.

Bodiam Castle, *Bodiam, Sussex. Three miles south of Hawkhurst, one mile east of A229.*

Set in the centre of a lily-filled moat with its exterior walls practically intact, Bodiam looks like the ideal medieval castle. Sir Edward Dallingrigge was granted a licence to build his castle on 20th October 1385 for the king, Richard II, was anxious to protect that part of Sussex against the French who were mounting audacious attacks on towns such as Rye and Winchelsea. After a sedate and unadventurous life the castle was purchased by Lord Curzon, who spent a great deal of money on its restoration and then bequeathed it to the National Trust.
Bodiam is square and very like the castles at Barnwell and Framlingham (qqv). There is no central keep, but a strong outer curtain wall with the living quarters and offices built on the inside, leaving a central open space. Bodiam has four round corner towers each with its own private staircase and privies. The main entrance is on the northern side and is a great, strong gatehouse which still has its iron-plated oak portcullis. The entrance leads directly into the central courtyard and facing the gateway on the south and east sides of the courtyard are the Lord's quarters. The castle's well is in the south-west tower and cannot be reached except by going through the lord's kitchen, and so was firmly under his control. Next to the kitchen, on the southern face of the castle, were the other kitchens, butteries, pantries and so on. Next came the hall with an access to the rear entrance and, at the south-eastern corner, the great chamber and then the solar—which is also on the eastern side—and finally the chapel. All the lord's chambers have direct access one to another, and on the western wall are another set of chambers which are also self-contained. These comprise another kitchen, situated at the centre of the wall, and two large halls. These living quarters were presumably intended for the servants and garrison and since there is no direct access from the retainers'

quarters to the gatehouse or to the lord's apartments, the chances of treachery or betrayal were greatly reduced. Although such an impressive looking castle it saw no action whatsoever, and for this posterity should be grateful, for the walls are untouched although the inside buildings are little more than foundations.

Open to the public April to September daily 10 a.m.– 7 p.m.; October to March, weekdays 10 a.m. to sunset. Admission (1972) 15p, Children 7p.

Bolam Castle, *Bolam, Northumberland.*

On top of Bolam Hill was a motte and bailey castle; a house was built on the site much later and a good deal of the stone was re-used.

Bolebec or Whitechurch Castle, *Whitechurch, Buckinghamshire. On the west side of the village on Market Hill.*

A mound of earth marks the spot today; until the late 18th Century there was a tower here. The castle dated from the post-Conquest period and was slighted during the English Civil War.

Bolesworth Castle, *Bolesworth, Cheshire.*

Built *circa* 1830 by William Coe, it is a two-storey building, turretted and castellated.
On private land.

Boleyn Castle, *East Ham, Newham, Essex. In Green Street.*

Mid-16th Century manor house, with hall and other remains including a three-storey tower. Some rebuilding was undertaken during the 17th Century.
On private land.

Bollitree Castle, *Weston-under-Penyard, Herefordshire. Three-quarters of a mile north of Weston-under-Penyard.*

A house of the late 17th Century added to and altered in 1770.

Bolsover Castle, *Bolsover, Derbyshire. Six and a half miles east of Chesterfield.*

This site was given to William Peverel by the Conqueror; the present tower is known as Little Castle and probably stands on the same foundation as the original one. It was built between 1613–46, copying an earlier style, for it has angle turrets and battlements, and even the interior is in keeping with this archaic style.

Open to the public:

	Weekdays	Sundays
March–April		
& Oct.	*9.30 a.m.–5.30 p.m.*	*2–5.30 p.m.*
May–Sept.	*9.30 a.m.–7 p.m.*	*2–7 p.m.*
Nov.–Feb.	*9.30 a.m.–4 p.m.*	*2–4 p.m.*

Admission 10p, Children 5p.

Bolton Castle, *Bolton, North Riding, Yorkshire. Three miles from Wensleydale.*

Bolton Castle was built quite late, the licence to crenellate being granted by Richard II to Richard, Lord Scrope in July 1379. The castle was not completed for some eighteen years; it was designed, and the building undertaken by a John Lewyn. He built the north-eastern tower and the tower next to it and part of the south wing.

Bolton Castle is similar to Bodiam (qv) in shape, for it consists of a rectangular wall with corner towers, a gateway and living quarters built around a central courtyard. The entrance, in the south-eastern corner, is extremely well defended with five doorways and a portcullis at either end. The inside towers are also fitted with a portcullis. Above the doorway is a machicolated section. The living quarters for the lord are against the eastern wall. The chapel is on the second floor. The entire south-eastern section of the castle is self contained with only one narrow doorway in the basement, and this is well protected. On the first floor is a narrow apartment beneath which is a vaulted cell, access being through a trapdoor in the floor. The top room itself would probably have been used for a prisoner of some consequence whilst lesser captives would have been consigned to the pit. There are also facilities for the restraint of captives on the north mid-tower.

Bolton's main claim to fame is that from July 1568 until January 1569 Mary, Queen of Scots was kept

prisoner there. During the Civil Wars it was held for the king by Colonel Scrope, who was finally forced to surrender after a lengthy resistance.
Open to the public daily except Mondays, 10 a.m.–dusk. Admission 12½p.

Bothal Castle, *Bothal, Northumberland.*

Licensed in 1343, this was an important castle on the Northumberland side of the river Wansbeck with a courtyard some 180 feet in length. The gatehouse was made strong enough to serve as a keep; it is square with flanking towers with a very long entrance passage way which has portcullis, gates and murder holes. This gatehouse survives; it has two semi-circular towers covering the archway, and retains its portcullis grooves. There are a number of sculptured shields on the walls. Other parts of the castle may still be traced from quite considerable masonry remains.
On private land.

Bottreaux Castle, *Boscastle, Cornwall. Three miles north-east of Tintagel on the B3263.*

The only remains, a mound known as Jordans, of a castle which probably dates from the reign of Henry II and was held by a John Hender during the reign of Elizabeth I.

Bourn Castle, *Bourn, Cambridgeshire.*

South of Cambridge, at the junction of the rivers Burne and Ouse, was this castle which belonged to the Peverel family, but it was destroyed by Ribald de Lisle during the reign of Henry III. The earthworks are now occupied by Bourn Hall.
On private land.

Bourne Castle, *Bourne, Lincolnshire. South of the town.*

Earthworks of an 11th Century castle with a moat, but little, if any, masonry remains.

Bowes Castle, *Bowes, North Riding, Yorkshire. South of the town.*

This was erected on the site of a Roman fort and

A peaceful career can be thanked for the magnificent preservation of Bodiam Castle's outer defences

much of the earlier masonry was incorporated into the Norman tower. The keep, 82 feet by 60 feet and 50 feet high, is rectangular with broad pilasters, and it has a forebuilding on the east side covering the entrance on the first floor. The main hall is on the first floor and has three fine large windows and a fireplace; it connects with the kitchen.
Open to the public weekdays 10 a.m.–5.30 p.m. and Sunday afternoons.

Brackley Castle, *Brackley, Oxfordshire.*

Traces of a castle to the south-west of the town.

Brailes Castle, *Brailes, Warwickshire. In Upper Brailes on Castle Hill.*

The remains of a motte and bailey castle, possibly belonging at one time to the Earl of Warwick.

Bramber Castle, *Bramber, Sussex. About a mile before Steyning on the A283.*

A Norman castle on the banks of the river Adur. It was owned by the Dukes of Norfolk from the 14th to the 20th Centuries and was destroyed in the English Civil War. The large mound is natural but the smaller one is probably pre-Conquest.

William de Braose was probably the builder of the late 11th Century tower keep, fragments of which survive. There are also some fragments of the curtain wall.
Open to the public Good Friday to October (except Mondays and Saturdays) 10 a.m.–dusk.

Brampton Bryan Castle, *Brampton Bryan, Herefordshire.*

This castle was built probably during the reign of Henry I (1100–1135); it left the Brampton family early in the 14th Century and became the property of Robert Harley. Part of the gatehouse dates from this period, but it was later lengthened southwards and an extra portcullis and towers were added. To the north of the gatehouse was the hall and between was a ditch. During Tudor times there were additions to the hall. In the Civil War it was held for the king.

Brancaster Castle, *Brancaster, Norfolk. On Rack Hill.*

A Roman fort known as Brandodunum, and part of the defence network of the Saxon Shore. A large square site, now partly covered by a road. It has rounded corners with turrets and earthen walls, probably of 2nd Century origin.

Brancepeth Castle, *Brancepeth, County Durham. Five miles south-west of Durham on the road by Nevills Cross.*

This castle belonged to the Neville family, but it was built by the Bulmer family. There are surviving sections of the curtain wall, which originally had eight curtain towers. The castle was heavily restored in the 19th Century; the "Norman" gatehouse is a reproduction, and most of the buildings around the courtyard are 19th Century.
On private land.

Brandon Castle, *Wolston, Warwickshire. North-west of the church.*

The earthworks and a few pieces of masonry of a 13th Century castle.

Dramatic ruins of Bramber, a castle of the Dukes of Norfolk, destroyed in the Civil Wars of the 17th Century. There are signs of pre-Norman Conquest earthworks on the site

Branksea or Brounsea Castle, *Poole, Dorsetshire.*

On a sandy island in the bay was a small castle built by Henry VIII, later extended by Elizabeth I and by Parliament. It was later converted to a fine dwelling place but in 1895 a serious fire caused great damage.

Braybrooke Castle, *Braybrooke, Northamptonshire. East of the village.*

Extensive earthwork remains, including moats.

Bredwardine Castle, *Bredwardine, Herefordshire. South-east of the church.*

A green hill displays fragments of masonry which formed the south end of the keep, which measured 70 feet by 45 feet. The bailey was oblong and there are traces of some earthworks.

Brewers Castle, *Dulverton, Somerset.*

Prehistoric earthworks opposite Mounsey Castle (qv).

Bridgnorth Castle, *Bridgnorth, Shropshire.*

A pre-Conquest castle which stood here was rebuilt by Robert de Belesme between 1098 and 1101. In the following year it was taken over by Henry I and given by him to Hugh de Mortimer. In 1155 Henry II again took it over and it became a Royal Castle: he rebuilt the keep between 1168–1189 and some of this still survives. The keep, 65 feet high, has the usual first-floor entrance and a very fine fireplace in the south wall; and the whole edifice is inclined by 15°. Part of the curtain wall also survives.
Open to the public daily, 10 a.m. to 4 p.m.

Bridgwater Castle, *Bridgwater, Somerset.*

Built by Walter de Douai early in the 13th Century. It was slighted in 1645. Here the Duke of Monmouth was proclaimed king, but now all has gone except a portion of the Water Gate near No. 12 West Quay. King Square is roughly at the centre of the site and there are traces of cellars below Castle Street.
The site is freely accessible.

Brimpsfield Castle, *Brimpsfield, Gloucestershire.*

The 13th Century castle was demolished in the 14th Century after its owner had rebelled against Edward II, and its keep and four towers are no more than mounds near the church. Masonry fragments do survive and in those of the gateway there are traces of the groove for the portcullis. One early castle was apparently built on a different site near the present Ermine Street.
The site is freely accessible.

Brimstage Castle, *Brimstage, Cheshire. At the end of the village.*

A hall with an attached pele-tower of four storeys connected by a newel staircase. It has battlements and machicolations and dates, probably, from the time of Henry V.

Brinklow Castle, *Brinklow, Warwickshire. East of the church.*

A motte and bailey castle site with the motte at the east end standing some 40 feet high, and with two baileys.

Bristol Castle, *Bristol, Somerset. North of St. Peter's Church.*

This castle was the rallying point of the conspirators who favoured the cause of William the Conqueror's son Robert. In 1130 it had a shell keep, and saw action when Stephen besieged it. Following the Civil Wars it was slighted and in 1656 it was further harmed when a roadway was cut through the site.
The keep stood between Cock and Bottle Lane and Castle Street, measuring roughly 100 feet square, and was of the 12th Century. Some parts of the city wall have survived.

Broncroft Castle, *Broncroft, Shropshire. One mile west of Tugford.*

This mid-19th Century house incorporates parts of an earlier building and the tower at the right of the entrance probably dates from the 14th Century. *On private land.*

Bronsil Castle, *Bronsil, Herefordshire. One mile east of the church, below Midsummer Hill.*

A licence was granted during the reign of Henry VI; the castle was rectangular with polygonal corner towers. There were two moats and the entrance was by way of a gatehouse on the west side, but now only the moat and part of some of the towers remain.

Brough Castle, *Brough, Westmorland. Eight miles south-east of Appleby, just off the main road to Barnard Castle.*

The Romans appreciated the strategic importance of this site guarding the point where roads crossed the Pennines, and so they established the fort of Verterae, which was occupied continuously until the end of Roman rule. As at Pevensey (qv) the Normans adapted part of the castle for their use, probably during the reign of William II in 1092; certainly masonry dating from the 11th Century is still in evidence. The first castle was destroyed by the Scots under William the Lion in 1174 but it was soon rebuilt. After a surprisingly short period —in 1245— it was reported to be in considerable disrepair, and during the late 13th and early 14th Centuries some drastic restorations had to be undertaken. The importance of the castle is stressed by the number of royal visits it received, and both Edward I and II are recorded as having spent time there. After the Battle of Bannockburn in 1314 the Scots burnt the town of Brough, a feat which they repeated five years later, but on both occasions the castle seems to have escaped damage.

Although originally a Royal castle, in 1204 Brough passed into the possession of the powerful Clifford family. During the Wars of the Roses the 9th Lord Clifford (known as the "Butcher", for obvious reasons) held the castle, but it passed for a while into the hands of Warwick, "the King Maker". In 1521 there was a major blaze at the castle which gutted the entire interior and so it remained for well over a century until Anne Clifford, Countess Dowager of Pembroke, Dorset and Montgomery, rebuilt it. In 1666 there was another fire in the Clifford Tower and although not a great deal of damage was caused, it is from this date that the decline of the castle begins. By 1695 the keep was a shell whilst the greater part of the stonework was being removed for use elsewhere. In 1763 the Clifford Tower was partly demolished and in 1792 the south-east corner of the keep fell down to be followed, in 1920, by the south-west corner. In 1923 the castle was handed over by Lord Hothfield to the Commissioners of H.M. Works.

The castle stands at the top of a steep escarpment overlooking the south bank of Swindale Beck, and the Roman fort was made with its short—northern —end resting on the escarpment. The Roman earthworks are still visible but all the stonework has disappeared. The Normans cut off a third of the fort at the northern end with a curtain wall, to give a roughly triangular bailey with the keep in the western corner. The castle is surrounded by moats but only a little of the original 11th Century masonry survives. At the south-east corner is the large, round tower known as Clifford's Tower, whilst there are three large buttresses on the northern wall. The main entrance was situated approximately at the centre of the southern wall, with the hall and other attendant buildings on the left of the gateway and extending westwards. Clifford's Tower was probably built originally in 1300 but the front part was restored by the Countess Anne. The hall block of 14th Century origin joins on to the side of the Clifford Tower with a broad extension forming the latrines. In front of the hall is a walled courtyard divided by a number of crosswalls. The hall was on the first floor supported by vaults which were probably rebuilt by the Lady Anne. The two vaults on the west side are equipped with latrines and were possibly used as prisons. Unfortunately Clifford's

The leaning ruins of the keep of Bridgnorth Castle, built on the site of a previous stronghold of Robert ("the Devil") of Belesme

Tower has no surviving interior construction. There is quite a long stretch of herringbone masonry, which dates from the 11th Century, still to be seen on the northern curtain wall. The keep was built by Henry II in place of the one destroyed in 1174 but the 11th Century keep was built on the site of a Roman barrack, and Countess Anne referred to it as the "Roman Tower". The basement was used as a store; on the first floor was the hall, and above this the private rooms of the lord. The main entrance was on the first floor at the east side and it is now approached by way of a wooden ladder. Between the keep and the gatehouse were the stables and the kitchen was at the north-east corner and these were all part of the Lady Anne's work, but now only the foundations remain.

Open to the public:

	Weekdays	Sundays
March–April	9.30 a.m.–5.30 p.m.	2–5.30 p.m.
May–Sept.	9.30 a.m.–7 p.m.	2–7 p.m.
Oct.	9.30 a.m.–5.30 p.m.	2–5.30 p.m.
Nov.–Feb.	9.30 a.m.–4 p.m.	2–4 p.m.

Brougham Castle, *Brougham, Westmorland. One-and-a-half miles east of Penrith.*

Brougham Castle, like so many others, had its position determined by the geographical factors of the countryside, for it stands not far from the junction of the rivers Eamont and Lowther. As early as the 1st Century A.D. Agricola established a Roman fort to guard this important crossing; the site of the Roman fort is to the south of this castle and is very large, covering over four acres. The fort was not a legionary one, but was used by auxiliary troops.

In the 13th Century the castle passed into the hands of the Clifford family and Robert Clifford, who built the great gatehouse, was killed at the Battle of Bannockburn in 1314. After the Middle Ages the castle was allowed to moulder away and in 1714 it was abandoned after all the timber and lead had been removed. In the 19th Century it passed to the Tufton family which, in 1928, placed the castle in the guardianship of the Commissioners of H.M. Works.

Of the surviving castle the oldest part is the keep which was built during the latter part of Henry II's reign. Early in the 13th Century a tall, three-storeyed tower, now destroyed, was built on the east of the keep and contained a chapel and rooms for the lord. Later that century more buildings were erected on the inside of the stone curtain wall, particularly on the eastern side. Late in the 13th Century the keep was heightened and a very strong gatehouse was built on the north-west side. At the same time a very strong tower was built in the south-west corner of the curtain wall. The outer gatehouse dates from the beginning of the 14th Century, and this was later heightened and a passage was built to join it with the inner gatehouse. Entrance is by way of the outer gatehouse, built early in the 14th Century, above the archway of which is an inscription stating that it was made by Roger, the fifth Lord Clifford. The groove for the portcullis can still be seen. On the south wall is a long inscription detailing the repairs carried out by Lady Anne Clifford and listing her titles. In the north wall a door leads into the guard room, which has a large fireplace in the north wall and a garderobe in the north-east corner. Below the floor is a vaulted store chamber which may have been used as a dungeon, and in the west wall is a 17th Century fireplace. The second floor consists

of one large room known, in the 17th Century, as the Painted Chamber. There is a small courtyard between the two gatehouses which contains a passage joining both houses on the north side. The inner gatehouse dates from the end of the 13th Century and the outer archway was fitted with a portcullis, the grooves of which can still be seen. The lower part of the keep, or Pagan Tower, was built about 1180, although the top-storey was added at the end of the 13th Century. When first built the ground floor could only be reached by stairs which led down from the first floor but a passageway was cut through the forebuilding towards the end of the 13th Century, to give direct access. The first floor of the keep was taken up by the hall, with a 12th Century doorway leading from the forebuilding, and originally there was a large fireplace in the south wall. The second floor was taken up with a large room with round-topped windows on the north and west walls and a short wall passage connecting with a stairway. Built into the ceiling is a Roman tombstone. The top storey, which was probably added by Robert Clifford, is of octagonal form and is completely surrounded by a wall passage. The Great Chamber to the east of the keep was built early in the 13th Century and was probably heightened at a later date. South of the Great Chamber was another building, known as the Great Hall, which probably dates from the 14th Century. South of the hall was the kitchen, again situated on the first floor, the ground floor being used for storage. To the west of the kitchen is a small courtyard with a well in one corner and a 17th Century doorway which opens on to a causeway crossing the ditch.

Running along the inside of the south curtain wall are the late 14th Century chapel with some adjoining buildings which were altered during the 17th Century and were probably used as lodgings for retainers. The large tower, known as the Tower of the League, in the south-west corner of the courtyard was built late in the 13th Century. Some other domestic buildings were by the west wall but these were largely destroyed at the time that Lady Anne Clifford was restoring the castle and are now turfed over.

Open to the public:

	Weekdays	Sundays
March–April	*9.30 a.m.–5.30 p.m.*	*2–5.30 p.m.*
May–Sept.	*9.30 a.m.–7 p.m.*	*2–7 p.m.*

Oct.	*9.30 a.m.–5.30 p.m.*	*2–5.30 p.m.*
Nov.–Feb.	*9.30 a.m.–4 p.m.*	*2–4 p.m.*

Broughton Castle, *Broughton, Oxfordshire. Three miles south-west of Banbury.*

This important castle was started by John de Broughton in 1301 and eventually passed into the hands of Lord Saye and Sele in the 15th Century. It was at this castle that the chief opponents of Charles I held their meetings when planning their opposition to the king. There is an extremely wide moat crossed by a bridge leading to a strong gatehouse on the south side, and much of the 14th Century work is still in a very good state of preservation. The great Hall and kitchens have had large windows fitted.

The small chapel is approached by a flight of stairs rising from a very long corridor and on the roof are two apartments—one known as the guardroom has a particularly fine chimney. There is one very large room also on the roof at the end, in which the regiment commanded by Lord Saye and Sele rested on the night before the Battle of Edgehill (1642). In the 15th Century Sir Thomas Wykeham built the walls inside the moat, heightened the gatehouse and added the domestic offices. During the 16th Century the Fiennes family had modifications made at the west end.

Open to the public on Wednesdays, April to September: also Sundays June 3rd, 10th, July 1st, 8th, August 5th, 12th, September 2nd, 9th, also Bank Holiday Mondays. Hours throughout 2–5.30 p.m. Admission 25p, Children under six years 20p.

Bruce Castle, *Tottenham, Middlesex.*

Situated by the side of the church are the remains of a Tudor house with additions made in the 17th Century. There is also a tall brick tower, 21 feet in diameter, but its purpose is unknown.

Buckden Castle, *Buckden, Huntingdonshire. Just off the A1, three miles south of Brampton.*

Late in the 15th Century, between 1472 and 1480, the Bishop of Rotherham built himself a new hall at Buckden. It was essentially residential, although the unsettled nature of the times prompted a cautious man to have some form of defence; Buckden is a compromise—a defensive and residential hall. It is somewhat like Tattershall (qv) in that it centres around a brick tower. although on a much smaller scale than that at Tattershall. The four-storey tower was in the centre of the main defensive complex with a moat running round it. A wall ran around the entire park, with its fish ponds, and a sort of inner bailey which contained the moated tower and a number of smaller buildings including St. Mary's Church. The tower is oblong with octagonal turrets at the corners. The various storeys are marked out by string courses in the stonework and there is a flat roof with embattled parapets on the tower and turrets. Buckden was visited more than once by Henry VIII, and when he divorced Katherine of Aragon in 1533 she was sent to Buckden.
On private land.

Buckenham Castle, *New Buckenham, Norfolk. Three miles south-west of Attleborough, north-east of the church.*

Traces of earthworks of an oval enclosure which housed a wooden castle of Ralph Guader. About 1136 the then-owners, the d'Albini family moved their site to New Buckenham, approximately one-and-a-half miles west of the village. Entrance is over the ditch by a modern bridge to the site of the gatehouse which breached the stone wall, long since gone except for a tower to the south-east, but there is no motte. There is another earthworks to the east complete with separate ditch and bank.

Buckingham Castle, *Buckingham, Buckinghamshire.*

On the motte of this castle, which had disappeared by the 17th Century, stands the church of St. Peter and St. Paul.

Bude Castle, *Bude, Cornwall.*

A house built by Sir Goldsworthy Gurney. He died there in 1853.
On private land.

Bungay Castle, *Bungay, Suffolk.*

This belonged originally to Roger Bigod but it later passed to the Howard family. The ruins are those of a castle built in the reign of Edward I; they form an octagonal enclosure with two circular towers and the keep, 54 feet square, but much distressed. The motte and other earthworks survive also. A castle well was in the north-west corner of the keep. *Open to the public at any time. Admission free.*

Burgh Castle, *Burgh, Suffolk. Three miles south-west of Great Yarmouth, off the A143.*

Burgh Castle is another of the Roman-built defences forming the Saxon Shore, and probably dates from the 3rd Century A.D. Known as Gariannonum, Burgh Castle housed a garrison of cavalry. Until 367 the Saxon Shore seems to have achieved its purpose and the Saxon raids were largely contained. Burgh Castle was manned throughout this period, and was occupied until the 5th Century A.D. when Roman rule in Britain ended. There is a burial ground to the east of the fort and the contents of some tombs indicate that after the Romans evacuated the fort it was taken over by the Saxons. During the early part of the 7th Century Sigeberht, King of the East Angles, became a Christian and gave to St. Fursa of Ireland land inside the Roman fort on which to build a monastery. This lasted for two centuries; early Saxon and Christian churches are found inside other Roman forts. When the Danes devastated England in the 9th Century Burgh appears to have been deserted, and remained so for at least two centuries. At the south-west corner of the fort there was once a large earthen mound covering part of the Roman wall and on the north and east side it was separated from the rest of the fort by a ditch. This mound was partly removed in the late 18th Century and finally destroyed in 1839. Recent excavations have shown that this was indeed the site of a motte and bailey castle, but no records of its existence have survived.
In 1846 the site was acquired by Sir John Boileau and to him must go the credit for its preservation, for it was intended to use the walls as a quarry. In 1929 the walls were placed in the care of H.M. Office of Works.

Like most Roman forts Burgh Castle was rectangular. The east wall was about 640 feet long and surviving parts of the north and south walls measure about 300 feet each; the western wall has disappeared. The east wall is eight feet thick resting on foundations eleven feet wide. The north and south walls are narrower to the west where they are only seven feet wide. The walls still stand to a height of some fourteen or fifteen feet, although originally there was probably a parapet above this level. They are built of rubble concrete faced with square flints and were not built in a continuous strip, sections being started simultaneously and then bonded together as they met. The junction of the various sections of the wall can be seen. The corners are rounded; there are bastions at the corners and spaced along the walls, but the method of construction and bonding suggests that they were added after the original walls. The bastions are designed mainly for use with ballista or catapults. In the middle of the east wall there is a gate which is nearly twelve feet wide, and there was also a narrow postern near one of the bastions on the north side. Only the walls are within the care of the Ministry.
Open to the public:

	Weekdays	Sundays
March–April	9.30 a.m.–5.30 p.m.	2–5.30 p.m.
May–Sept.	9.30 a.m.–7 p.m.	2–7 p.m.
Oct.	9.30 a.m.–5.30 p.m.	2–5.30 p.m.
Nov.–Feb.	9.30 a.m.–4 p.m.	2–4 p.m.

Burwell Castle, *Burwell, Cambridgeshire. Four miles from Newmarket.*

To the west of the church are minor fragments and earthworks, all that remain of a castle belonging to the Tiptoft family, built in 1143.

Burwen's Castle, *Elslack, West Riding, Yorkshire.*

A Roman fort of the period of Agricola, 1st Century A.D., approximately 600 feet by 300 feet and now cut through by the railway.
On private land.

Bury Castle, *Bury, Lancashire. Castle Street, at Castle Croft.*

The structure, discovered during digging in 1865, was 82 feet by 63 feet with outer walls 120 feet by 113 feet; its date of building is uncertain— probably the reign of Henry II. It was in ruins by the 16th Century and the site is now occupied by Castle Armoury, built in the style of a Norman keep.

Bywell Castle, *Bywell, Northumberland.*

Granted to Guy de Baliol by William II, this castle is another example of a motte and bailey castle with the main tower serving as a keep and a gate-house. It is rectangular, approximately 60 feet by 40 feet, machicolated and was fitted with a port-cullis and gates. Unlike most towers the staircases are external and protected by heightened battle-ments.
On private land.

Burgh Castle, a surviving bastion of Roman defences on the "Saxon Shore"

Cadbury Castle, *South Cadbury, Somerset.*

An Iron Age earthwork of considerable size, eighteen acres, with strong defences of four banks and ditches; some of the ramparts rise nearly 30 feet high. It is romantically associated with King Arthur.

Cainhoe Castle, *Clophill, Bedfordshire. A quarter-of-a-mile west of the village.*

Some fragmentary remains of a keep and traces of baileys, that on the west being the earlier.

Caister Castle, *Near Caister-on-Sea, Norfolk. Four miles north of Great Yarmouth off the A1064.*

There are references to a moated manor house on this site during the reign of Edward I, but it is with the Fastolf family that this present castle is concerned. Sir John Fastolf was licensed to build this castle between 1432/1435, and it was this man who is supposed to be the model for Shakespeare's Sir John Falstaff. Sir John died in 1459 and left his lands to John Paston, head of a family about whom much is known because of their voluminous surviving correspondence. In 1469 the castle was besieged and captured by the Duke of Norfolk because of a dispute over the ownership of the castle. One of the Paston brothers was present at the "Battle of Caister", and he said that there were only thirty defenders holding against an army of 3,000—although some medieval exaggeration is probably at play here. During the siege cannon were used, and there was some considerable damage inflicted upon the castle. The Pastons had to cede the castle to John Mowbray, Duke of Norfolk, but they finally regained possession in 1476. The Paston family actually retained it for well over 200 years finally selling the castle in 1659, after abandoning it in 1600.

Caister Castle is of particular interest since it is built of brick, at that time a comparatively new material for castle building. The main part of the castle consists of a rectangular building which encloses a courtyard, at the north-west corner of which is a tall, slender, round tower. In the middle of both east and west fronts are gatehouses; that on the west is covered by a walled forecourt at the south-west corner of which is a low, round, bastion tower. On the east side is another large forecourt, also walled, with round towers at the two angles and a range of buildings along the north, south and east sides. Central buildings and the forecourt are encircled by a wide ditch with a cross cut separating the two portions. The western forecourt had a wide, low arch which led to the barge ditch, an artificial channel which runs through to the river. Only part of the wall survives in the eastern forecourt, and the buildings in the western court have been modified to form a modern country house. The principal survivor of the central building is the five-storeyed tower, 23 feet in diameter but rising to over 100 feet, and at the top of the tower is a machicolated parapet. The parapet is not fitted with the conventional arrow-slits but with circular holes to accommodate handguns. The eastern forecourt of the castle is built of a different kind of brick which has a lot of flint rubble in it; its walls are thinner and its loopholes are of a different type, and it may well be that this is the last remaining part of the original manor house.

Open to the public May 13th to September 30th. Daily 10.30 a.m.–5 p.m. October 7th, 14th, 21st, 28th Sundays 2–5 p.m. Admission 25p, Children 10p.

Callaly Castle, *Callaly Castle, Northumberland.*

On the north side of the small river are traces of a motte and bailey castle, the earliest on this site, built in the 12th Century. This site was abandoned and a start was made on a new castle south of the river, on the top of Castle Hill. A tower, approximately 40 feet square, was erected and fitted with

two turrets. Part of this tower was incorporated into the modern house.

Calshot Castle, *Calshot, Hampshire.*

A circular tower of two storeys with a circular gun terrace and domestic buildings at the back; all built by Henry VIII as part of his coastal defence programme.

Caludon Castle, *Coventry, Warwickshire. In Stoke.*

Licensed in 1304; a piece of surviving wall is of 14th Century date and was probably part of the hall. There is also a moat.

Camber Castle, *Winchelsea, Sussex. Two miles north-east of the town.*
This was one of Henry VIII's coastal defence forts of 1539/40; it has one large, round central tower surrounded by several smaller semicircular towers with connecting curtain wall.

Cambridge Castle, *Cambridge, Cambridgeshire.*

North of the river, on Castle Hill, William I built a castle, destroying 27 houses to do so, in 1068. There was fighting around the castle during Stephen's reign. John strengthened it, but in 1215 it was captured by his enemies. Henry III had a ditch, King's Ditch, dug around the town. By the 15th Century it was largely in ruins, although it did serve as a prison for a while during the 14th Century. During the Civil War it was repaired and strengthened but in 1842 the gatehouse was demolished to make way for the County Courts. Only a 40-foot-high motte survives together with traces of the 17th Century fortifications.

Canfield Castle, *Great Canfield, Essex.*
To the east of the church, a fine example of a motte and bailey castle site with moat.

Canterbury Castle, *Canterbury, Kent. South-west of the city.*

The first castle in this area was built by the Danes;

under William the Conqueror a new one, known as Lodam's Castle, was erected on this site. The keep is the third largest in England. Throughout its working life this was a royal castle, and under Henry II the defences were extended and increased. Towards the end of the reign of John the castle was invested by Philip of France and surrendered to him after—presumably—suffering some damage, for shortly afterwards money was being spent on its repair. Its importance declined somewhat over the centuries, and it was used as a county prison and a headquarters for the local Sheriff. It continued in use as a prison up to Tudor times but by the end of the 16th Century seems again to have been very greatly neglected.

The castle stands at the south-west of the city and covers an area of over four acres. The city wall is actually 50 feet beyond; there were a deep ditch and a barbican, thick walls and four towers protecting the keep. The drawbridge was not demolished until 1792. The keep, which is fairly complete, measures some 80 feet by 88 feet with walls which are eleven feet thick and some 50 feet high. The wall is strengthened with the typically Norman pilasters found on many other castles of the same period. Again typical of its period is the entrance situated on the second floor, north end and guarded with a forebuilding. The castle remained crown property until the time of James I.

Cardinham Castle, *Cardinham, Cornwall. To the north-east of Bodmin.*

There are some fragmentary traces of the foundations of this castle, which was the home of the Dynhams or Dinhams, roughly half a mile from the church.

Carlisle Castle, *Carlisle, Cumberland.*

Following the Battle of Hastings resistance to the Normans largely collapsed, but in some places, particularly in the north of England, it did continue; and Carlisle, or Caerlluel, was one such place. William took an army north and defeated Dolfin who ruled the land, and to ensure future peace fortifications were set up and some English peasants were brought in to colonise the territory. In 1092 William II began the castle, which was situated on a bluff rising well above the river Eden. During the troubled reign of Stephen (1135–1154) King David of Scotland supported Queen Matilda who was attempting to reclaim the throne from Stephen. In gratitude Cumberland and Westmorland were ceded to the Scots, and Carlisle became a Scottish city. It was in the castle of Carlisle that King David (1084–1153) died, but four years later Henry II received back the castle. In 1174 the castle was besieged by a Scottish force and after three months the governor, Robert de Vaux, was about to surrender when he was saved from this indignity by an English victory at the Battle of Alnwick. Not for long was Carlisle left in peace, for Alexander of Scotland attacked the castle twice more and, on the second attempt, succeeded. Whilst Edward I was engaged on his Scottish campaigns Carlisle became, in many ways, the seat of government, but with his death the castle settled down to quieter times. Following the Battle of Bannockburn (1314) the Scots regained hope and mounted yet another attack, and soon the castle was again under siege. Every known method of Medieval attack was used, including catapults, a "sow" to breach the wall, and scaling ladders. A siege tower was made but, because of its weight, it got stuck in the mud. All means failed and the Scots reluctantly raised the siege.

Sir Andrew de Harcla, Earl of Carlisle and Lord Warden of the Marches fell from royal favour, and in 1322 the king ordered him to report to York. He refused and was arrested by the Sheriff of Cumberland, degraded from his knighthood and then hanged, drawn and quartered. His head was spiked on London Bridge while his quarters were displayed at York, Carlisle, Shrewsbury and Newcastle.

Twice during the reign of Richard II Carlisle successfully defeated Scottish invaders. All these sieges left their mark and when Richard, Duke of Gloucester took over the castles of Penrith (qv) and Carlisle considerable repairs were necessary. During the reign of Henry VIII further work was carried out under the control of Stephen von Hashenperg who, because of his Teutonic origin, was known as "the Almain". Some of the repairs and modifications were so that the castle could house a new weapon—artillery. Although a survey carried out early in the reign of Queen Elizabeth reported that the fortress was partly in ruins, it was in Carlisle Castle, ruined or not, that Mary,

Queen of Scots was housed for two months in 1568 in the private apartments which stood in the south-east corner. By this period Anglo-Scottish relations had become more peaceful, but Carlisle still saw its moments of violence. In 1596 Lord Scott of Buccleugh attacked the castle with 200 men to rescue one of his followers who had been imprisoned for cattle-raiding. The castle knew peace until 1644 when it became the refuge for the Royalist Sir Thomas Glenham, who had just lost York. Glenham was pursued by the Roundhead General Leslie, and the castle was once again under siege. When news of the great victory at Naseby (1645) reached the defenders, who were already starving, they surrendered. In 1648 the castle was again secured for the king by Sir Philip Musgrave, but following the victory at Preston the castle was soon in Roundhead hands.

This time the peace of the castle was to continue for 100 years, until the Jacobite rebellion of 1745. The castle—with a very scratch garrison of "invalids" and local, more or less untrained, militia—held out for seven days before surrendering. The Duke of Perth took over the castle and the next day Bonnie Prince Charlie proclaimed his father King of England at Carlisle Cross before moving on and leaving 100 men to garrison the castle. The upsurge of victory carried Charles forward as far south as Derby, but before Christmas he was back again in Carlisle, being chased by the brutal Duke of Cumberland. It was decided that the castle would be held against the English and some 400 Highlanders were left behind to defend it. However, artillery and careful planning by Cumberland soon reduced the castle and for many of the Scots captured after the Battle of Culloden in 1746, Carlisle became their prison and death-house.

Although Carlisle Castle survived every type of military attack it succumbed to civic planning, and in the 19th Century much of the outer ward was razed when barracks and other buildings were erected. Only bits of the wall and the tower in which Queen Mary was imprisoned have survived. The keep, which houses the Regimental Museum of the Border Regiment, was taken over in 1927 by the Commissioners of H.M. Works.

The city of Carlisle rises 60 feet above the river Eden and it is protected on each side by smaller tributaries, the Petteril and the Caldew. The city walls, which enclosed an area of 45 acres, have largely disappeared and the three town gates have also gone. Much of the work on the earlier castle was carried out by William II, although some Scottish authorities say that David I of Scotland set out a towered castle with inner and outer wards and ditches as well as increasing the height of the city wall. In 1529 the castle was described as being ruinous but by 1541 work ordered by Henry VIII had been carried out; this included a bulwark outside the buttresses designed to protect the north-east corner and consisted of two circular block houses linked by a wall. The castle was roughly triangular with an outer and inner bailey, with the side walls extending southwards about 120 yards to join with the city walls. On the east side was a solid square bastion which appears to date from the 12th Century. The western wall is of about the same date and the masonry shows evidence of considerable repairs.

The solidly built keep is rectangular with corner towers, with a spiral staircase, reaching all floors, set in the north-east tower. It was probably built during the third quarter of the 12th Century and was known during the 18th Century as Queen Elizabeth's Tower, although it predates her by some 400 years. It measures 67 feet from north to south and 60 feet from east to west and was some 65 feet high. Along the east wall there was a fore-building which contained a straight staircase leading up to the original entrance on the first floor. The entrance was protected by a portcullis. Much restoration has been carried out; the roof and parapets are fairly modern and both the western towers have been rebuilt. Early in the 18th Century the south wall was reduced in thickness and refaced. The present entrance dates from the 13th Century with some restoration carried out during Tudor times. The slots for the portcullis can still be seen and there was also a drawbridge. On the left of the entrance passage is a staircase within the thickness of the wall which leads up to the first floor. At the end of the passage a few stairs lead down to the lowest floor; this was originally a single room, probably a store, but at some date has been sub-divided into three rooms and a vaulted passage. The first floor was also originally one chamber but was divided into two, probably during Tudor times. On the north-east corner is a chamber which originally held the portcullis when in the raised position. The second floor is reached by a newel stair and above the rooms the massive floor timbers of the top storey can be seen. Fitted into the eastern wall is a suite of prison cells used during the 15th Century and on the walls and on the back of the door are a series of carvings executed, no doubt, by the various prisoners. Some are fairly simple drawings and scratched representations of animals, but another group are far more elaborate and include shields of arms, dragons, knights in 15th Century armour and a whole range of similar figures. The top floor, also divided at some time, is reached by a modern staircase within the west wall. The roof forms a gun platform and was covered by flagstones in 1812. Beneath the north wall is a 78-foot-deep well which probably dates from the time of William II.

Near the centre of the south-west wall stands the Tile or Richard Tower, with its two storeys. The lower section was built at the same time as the curtain wall but the upper part was added in the 15th Century and was made with small, thin bricks hence the name. In front of the south wall was a deep ditch as well as an inner one.

The inner ward was approached through William de Ireby's Tower, which probably had three storeys. The original drawbridge over the wide ditch has now been replaced by a modern stone one. The inner bailey is cut off in the south-eastern corner by a wall forming an inner ward, but the main part of the bailey has been raised by at least five feet early in the 19th Century and modern buildings cover most of the curtain wall. The inner ward was protected by a curtain wall and a wet ditch which is now drained. The inner ward is approached through the gateway, or Captain's tower, again of three storeys, which was rebuilt some time around the middle of the 14th Century. It originally had a portcullis and probably a drawbridge as well.

Open to the public:

	Weekdays	*Sundays*
March–April	*9.30 a.m.–5.30 p.m.*	*2–5.30 p.m.*
May–Sept.	*9.30 a.m.–7 p.m.*	*9.30 a.m.–7 p.m.*
Oct.	*9.30 a.m.–5.30 p.m.*	*2–5.30 p.m.*
Nov.–Feb.	*9.30 a.m.–4 p.m.*	*2–4 p.m.*

Admission, summer 20p, winter 10p, Children and OAPs 5p.

Carn Brea Castle, *Carn Brea, Cornwall. Near Redruth.*

There are the remains of a tower roughly twenty feet square and rising to a height of 40 feet. It originally had two timber floors with the entrance in the rock. It stands at the east end of Carn Brea hill; to the north-west are some further earthworks and on the west, near the summit, are the traces of a circular fortification known as the Old Castle. *On private land.*

Carisbrooke Castle, *Newport, Isle of Wight. One-and-a-quarter miles south-east of Newport.*

Like Porchester and Pevensey (qqv), Carisbrooke stands on the site of an earlier Roman fort, and when the island was invaded by the Saxons in A.D. 530 a battle was fought here. Following the Norman Conquest the land was given to William FitzOsbern, but it did not stay long in this family for it passed to William's son Roger who, in 1078, was stripped of his possessions following a rebellion against the king. For the next 25 years or so Carisbrooke remained a royal castle; in 1100 it was given to Richard de Redvers, who added the first stone buildings, and it stayed within this family until the early part of the 14th Century. During the anarchy under King Stephen Carisbrooke was a stronghold for the Empress Maud, and following the defeat of her troops at Exeter in 1136 her supporter, Earl Baldwin, withdrew to the castle, where he held out until lack of water forced eventual surrender. Baldwin was exiled, but returned to England in 1153, and it was at this date that the building of the keep was begun. During the latter part of the 13th Century the castle underwent some major restoration and modification under the direction of the last of the Redvers. Following the death of the Countess Isabel the castle was once again in royal hands and remained so until the middle of the 14th Century. Richard II granted the castle to the Earl of Salisbury, who added the great hall and a series of domestic buildings. In 1377 a raiding force of French landed on the Isle of Wight and attacked the castle but, under the command of Sir Hugh Tyrell, the garrison successfully resisted and the French withdrew. During the wars of the Roses Carisbrooke seems to have had somewhat unlucky associations, for no less than three of the Lords of Carisbrooke were beheaded for treason. During the reign of Elizabeth I, when it was feared that Spain might attempt an invasion, the castle was repaired and brought into a state of readiness. Although not directly involved, the castle witnessed the battle against the Armada in 1588. Following this event further improvements to the defences were carried out, some under the control of Federigo Gianibelli, an Italian architect of repute.

Towards the end of the English Civil War Charles I surrendered to Parliament and was held for a while at Hampton Court. The Parliamentary party was seriously divided and the king took advantage of this disorder to leave Hampton Court and make his way to the Isle of Wight. Somewhat reluctantly, and fearing the intentions of the Parliamentary commander of the castle, Charles crossed the Solent, and took up residence in the castle. At first he was treated as an honoured guest but on discovery of his agreement with the Scots—that they should invade England to set him back on the throne—he became a prisoner. His servants were dismissed and he was placed under restraint, but the king was not a man to give up easily and he made his plans to escape. The first attempt proved an abysmal disaster, for he found that he could not get through the window, and the second one was betrayed by one of the guards who had been thought safe since he had accepted a bribe. On the 30th November 1649 Charles left Carisbrooke to make his way to London, where he was tried, found guilty of treason and executed.

After King Charles had left the island it was rather neglected and little of note occurred. Carisbrooke became very sober, and in 1896 Her Royal Highness Princess Beatrice made it the home where she was to stay for the next 55 years.

At present the gatehouse houses an exhibition to commemorate the Governors of the Isle of Wight from 1066 to the present. In 1944 the Governor's residence of the Castle was taken over as a museum for the Isle of Wight and today houses a number of exhibits of particular interest, including a number of items associated with Charles I.

The castle is roughly rectangular with a gatehouse, a keep and a motte and bailey. The entrance to the castle is by way of a large, well-defended gatehouse complete with machicolations above the pointed arch. The gateway is flanked by two towers which were built about 1335, although later extended and heightened. A passageway leads from the gateway through to the entrance which is guarded by an original pair of oak doors; there was another inner gatehouse which has now disappeared. On the right hand side are a group of domestic buildings, and the very large window which can be seen is part of the great chamber which served as a bedroom to Charles I. Beyond the domestic offices is the chapel of St. Nicholas; a church has been here since the Domesday inquest, although the present building dates only from the early part of this century and was built as a memorial to Charles I. It is now also a memorial to the war dead of the Isle of Wight.

Beyond the chapel and entered by way of a very fine wrought iron gate is the privy garden which is not open to the public. Near the centre of the bailey is the well house containing the wheel used to draw up the buckets of water. The well dates from the late 11th or early 12th Century and the house and wheel were built in 1587. Since the well is 161 feet deep the length of rope was considerable and heavy, and therefore a treadwheel-like device was built so that donkeys could be used to draw the water. The castle is officially allowed five donkeys, and each does two hours work a day. In order to turn the wheel sufficiently to draw up one bucket of water the donkey walks the equivalent of 300 yards. The great, oak framed 16th Century wheel turns the operating shaft and so draws up the water. At the eastern end of the bailey, not quite in line with the main gateway, is a gap in the curtain wall, and behind this is an open space known as The Old Barbican where Charles I spent some of his time playing bowls. A path skirts the motte and steps lead up to the keep. This was first built in the 12th Century but was originally much higher, and it is known that at least one portcullis backed up the heavy gate. In addition to the well in the well house there is a second one in a room in the keep, which is probably the older of the two.

Open to the public from 9.30 a.m. on weekdays and from 2 p.m. on Sundays until 7 p.m. May to September, 5.30 p.m. March to April and October, 4 p.m. November to February. Admission, summer 20p, winter 10p, Children and OAPs 5p.

Cartington Castle, *Cartington, Northumberland. North of Rothbury.*

The masonry remains were largely restored in the 19th Century but it is possible to trace the founda-

tions of several other buildings. The castle had a square courtyard with a large 14th Century tower on the east end of the northern range of buildings. At the other side, the south, there are two towers, one of which houses a garderobe. The hall was on the west and seems to have been sub-divided during the late 15th Century.
On private land.

Castle Acre, *Castle Acre, Norfolk. Four miles north of Swaffham on the north bank of the river Nar.*

There is a large circular mound with surrounding ditch, and to the south another horseshoe rampart and ditch. Like Pevensey (qv) this was originally a Roman site and measured 350 feet by 420 feet with 20-foot-high banks. They kept the Roman road running north to south through the camp and put gatehouses at either end where it crossed the ditch, the present Bailey Street. On the motte the Normans put a shell keep from which radiated some walls to unite with the main curtain wall. Traces of some of the domestic buildings may still be seen, and the north gatehouse still remains with its two flanking towers and portcullis room and grooves. In 1085 Earl William de Warrenne founded a monastery at Castle Acre within the castle walls, but later the priory and monks were removed outside the walls.
Open to the public at any time. Admission free.

Castle Ashby, *Castle Ashby, Northamptonshire. Situated at the end of a very long drive near the church.*

A castle stood here from the 11th Century, but by the 16th Century it seems to have been completely flat. In 1574 the first Lord Compton started work on the present building. It stands around an open courtyard and has a number of 17th Century additions and alterations, but the whole is still in a fine state of preservation.

Open to the public Good Friday to Easter Monday, then all Sundays and Bank Holidays April to September. Also Thursdays and Saturdays June to August 2–5.30 p.m. Admission to Houses and Terraces 40p, Children 20p, Gardens and Terraces 15p.

Carisbrooke Castle – King Charles's detention here was only one incident in an eventful history

Castle Batch, *Weston Supermare, Somerset. North-east of Warle, near Warlesbury Camp.*

An earthwork ring with a moat.

Castle Bourne, *Belbroughton, Worcestershire. One-and-a-half miles east of Belbroughton.*

A late 18th Century folly with two round towers and a short length of wall.

Castle Bytham, *Castle Bytham, Lincolnshire.*

Large-scale earthworks with wide ditches, large bailey, probably dating from the 11th Century but demolished in 1221. Almost all the masonry has disappeared.

Castle Carlton, *South Reston, Lincolnshire. Half-a-mile north-west of the valley, at Carlton Hill.*

Motte and two baileys with surrounding ditch. All

that is left of a castle of Hugh Bardolf, Justicar of Richard I.

Castle Cary, *Castle Cary, Somerset. North-west of Wincanton, on the B3152 which joins the A371 and A359.*

To the north-east of the church are the scanty remains of a castle built by Walter de Douai; mounds and indications of a large keep and ditch survive.

Castle Combe, *Chippenham, Wiltshire. On B4039, six miles north-west of the town.*

Built by Walter de Dunstanville in 1270, the castle was neglected by the 15th Century, and now only a few fragments of masonry from the two-storey keep remain.

Castle Dore, *St. Sampson, Cornwall.*

Standing a little way outside the village is an earthwork probably dating from the Iron Age. Excavations have discovered numerous fragments of pottery and traces of potholes indicate a large timber building, probably of the 5th Century. The potholes suggest something within the region of 100 feet by 40 feet wide. There were two ramparts, with huts and chambers near the entrance.
On private land.

Castle Drogo, *Drewsteignton, Devonshire. One mile south-west of the village.*

Built between 1910 and 1930 by Sir Edwin Lutyens, predominantly Tudor in the general exterior appearance.

Castle Eden, *Castle Eden, County Durham. North of Hartlepool.*

There is no trace of an earlier castle; the present one was built in 1780 and remodelled in 1823.

Castle Frome, *Castle Frome, Herefordshire. Quarter of a mile east of the church.*

Traces of a bailey with a motte 150 feet in diameter and fifteen feet high.

Castle Godwyn, *Painswick, Gloucestershire.*

Built during the second quarter of the 18th Century, with some battlements but some classical features as well.
On private land.

Castle Goring, *Goring, Sussex. On A259 between Worthing and Littlehampton, about one mile west of Goring.*

Goring Castle, seen among the trees from Highdown Hill, is the large house built *circa* 1790 by Sir Bysshe Shelley.
On private land.

Castle Howard, *Malton, North Riding, Yorkshire. Four-and-a-half miles south-west of Malton.*

This property has belonged to the Howard family since 1571, although there was rebuilding in 1683, and after a damaging fire in 1693. The present magnificent mansion was built for the 3rd Earl of Carlisle between 1699 and 1726, and there is some dispute over whether Hawksmoor or Vanbrugh should receive the credit. A "castle" in name only, it is a building of palatial proportions and richness, visible for miles in a superb parkland setting and boasting some fine pictures, furniture, and a collection of historic costume.
Open to the public Easter Sunday to first Sunday in October, 1.30–5 p.m., grounds 12.30–6.30 p.m.; Bank Holiday Mondays, 11.30 a.m.–5.30 p.m. Admission: house, garden and costume galleries 50p, Children 30p; house and gardens 35p/20p; gardens 20p/10p.

Castle Malwood, *Munstead, Hampshire. One mile north of Munstead.*

A yellow brick building of 1892.

Castle Nick, *Castle Nick, Northumberland.*

This is Mile Castle No. 39 of the Roman Wall; it measures 70 feet by 50 feet, with a gateway of small masonry. It can be seen from Hotbank and Peel Crag.
On private land.

Castle Rising, *Castle Rising, Norfolk. Four miles north-east of Kings Lynn.*

This site is now two miles from the sea but when built it was directly on the shore. Like Castle Acre (qv) this was originally a Roman fort. William I gave the lands first to his half-brother Odo and then to d'Albini, and it was d'Albini's son who probably started the castle. Traditionally it was here that Isabella, the "She-Wolf of France", mother of Edward III, was imprisoned. Only the keep has survived and a few foundations of Henry VII's time, for it was in poor condition as early as the reign of Edward IV (1461–1483). The keep is 75 feet by 64 feet and 50 feet high with a good forebuilding on the east side with a staircase leading up to the second floor. A wall divides the keep from east to west and on the outside there are pilasters. There is a basement with a kitchen and well on the north side and in the north-east corner a spiral staircase leads to the upper floors. The keep is entered up a flight of stairs on the east face with a door halfway up, and the sockets for the bars to bolt it can still be seen. At the top of the stairs is a lobby and beneath this is a prison cell. On the north side of the keep is the hall, and at the west two small apartments; from the hall there is access to the lodging apartments with numerous small chambers.

Open to the public:

	Weekdays	Sundays
March–April	*9.30 a.m.–5.30 p.m.*	*2–5.30 p.m.*
May–Sept.	*9.30 a.m.–7 p.m.*	*2–7 p.m.*
Oct.	*9.30 a.m.–5.30 p.m.*	*2–5.30 p.m.*
Nov.–Feb.	*9.30 a.m.–4 p.m.*	*2–4 p.m.*

Castle Sleads, *Dalton, North Riding, Yorkshire. Half-a-mile south-west of the village.*

This is a four acre, Iron Age hill fort with some stone-faced ramparts and a wide ditch.
On private land.

Castle Spofforth, *Spofforth, West Riding, Yorkshire. Five miles south-east of Harrogate.*

William de Percy arrived in England in 1067 and was granted considerable holdings by William the Conqueror, amongst them Spofforth. It was here that he set up his headquarters and it was here that the Percy family founded their fortunes. The male line died out but continued through the female side of the family from the late 13th Century, when the husband of the heiress had to agree to take the name of Percy. Henry, the son of this marriage, obtained from Edward II in 1308 a licence to fortify his house, but Spofforth was never a complete castle with curtain walls and keeps and was seldom more than a fortified manor house. In 1408 Spofforth passed from the Percy family but they recovered it later. After the Battle of Towton in 1461 the Yorkists plundered the area and burnt and seriously damaged the castle. The family suffered many ups and downs and in 1489 the then-owner, Lord Herbert, was murdered by a mob at Topcliffe and the castle was then neglected. In 1559 it was restored and used as an occasional dwelling by the then-Lord Percy, but in the 17th Century the castle seems to have been totally abandoned and fell into ruins.

The castle stands on the west slope of the village on some high ground but little now remains except part of the western set of buildings. The undercroft below the hall is the oldest part and probably dates from the first half of the 13th Century. It has only three walls, the fourth being formed from the rock itself. The building has two storeys which contained the principal apartments, the hall at the south end and the family's private chambers at the north. The main room in the cellar is at the northern end, which contains a large fireplace; originally there were windows on the west and north walls, but there have been extensive alterations. From the north-east corner a doorway leads off into a smaller chamber and a second door at the south-west corner leads to another room on the south, probably intended as some sort of lobby. On the upper floor there is a very large room with fine, light windows. Although none survives the room must have contained a fireplace. At the northern end of the hall is a small room which is thought to have been the original chapel, later modified to serve as an ordinary room. There is yet a further room at the very northern end. The hall as it stands is mainly 15th Century. Within the castle precincts there are a number of mounds beneath which are the foundations of other buildings which have not yet been excavated.

Open to the public:

	Weekdays	*Sundays*
March–April	*9.30 a.m.–5.30 p.m.*	*2–5.30 p.m.*
May–Sept.	*9.30 a.m.–7 p.m.*	*2–7 p.m.*
Oct.	*9.30 a.m.–5.30 p.m.*	*2–5.30 p.m.*
Nov.–Feb.	*9.30 a.m.–4 p.m.*	*2–4 p.m.*

Castlethorpe Castle, *Castlethorpe, Buckinghamshire. To the west of the church.*

A 36-foot-high motte with a well preserved inner bailey and an outer one with a rampart on the west, the whole encircled with a ditch 60 feet wide.

Castle Toll, *Newenden, Kent.*

A large, early earthworks and a motte and bailey site is to be found one and a half miles north-east of Newenden.

Castleton Castle, *Castleton, North Riding, Yorkshire.*

Situated on Castle Hill is a Norman motte although on this occasion there is no trace of a bailey. The motte is of horse-shoe shape and there are traces of a stone building of *circa* 1160.

Caus Castle, *between Stoney Streeton and Rowley, Shropshire. Ten miles west of Shrewsbury.*

Built by Roger FitzCorbet above the valley of the Rea, in the 11th Century, it was taken and burnt by the Welsh in 1134 but later repaired. It formed

an impressive site, with baileys and a shell keep with strong walls. It saw action during the English Civil Wars, being held for the king, but surrendering after a week's siege. Only mounds and fragments survive as well as traces of the keep and well.

Cave Castle, *South Cave, East Riding, Yorkshire.*

Built early in the 19th Century and altered in 1870, it has turrets, gatehouse and battlements.
On private land.

Caverswall or Careswell Castle, *Blythe, Staffordshire. One-and-a-half miles north of Blythe Bridge railway station.*

Licensed in 1275 to Walter de Caverswell, but most of the present building dates from the 17th Century. It is three-storeyed and battlemented with one tall tower imitating medieval style.

Cawood Castle, *Cawood, West Riding, Yorkshire.*

Originally just a palace of the Archbishop of York, it was fortified during the reigns of Henry IV and Henry VI. The surviving gatehouse dates from the period of Archbishop Kempe (1426–51); it has a broad entrance with a low arch. At the corners are turrets and above the entrance was the courtroom of the manor.

Chartley Castle, *Hoxon, Staffordshire. One mile north of Hoxon. Near the parish church of Stowe.*

Above the present mansion are the remains, two circular towers and a curtain wall, of a castle probably of the 13th Century. It was decayed by the 16th Century but the walls are still twelve feet thick and the keep was 50 feet in diameter. Mary, Queen of Scots stayed in the nearby manor house prior to going to her death at Fotheringhay.
On private land.

Cheney Longville Castle, *Cheney Longville, Shropshire.*

Although licensed in 1395, little remains beyond the courtyard; the present house has no crenellation.

Chester Castle, *Chester, Cheshire. South-west corner of the city walls.*

The remains of the original castle are limited to Caesar's or Agricola's Tower which, for many years, was used as a powder magazine and stands partly on the old Roman walls. There are two wards, the upper on high ground with some remains of the Norman towers at each corner. A building used for a long time as a courtroom was known as Hugh Lupus Hall; it measured 99 feet by 45 feet and was 50 feet high. This was demolished in 1830 and the gatehouse and towers were also removed. Chester town walls are still in good repair and at the north-west corner stands the Water Tower, circular, with a diameter of 30 feet and standing 72 feet high. In 1643 Chester was besieged and was to remain so for nearly three years; the town refused no less than nine calls for surrender before giving in on February 3rd 1645.
Open to the public at the discretion of the military authorities.

Chiddingstone Castle, *Chiddingstone, Kent. Five miles east of Edenbridge via Bough Beech and Hever.*

Although the castle was built during the 18th and 19th Centuries, the interior incorporates part of a manor house of the late 17th Century, much of it retaining the original panelling. It houses a very fine collection of antiquities and a particularly outstanding collection of Japanese swords.
Open to the public Easter Saturday to October 31st daily except Mondays 2–5.30 p.m.; Saturdays and Sundays and Bank Holiday Mondays 11.30 a.m.– 5.30 p.m. Admission 30p, Children 15p, Fishing 50p. Special rates for parties of 20 on application.

Chidiock Castle, *between Bridport and Lyme Regis, Dorsetshire.*

This castle was situated in a field by the new church. It saw some fighting during the Civil War but by the 18th Century it had practically disappeared and today only traces of the moat remain.

Chilham Castle, *Chilham, Kent. Five miles south-west of Canterbury.*

The original castle, situated on a hill and surrounded by a deep ditch, covered some seven or eight acres. There are traces of an early Roman camp in the grounds. The land was ceded by the Conqueror to his half-brother Odo. The surviving castle consists of part of the three-storey keep and the north-west angle; the present Chilham was built in 1616 by Sir Dudley Digges. Chilham is the seat of Viscount Massereene and Ferrard; features of interest open to the public include displays of falconry and a museum of relics of the Battle of Britain.
Open to the public: gardens only, May to October daily 2–6 p.m. except Mondays and Fridays. Admission (1972) 25p, Children 15p, Children under five free.

Chillingham Castle, *Chillingham, Northumberland.*

This building dates from the 13th Century, when it is recorded that it was sacked by the Scots on one of their numerous visits. A licence was awarded in 1344, and the south-west section certainly dates from this period. The castle has four corner turrets and was square, with a central courtyard, entrance on one side (south or west), the Great Hall to the east and a plain wall on the north. On the west were the domestic buildings, sufficient to accommodate 100 horsemen. In the 17th Century it was converted to a residence and in the mid-18th Century the grounds were carefully landscaped.
On private land.

Chipchase Castle, *Chipchase Castle, Northumberland.*

A mid-14th Century castle, 50 feet by 35 feet by 50 feet high, the turrets rising a further ten feet. There are machicolations on walls and turrets. There were four floors, each a separate room with small chambers set into the walls. Entry was on the east side with a strong door and portcullis, and

on this side a 17th Century mansion was added.
On private land.

Chipping Norton Castle, *Chadlington, Oxfordshire.*
North of the churchyard.

Mounds showing the position of the earthworks
of a castle belonging to the FitzAlans of Clun,
which was apparently destroyed by Stephen in
1145.

Chipping Ongar Castle, *Chipping Ongar, Essex.*
To the east of the town.

A high motte with a moat, still with masonry
remains of the castle. Probably built during the
reign of Henry I (1100–1135). The land at the time
of Domesday was held by Eustace, Count of
Boulogne but it later passed into the hands of the
Crown. It was apparently pulled down during the
reign of Elizabeth (1558–1603) and a house was
built which was, in turn, destroyed in 1774.

Cholmondeley Castle, *Cholmondeley, Cheshire.*

The old building dated from the late 16th Century
and was remodelled by Vanbrugh early in the 18th
Century. However, most of it was demolished to
make way for the present house built in 1801–30.
It is well castellated.
On private land.

Christchurch Castle, *Christchurch, Hampshire.*

The manor of Twineham, in which Christchurch
stands, was a royal one, but in 1100 Henry I
granted it to his cousin Richard de Redvers. The
great motte dates from his ownership although the
castle hall was probably built about 1160–80. The
manor belonged to the Earls of Devon until the
late 13th Century when, once again, it became
Crown property. Although many of its owners met
violent ends (for example, the Countess of Salisbury, who was beheaded in the Tower in 1541, and
the Lord Protector, Edward Duke of Somerset,
who was executed in 1552) the castle saw little
action until the English Civil War. It was held for
the king by the governor, Sir John Mills. In April
1644 a meeting was called to discuss the Royalist
plans, and a group of Roundhead cavalry, under
Sir William Waller, surprised and captured most
of the leading Royalists. Nearly a year later, on
January 15th 1645, Lord Goring attacked and
captured the town although the Parliamentary
garrison held out in the castle and the church.
Goring did not have a chance to attack the castle,
for a false alarm that a relief force was on the way
caused him to withdraw. In 1650 Parliament
ordered that the castle should be demolished but
the order was not immediately carried out. In 1946
the castle hall was given to the then Ministry of
Public Buildings and Works, and in 1953 Sir
George Meyrick placed the remains of the keep
and mound also under the Ministry's guardianship.

The castle hall stands in the garden of the King's
Arms Hotel, to the north of the Priory church, by
the side of a mill stream running from the River
Avon. It was probably the home of the constable
of the castle and has two rooms on the first floor
fitted with fairly large windows. A wall divides off
the solar, or private room, from the more public
section known as the hall. As the east wall fronted
the river and formed part of the curtain wall of the
castle, it is considerably thicker than the other
walls. An interesting architectural feature is the
very tall, circular Norman chimney. During the
13th Century a privy tower, or garderobe, was
added at the south-east corner but only the arches
over the stream are preserved. The ground floor
was probably used for a store; it is some 68 feet
long and 24 feet wide and is entered only from the
bailey.

The few remains of the keep stand to the west of
the hall and are on top of a motte about 27 feet
high. Unlike most keeps it is oblong rather than
square, with internal measurements of 30 feet by
27 feet, and the walls were about nine feet thick.
It rose for at least three storeys, most probably
with the entrance on the first floor. It was probably
built early in the 14th Century.

Open to the public:

	Weekdays	Sundays
March–April	*9.30 a.m.–5.30 p.m.*	*2–5.30 p.m.*
May–Sept.	*9.30 a.m.–7 p.m.*	*2–7 p.m.*
Oct.	*9.30 a.m.–5.30 p.m.*	*2–5.30 p.m.*
Nov.–Feb.	*10 a.m.–4.30 p.m.*	*2–4.30 p.m.*

Chun Castle, *Morvah, Cornwall.*

Above the small village, 700 feet high, stands a hill fort in the shape of an oval with two lines of stone walls, one twelve feet thick.

Clare Castle, *Clare, Suffolk. About eight miles west of Haverhill.*

Only a few fragments remain of a castle which was built on the site of earlier earthworks. There were two baileys separated by a ditch, and a mound 100 feet high in the north-west corner of the inner bailey; the whole was surrounded by wet ditches. Part of the keep, which was polygonal with buttresses, survives; there are traces of a curtain wall also. Clare was given to Richard FitzGilbert by the Conqueror, and at a much later date it was a royal castle.
Open to the public at all times.

Claxton Castle, *Claxton, Norfolk. Seven miles south-east of Norwich.*

This castle was licensed in 1341 and 1377. There are slight remains of one long wall with three round towers which were built in red brick.

Clearwell Castle, *Clearwell, Gloucestershire.*

Known until early this century as Clearwell Court. It is a battlemented house of mid-18th Century origin with later repairs and alterations.
Open to the public April 1st to October 28th, Wednesdays, Thursdays, Fridays, Saturdays, Sundays and Bank Holiday Mondays 11 a.m. to 5.30 p.m. Admission Adults 25p. Children 15p.

Clifford Castle, *Clifford, Herefordshire. Two-thirds of a mile north-west of the church.*

This castle was built by William FitzOsbern, Earl of Hereford, but it later passed to the Clifford family. It covers more than three acres and has a motte at the west end of the bailey on which stood a polygonal shell keep with five semi-circular projections spaced around the wall. There is a 13th Century gatehouse with round towers, and there are remains of the great hall.

Clifton Castle, *Masham, North Riding, Yorkshire. Two and a half miles north-north-west of the village.*

This was designed by John Foss 1802–10, but despite its name it bears only the faintest resemblance to a castle.
On private land.

Clinch Castle, *Ingram, Northumberland.*

A Roman fort.

Clitheroe Castle, *Clitheroe, Lancashire.*

On the summit of a limestone hill. The site was given to Roger de Poictou following the Battle of Hastings but was confiscated by King Stephen (1135–1154). It was slighted by Parliament in the mid-17th Century. The surviving keep is square with flat, square, corner towers, one containing a spiral staircase. It is only 35 feet square and is said to be the smallest in England. The bailey has part of the south wall remaining, although the circular gate tower has gone.

Clun Castle, *Clun, Shropshire.*

The tall Norman keep was protected by the river on the north and west sides; there are extensive earthworks on this site as well as two semi-circular towers.

Cockermouth Castle, *Cockermouth, Cumberland. At the junction of the Derwent and Cocker rivers.*

This castle was situated at the junction of two rivers and so was protected on three sides. It was built by William de Fortibus in the mid-13th Century. Part of the west tower, some parts of the north and south curtain walls and a part of the original gatehouse all date from this period, but the rest is mostly mid-14th Century. On the east is the outer gatehouse with its barbican, and in the south-west corner is a spiral staircase. Most of the buildings in the outer ward are 18th and 19th Century additions but in the south-east corner is a square tower, the Flag Tower. The inner and outer wards are separated by a late 14th Century ditch. The inner gatehouse was fitted with a drawbridge and also has machicolations and, internally, doors lead off to some small rooms which were probably prison cells. The kitchen tower is in the north-east corner of the inner ward with a staircase leading down to its basement. On the west is Great Hall with a solar and another chamber.

On private land, but open to the public Mondays to Fridays 10 a.m.–5 p.m. if convenient.

Codnor Castle, *Codnor, Derbyshire. One mile east of Codnor.*

Built by Lords Grey of Codnor in two parts; the lower section is separated by a wall with two circular towers at the ends and a gateway with two turrets. In the upper court were the living quarters. Both structures appear to date from the 13th and 14th Centuries.

Cogges Castle, *Cogges, Oxfordshire.*

South-west of the church by the side of the river Windrush, traces of a moat and ramparts.

Colchester Castle, *Colchester, Essex.*

Colchester has been inhabited for a very long period of time and there is evidence of a settlement at least as early as the 5th Century B.C. By the 1st Century A.D. the settlement had increased in importance and had become the capital of King Cunobelin or, to give him his Shakespearean title, Cymbeline. Led by the Emperor Claudius the Romans invaded Britain in A.D. 43, and had soon subjected Essex and had established themselves in Colchester, known by them as Camulodunum. It was made a colony, which was essentially a settlement for legionaries who had served their term of service and were then given a grant of land and permitted to settle down. The town

flourished, and one of the most important buildings within the town was the temple of Claudius which had been built in honour of the victorious Emperor. In A.D. 60 Queen Boudicca (Boadicea) led her tribe—the Iceni—in a very serious rebellion against Roman rule. The rebels overwhelmed the Roman army and sacked Verulamium (St. Albans) and Camulodunum (Colchester). No doubt many of the veterans fought bravely but they were unable to prevent the storming and sacking of the town. Tacitus reports that many fled to the temple, but within a few days this also had been captured and burnt. The foundations of the temple survived and bear to this day marks of the great fire.

Following the final withdrawal of the Romans in the 5th Century A.D., the town suffered a number of raids from the Saxons and Vikings and never really regained its position of importance. During the 13th Century Colchester did become an important port, with ships plying to Winchelsea and France with oysters as one of the prime products handled. Following the Norman Conquest it was decided to erect a castle there, an event which seems to have taken place around 1080–85. The very substantial surviving foundations of the Emperor Claudius' temple were selected by the architect as a suitable base for his new castle. The castle belonged to Eudo, who was steward to William I and Henry I, although it did later become Crown property. During the barons' revolt against King John one of the previous constables of the castle, William de Lanvalei, was given back command. In 1215 the French, who with papal approval were opposing King John, landed some 7,000 men in Suffolk and a force under the Earl of Winchester occupied the castle. King John and Savaric de Mauleon led their armies in a determined attempt to drive out the French.

Following this brief spell of military glory the castle appears to have lapsed into the role of prison. This was its prime function right up to the English Civil War. Colchester was held for King Charles although, judging by subsequent events, the people of the town did not necessarily support this position. The Cavaliers held out for some three months, defying all efforts by Lord Fairfax and Parliament's army to break in, but eventually, in August 1648, they surrendered. For various reasons the two Royalist leaders, Sir Charles Lucas and Sir George Lisle, were especially detested by Parliament, and they were accused of various crimes and put on trial. They were detained in the long vault near the well house and, after being found guilty, they were sentenced to be executed by a firing squad. They were shot on the 28th August 1648, and a stone commemorates this vindictive execution. Another small monument in the grounds of the castle is dedicated to the memory of James Parnell, a nineteen-year-old Quaker prisoner who, as a direct result of illtreatment and downright cruelty died whilst imprisoned in the castle. Following the Civil War the castle was rather neglected and in 1683 a local ironmonger was given permission to demolish the building; but, fortunately for posterity, the job was too much for him and he was unable to complete the task.

The castle is unique in one respect, for it has the largest keep in Britain and indeed in the whole of Europe, measuring some 151 feet by 110 feet. It is basically rectangular in shape with towers at each corner and a semi-circular apse on the south-eastern corner. When built it was three storeys high but, thanks to the efforts of the ironmonger, the top storey has now disappeared. The first keep was heightened, for on the eastern side the masonry clearly shows that there were originally battlements which were later filled up. On the south-east corner, rather in the manner of the Tower of London, the semi-circular apse of the chapel projects. The great size of the walls required considerable strength in the masonry and the face of the keep is strengthened by half pillars, or pilasters. Naturally when the Normans were building the castle they used the materials which were to hand and in consequence a lot of the Norman building actually incorporates Roman materials. In the tower adjoining the gateway is a very fine spiral staircase which, in common with most of those built into castles, spirals clockwise. Spiral staircases are made in this way so that anybody climbing the staircase has his right—sword—arm on the same side as the central pillar, the newel. This inevitably cramped his movement while the defendant, presumably facing down towards the attacker, was far more advantageously placed.

In the tower at the north-west corner there is a small postern gate at first floor level. Inside, the tower is divided into three sections by two walls running roughly from north to south. Two of the divisions are quite narrow whilst that at the west is the widest. The fine, large fireplaces are Norman and differ from the normal type in that the flues do not go up chimneys but slope backwards with double openings in the outer wall. In the basement was the well, and there are a number of garderobes, or privies, dotted around the walls. Of considerable human interest are the mementoes of past visitors and prisoners in the keep, for there are numerous carvings and graffiti on the wall at various points. The inside of the keep was empty and dilapidated for many years, and the building lacked a roof, but in 1932 the great hall was roofed and fitted with galleries which house the interesting collection of local relics. In the 13th Century the entrance was reinforced by a barbican but all other external defences have largely disappeared, although there are ample remains of the banks and ditches to the north. These, presumably, would have run all the way around the castle and there are also traces of walls extending from the south-west corner of the main keep. In many ways the keep at Colchester resembles the White Tower of the Tower of London and it is possible that the same architect was concerned in both ventures.

Open to the public weekdays 10 a.m.–5 p.m.; Sundays (summer only) 2.30–5 p.m. Admission free: tour of vaults and cells—weekdays only—10p.

Colcombe Castle, *North of Colyton, Devonshire.*

The remains of a castle of the Courtenay family, the Earls of Devon: originally 13th Century: the remains suggest that there were extensive buildings with the kitchen at the north end.

Colebridge Castle, *Edgerton, Kent.*

Very little survives of this small castle which lies at the base of a hill near Edgerton and for which a licence to crenellate was granted in 1314.

Compton Castle, *Compton Pauncefoot, Somerset. Just south-east of Castle Cary (qv), just south-west of Wincanton.*

Built about 1825 for Hussey Hunt, with lawns stretching down to a lake, in castellated style but with some 17th Century work in the courtyard. *On private land.*

Compton Castle, *near Marldon, Devonshire.*

The original manor house was probably built in the 14th Century but there were modifications at later dates. It later became the home of Sir Humphrey Gilbert, the discoverer of Newfoundland. Considerable alterations were carried out over the period, and in 1808 the entire estate was sold off in lots and Mr. John Bishop purchased the castle and converted it to a farmhouse. The hall was destroyed; there is no moat, but the north front with the gatehouse still remains complete with its machicolations over the doorway and a marked symmetry in design.

Open to the public: April to October, Mondays, Wednesdays, Thursdays, 10.30 a.m.–12.30 p.m. and 2–5 p.m. Admission 20p, Children 10p.

Conisbrough Castle, *Conisbrough, West Riding, Yorkshire. Four-and-a-half miles south-west of Doncaster.*

The very name is probably derived from the Anglo-Saxon word Cyningesburh, which means the king's burh—a fortified settlement of the king—and this seems to suggest that there were fortifications here long before the Norman Conquest. At the time of the Domesday survey the land was held by William de Warenne, first Earl of Surrey but his wooden castle was probably converted to masonry by Hamelin Plantagenet, the half-brother of Henry II. Although the castle saw little military action it had a chequered ownership and from the 14th Century onwards was frequently in the hands of the king. From the mid-15th Century it seems gradually to have been abandoned and by Tudor times it was largely derelict. A survey of 1538 declared that bridge, gates and much of the curtain wall had fallen and the keep had also suffered, indeed it was in such a poor condition that during the English Civil War it was not even considered possible to defend it.

The main castle buildings are set on the top of the hill, whose sides were steepened by cutting away some of the earth. The outer bailey was defended only by a bank and ditch and the present entrance probably occupied the site of the original gateway which was defended by a drawbridge. The inner ward is roughly oval-shaped and was circled by a tall curtain wall. The bottom parts of the walls and tower slope in such a way that stones dropped from the top of the walls would be likely to bounce off at the correct angle to cause maximum damage to besiegers. From the curtain walls projected half-round towers, some of which still survive on the south wall. The northern wall had only buttresses, since the lie of the land was nearly sufficient protection. There are still some traces of the domestic buildings which were on the inside of the castle curtain wall and the foundations of some may be traced. The keep, probably built by Hamelin Plantagenet, is one of the best surviving examples of 12th Century architecture. It is essentially a cylindrical tower with a splayed base and is fitted with six large, wedge-shaped buttresses which are later than the keep itself. The present steps are modern and the original entry was on the first floor, guarded by a heavy door which was bolted by two draw bars, the holes of which can still be seen. The walls are fifteen feet thick and enclose a passage which leads up to the first floor room. The only way down to the basement was by means of the hole in the centre of the floor. The well was set in the centre of the ground floor but this is now blocked. On the east side there is a wide staircase which leads up to the great chamber which contains a very large fireplace. Near this is a wash basin recessed into the wall and opposite is a small garderobe. The third floor, reached by a staircase in the wall, was probably used as the lord's bedroom. The chapel is set into one of the buttresses, being of an elongated hexagonal shape. From the third floor a vaulted staircase leads from an offset garderobe up to the wall walk and parapet at the top of the tower, which originally had a conical roof.

Open to the public:

	Weekdays	*Sundays*
March–April	*9.30 a.m.–5.30 p.m.*	*2–5.30 p.m.*
May–Sept.	*9.30 a.m.–7 p.m.*	*2–7 p.m.*
Oct.	*9.30 a.m.–5.30 p.m.*	*2–5.30 p.m.*
Nov.–Feb.	*9.30 a.m.–4 p.m.*	*2–4 p.m.*

Cooling Castle, *Cooling, Kent. One mile east of Cliffe.*

The licence to crenellate the building was granted in 1380, and it consists of two rectangular enclosures with circular corner turrets and a moat. The east ward has a large gatehouse at the south-

west corner, complete with projecting barbicans. The gatehouse survives in almost perfect condition, with its two semi-circular towers, its portcullis and fine machicolations. The gateway itself is fifteen feet high and was closed with strong doors. During the latter part of the 19th Century a number of farm buildings were erected on the site. The western, or inner bailey was very much smaller than the other. In the north-east corner of the bailey stood the great hall. Part of the walls which survive are between fifteen and 27 feet high. This castle was attacked by Sir Thomas Wyatt during his rebellion.
On private land.

Corby Castle, *Corby Castle, Cumberland.*

The beginning of this edifice is of uncertain date, but it began as a pele-tower of the Salkeld family built either in the 13th or 14th Century. The remains stand on the right of the site by the entrance to the house; in the early 17th Century it passed to the Howard family and they added a large range of three-storey buildings.
On private land.

Corfe Castle, *Corfe, Dorsetshire. Midway between Wareham and Swanage.*

The castle stands on an isolated hill and the ruins cover an area of more than three acres. In Norman times the upper bailey formed a motte and on it William the Conqueror built the usual wooden tower, which was replaced by a stone keep by Henry I. Even before this the motte had been encircled by a stone wall and a stone hall had been built in the middle, or western, bailey, and part of this wall survives. Henry II and Edward I had the whole area enclosed within stone walls and towers together with two gatehouses, one in the outer and one in the middle ward. On the old Norman motte Henry III built himself a beautiful palace. As the castle and town were royal, every Saturday the citizens of Corfe had to carry beer and bread from Wareham to Corfe for the constable's use. During the Civil War the castle was twice besieged by Parliament's forces. In 1643 it was defended by Lady Banks, the owner's wife—and successfully,

although the siege was conducted with great determination, including the use of a wooden protective device known as the "sow". The garrison, from the flanking towers, fired at the legs of the men pushing the "sow" up to the wall; nine out of the eleven inside were wounded and one was killed. Next the besiegers brought up heavy guns, including some which they mounted on the church tower; they melted down the lead from the roof to make bullets. Another battery was planted on the west side of the castle, where the earthworks remain today. Marines were brought in to assail the castle but they were beaten off, and finally, on August 4th 1643, Sir Walker Earle called off the siege. For three years the castle was left untroubled, until 1646, when Lady Banks was in London and the castle garrison was commanded by Colonel Anketil; but this time the castle was betrayed. Goods to the value of £1,300 were removed by Parliament's men. On March 5th 1646 Parliament ordered that the castle should be demolished. Gunpowder was used to blow up the walls and two-thirds of the keep were blown away, but 60 feet of it still stands unsupported. Many other towers of the castle suffered even worse damage.
The ruins are open to the public.

Cotherstone Castle, *Cotherstone, North Riding, Yorkshire.*

Situated to the north of the village at the junction of two rivers with a steep escarpment to the north. The licence to crenellate was granted in 1200–01, but little remains and there is no trace of a bailey.

Cottingham Castle, *Cottingham, East Riding, Yorkshire. Also known as Baynard's Castle. Three miles from Beverley.*

Little remains except the motte which can be seen from the West Green, and part of the moat behind houses in West End Road and Northgate. It was built about 1320 and was then known as Baynard's Castle; it was destroyed by fire during the reign of Henry VIII.

On private land.

Coupland Castle, *Millfield, Northumberland. Two miles south of Millfield.*

One of a chain of forts recommended in 1584 to protect the border; it is "L"-shaped and has a staircase in the short arm of the "L". The inside was restored in the 19th Century and the house was built *circa* 1820.
On private land.

Cow Castle, *Simonsbath, Somerset.* On a steep hill, with a rampart, is this earthwork in a very poor state of preservation.

Cowes Castle, *Cowes, Hampshire.*

The Royal Yacht Squadron buildings occupy the site of one of Henry VIII's two castles on the island; the semi-circular platforms facing the sea are part of the original castle although the rest is by Salvin, *circa* 1856.

Cowton Castle, *South Cowton, North Riding, Yorkshire.*

An oblong tower built for Sir Richard Conyers in the late 15th Century.
On private land.

Cranbrook Castle, *Drew Steignton, Devonshire. One mile south of village.*

An Iron Age earthwork near the banks of the river Teign, more than 1,000 feet above sea level.

Crayke Castle, *Crayke, North Riding, Yorkshire.*

This belonged to the Bishop of Durham and stands on the site of a Norman motte and bailey castle. The remains are of 15th Century origin but there are 19th Century additions.
On private land.

Croft Castle, *Leominster, Herefordshire. Five miles north-west of Leominster.*

This was the home of the Croft family who headed the plot to put Lady Jane Grey on the throne. There are some remains of the 14th Century castle, which was quadrangular with circular, corner towers. In 1645 it was damaged by the Royalists and in 1746 it lost its north end. Some restorations were carried out, and the porch dates only from 1914.
Open to the public Easter Saturday to the end of September, Wednesdays, Thursdays, Saturdays, Sundays and Bank Holiday Mondays. Also Saturdays and Sundays during October. 2.15–6 p.m. Admission 20p, Children 10p.

Cromwell's Castle, *Tresco, Scilly Isles.*

This is the remains of a 17th Century gun tower built to defend the town of New Grimsby. Some alterations were undertaken during the period following the Civil War and much of it was made up with stones extracted from another castle. (See King Charles' Castle.) It is a low, round tower with very thick walls and is situated at the foot of a hill.
The ruins are freely accessible.

Cropton Castle, *Cropton, North Riding, Yorkshire.*

To the west of the church lies a triangular bailey with a large motte, 150 feet in diameter and 50 feet high, at the west end; there are traces of the foundations of a large hall.

Crowhurst Castle, *Crowhurst, Sussex.*

The small remains of a two-storey building 40 feet by 23 feet, with a porch on the south-east corner over which is a small room. The castle dated from 1251, but a Norman castle predated this.

Cynwit Castle, *Cannington, Somerset.*

Situated on a hill; the earthworks from which King Alfred's men fell upon the Danes. There are indications of occupation during the Iron Age, and a number of skeletons have been excavated.
On private land.

Dacre Castle, *Dacre, Cumberland.*

Another 14th Century pele-tower but with twin projections; that on the south-west contained the garderobes whilst the other, to the north-west, housed the staircase. In the very early 18th Century windows were let into the walls. There is a good basement and the hall occupies the main floor with a solar above—known as the King's chamber.

Dally Castle, *one mile south of Greystead, Northumberland.*

Set on a high ridge with a moat at either end, this castle was built in 1237 but suffered a common fate in supplying raw materials for local building. Now only foundations are visible, together with some fragments. There were two main blocks, one of which is rather obscure.

Dalton Castle, *Dalton, Lancashire.*

A two-storey tower occupies the site of an Agricolan Roman fort; it seems to have served more as a place of refuge than a true castle, probably being erected during the time of Edward III (1307–1322). In the 16th Century a commission ordered its repair and it was used as a prison for the whole of Furness. During the latter part of the 19th Century it was the armoury of a local Rifle Volunteer group.

Danby Castle, *Danby, North Riding, Yorkshire. One mile south-west of the village.*

Some ruins of late 14th Century buildings; a courtyard 50 feet by 22 feet, with a much later farmhouse added.
On private land.

Dartmouth Castle, *Devonshire. One mile south-east of Dartmouth, off B3025.*

Following the Conquest in 1066 many Norman lords were given lands within this area. Dartmouth's importance increased, and it was from here that the fleet carrying the English to the Second Crusade gathered before setting sail. It was also an important port for the wine trade from France; it declined somewhat after Gascony was lost to the English, but by Tudor times its prosperity was again increasing. The importance of the town naturally made it a potential target for French raids; in 1336 Edward III gave orders that defensive precautions were to be taken, and in 1338 the townspeople under the leadership of John Horley, the Mayor, were building a small fortress by the sea. The curtain wall and ruin of a tower near the present car park are probably the remains of this building, which may have consisted of no more than a deep ditch and a thick curtain wall with two or three towers flanking it. It does not seem to have been in use for very long and by 1539 it was described as deserted.

In 1402 one of the leading citizens, John Corp, was granted a licence to crenellate but little is known about this, although there was a tower on Paradise Point, demolished in the middle of the 19th Century. The fears of Dartmouth people were realised in 1377 when there was a French raid on the coast, and in 1404 six thousand French, under Du Chatel, attacked Dartmouth itself. During the 15th Century it seems that a chain, or boom, was stretched across the harbour mouth but it was not until 1481 that the construction of the present castle began. The townspeople again seem to have been the prime movers and Edward IV made some allowance to them for this public spirited act. The stronghold consisted of a circular tower with a rectangular one built alongside and eventually united to the round one. The process of building was slow and was still going on at least in 1495. Although the castle was incomplete during this period it was at least protected, for there are records of powder and shot being purchased and in 1491 four watchmen were being paid to keep the castle.

Dartmouth is the first castle known for certain to have been designed to depend entirely on guns for protection. (By 1390 gun ports are found on the west gate of Canterbury, but these were adaptions.)

Guns were placed in the basement near the water-line with accommodation for the garrison on the two floors above. The windows are splayed to allow some lateral movement of the gun barrel, and the bottom of the window is level with the floor—for the cannon of this time were simply barrels secured to a solid wooden base-board. In 1567 the rock floor of the basement was dug out and this may well have been to accommodate improved types of guns. In 1545 there is mention of a "Lamberd's Bulwark," this was a battery of guns situated at the top of the cliff above the beach, the site now being occupied by the granite 19th Century battery. The French threat disappeared during the 16th Century, but that of pirates from Morocco was still very strong, and defences were maintained. During the English Civil War the town of Dartmouth declared for Parliament but the castle was captured by Prince Maurice in 1643, after a siege of one month. Five hundred men were left to garrison the castle; when news of the Battle of Naseby reached them it was obvious that the castle would soon be attacked by Parliament and extra earthworks were formed on the high ground by the side. Mount Ridley above Kingswear and Gallant's Bower above Dartmouth Castle are examples. In January 1646 Sir Thomas Fairfax decided to attack the castle, and at 11 a.m. on Sunday 18th the attack opened. Despite heavy fire from the defences casualties were extremely light, and by Tuesday morning all the defences had surrendered. The new fort of Gallant's Bower was ordered to be demolished but the original castle was kept in repair.

The Dutch threats following the Restoration led King Charles II, in 1672, to order an additional block house, or fort, and the Elizabethan Lamberd's Bulwark was rebuilt using stone. However, as the Dutch threat passed the defences were allowed to fall into disrepair. Desultory repairs continued, and the last major defence efforts were made in 1861, again probably as a result of the supposed French threat. A strong battery was built on the site of the Maiden Fort, the one known as the Old Battery, and even as late as 1940 a brick position for a 4.7-inch gun was built on one of the two upper buildings of the Old Bailey. The emplacement was deliberately disguised to blend with the rest of the castle. The War Department handed over the castle to the Commissioners of Works in 1907 and in 1909 and 1959 the last parts were made

over to the Ministry as a National Monument. On the headland to the left of the car park is the Old Battery; this is the one that was built in the 1860s. On either side of the main castle are the gun platforms with embrasures altered during the 18th Century. The bridge leading to the tower is modern, for it was originally entered from the lower road by a bridge over a ditch. The round tower was built of large rubble; work was stopped before the tower was finished and the square tower was begun beside it. This is obvious from the different sizes of stones, which are largely of slate. The door to the castle is in the square tower at a slightly higher level than the original although essentially in the same position. The castle has three storeys with the entrance directly into the ground floor. The room is square, with eleven small openings for hand-guns, and all the other openings were made at a later date. The three overlooking the river are probably Elizabethan and were cut to allow the insertion of cannon within the room. The join between the two towers is clearly visible where it has been butted in with rough materials. The round tower room has small openings which were probably intended for muskets, whilst the very large timber-framed opening suggests that the chain which was stretched across the harbour mouth passed through it over a pulley; the various positions for the axles of different pulleys can still be seen. The chain would probably have been pulled in by some form of capstan, the housing for which can be seen in the holes at the back of the room. Whenever the chain was in use the far end was fixed on the Kingswear side. The basement is very small; the ceiling was lower by three feet and the rock floor was higher by fifteen to eighteen inches. The ledges for the beams can be seen, and there are seven openings for the guns in the wall facing the sea; these are the earliest examples of this type of gunport known in England. Hinged shutters were fitted on the outside and these could be closed when the guns were not run out. This part was used during the 19th Century as a guard-room, although later it became a coal store. The round tower room has been altered considerably, with some of the walls being cut back. The upper openings are narrow and were intended for muskets, with a small fire step for the gunner to stand on. The lower openings are gun ports similar to those in the square tower. This room was eventually used as a magazine. Following up the stairs, the first floor or main living room is reached. This is now open and the partition which originally divided it into three has gone. This room was known in the 19th Century as the Governor's room. There is a fireplace and also a latrine which opens out on to the rocks below. In the square tower there may have been one long room. The roof is approached by a newel staircase which is reached through a pointed arch. The original roof was about level with the lowest of the lead gullies. On the side facing the land the battlements are higher because extra protection was needed since the castle was overlooked by the higher ground. There are four machicolations over the castle entrance.

Open to the public:

	Weekdays	Sundays
March–April	*9.30 a.m.–5.30 p.m.*	*2–5.30 p.m.*
May–Sept.	*9.30 a.m.–7 p.m.*	*9.30 a.m.– 7 p.m.*
Oct.	*9.30 a.m.–5.30 p.m.*	*2–5.30 p.m.*
Nov.–Feb.	*10 a.m.–4.30 p.m.*	*2–4.30 p.m.*

Admission (1972) 5p, Children and OAPs half-price.

Daws Castle, *Watchet, Somerset.*

A very minor section of a prehistoric earthworks, off the Blue Anchor Road.

Deal Castle, *Deal, Kent. One mile north of Walmer Castle and seven miles north-east of Dover.*

Henry VIII was well aware that plans were in hand to attack England, and he prepared to defend the country against French invasion; to this end he constructed a network of forts to protect the most vulnerable areas. Numerous castles were built along the coast including five between the Thames at Tilbury and Gravesend. Three were at Dover, one of which, Moats Bulwark, before the castle, is still complete. Others were at Southampton, the Isle of Wight and near Falmouth. The castle at Deal was built between 1538 and 1540, and together with the castles at Sandown and Walmer was placed under the control of the Lord Warden of the Cinque Ports. This castle was, for its period, of

Dunstanburgh Castle, largest in Northumberland, covering nine acres on the North Sea coast

revolutionary design, with its rounded surface to deflect cannon balls and its general siting, construction and position. After some fifty years, in 1595, the castle was in need of repair and another twenty years (1615) saw it described as being in a dangerous condition.

During the Civil War the castle was held for Parliament; for the greater part of the war it remained untroubled, until 1648 when the men of Kent, dissatisfied with Parliament, broke into open rebellion. The rebellious crowds marched to London, but finding no popular support, melted away. Deal Castle was taken over by the rebels when part of the Navy proclaimed itself Royalist. Following the dispersal of the rebel army some of the other Royalist castles surrendered, but Deal held out against the Roundheads. In August a Royalist force tried, unsuccessfully, to lift the siege and suffered heavy casualties, and shortly afterwards Deal surrendered. Despite sundry alarms and excursions during the next three centuries little of military note happened to the castle, until during World War II it was struck by a German bomb and one of the bastions was destroyed.

Essentially Deal Castle consists of a number of circular edifices placed one within the other. The inner keep has six large semi-circular bastions spaced around a central circular space, and around this central block is the curtain wall with another six curves, the whole so arranged as to cover any gaps between bastions. The outside bastions level with the first floor of the keep are battlemented, but this was a feature added in 1732. The outer wall is Tudor but the bridge at the entrance is modern. The entrance was well protected with drawbridge, portcullis, and an iron-studded and barred door which is still in position. The keep was used as the living quarters for the garrison of a Captain and twenty-four men. In the basement were kept the stores whilst on the ground floor was a kitchen, bakery and living quarters for the men. On the first floor were the captain's quarters. There is a good museum of local archaeology housed in the gatehouse.

Open to the public:

	Weekdays	*Sundays*
March–April	*9.30 a.m.–5.30 p.m.*	*2–5.30 p.m.*
May–Sept.	*9.30 a.m.–7 p.m.*	*9.30 a.m.– 7 p.m.*
Oct.	*9.30 a.m.–5.30 p.m.*	*2–5.30 p.m.*
Nov.–Feb.	*10 a.m.–4.30 p.m.*	*2–4.30 p.m.*

Deddington Castle, *Deddington, Oxfordshire. East of the town.*

Some mounds mark the site of this castle, which was probably built in the late 12th Century and was demolished in the 16th Century; but sufficient survived to allow it to be held by the king, and it saw action during the Civil War. In 1312 Piers Gaveston, the favourite of Edward II, was held here and snatched away by his chief enemy, the Earl of Warwick, to be taken to Warwick and beheaded.

Denbury Castle, *Denbury, Devon. Half a mile west of the village.*

Prehistoric earthworks.

Desborough Castle, *West Wycombe, Buckinghamshire. To the south-east of the town.*

A one-acre hill fort, probably of Iron Age origin.

Devizes Castle, *Devizes, Wiltshire.*

The earthworks are probably pre-Conquest. Henry I was responsible for the first big castle here, and it was enlarged by Bishop Roger, who erected a shell keep and mural towers. There was a ditch, drawbridge and a barbican. In 1106 Robert, son of William I, was held prisoner here for a while. By the 16th Century the castle was already in ruins and was being used as a source of raw materials for local building. In 1645 the gatehouse suffered attack but soon surrendered. In 1842 the house was largely rebuilt under the direction of H. E. Goodridge. Two towers with some fine windows and the original moat still survive.
On private land.

Dilston Castle, *Dilston, Northumberland.*

In the 13th Century a manor house, but the tower which is here today was built in the 15th Century. It is rectangular, 39 feet by 23 feet; at the south end there was an added extension, thirteen by eighteen feet which rises to the same height as the

two-storeyed tower but is, in fact, of three storeys. There is a 17th Century chapel and by it an archway dated 1616. In 1805 the vault was opened and the head and body of the Earl of Derwentwater were found; he was executed for supporting Bonnie Prince Charlie.
On private land.

Doddington Castle, *Doddington, Cheshire. Four miles south-east of Nantwich.*

A licence to crenellate was granted in 1405 to John de Delves for a tower in Doddington Park, and the surviving remains probably date from this period. Sir John Delves was granted a licence in 1365, and it is known that there was a two-storey keep with battlemented turrets on the site. In 1643 Doddington Hall was besieged and taken by the Royalists but it was soon recaptured by Parliament.

Doddlestone Castle, *Doddlestone, Cheshire. South-west of Chester.*

West of the church—a rectangular enclosure with a moat, and a motte with its separate moat. Originally the home of the Boydel family.

Donnington Castle, *Newbury, Berkshire. One-and-a-half miles north of Newbury.*

Sir Richard de Abberbury was granted a licence to crenellate Donnington in 1386, but this would seem to apply to the gatehouse which appears to have been added to an earlier building. Later he was also given permission to start some alms-houses in the village. The castle stands on a hill overlooking the river Lambourne and, in keeping with the fashion of the time, it was rectangular with four round towers. Midway along the east front was the gatehouse of Sir Richard with its two round towers, and this is the only part of the castle that has survived. In 1415 the castle was sold to Thomas Chaucer, son of the poet, but eventually it passed into the hands of William de la Pole, Duke of Suffolk. However, the family later ran foul of Henry VII and Donnington was forfeit to the Crown.

When the English Civil Wars started Donnington was owned by John Packer, who opposed the king, but it was seized by the Royalists and after the First Battle of Newbury it was fortified and garrisoned by Colonel John Boys. On 31st July 1644, a Roundhead force sent by General Devereux demanded the surrender of the castle; this was courteously but firmly refused. Troops commanded by Lieutenant-General Middleton attacked but suffered heavy losses, and it was decided that a siege would achieve the capture with far fewer casualties. A heavy bombardment did extensive damage, but still the garrison refused to surrender and even mounted strong sorties, capturing weapons and stores. Charles I took an army towards Newbury, raised the siege, and knighted John Boys, the commander of the castle. On 27th October 1644 the Second Battle of Newbury was fought, but it was indecisive. The Royalist army slipped away to Oxford but left the king's treasure and his guns in the castle. Again Parliament besieged the castle, and threatened that if it was not surrendered then not one stone would be left standing. There were delays in mounting the attack, and there was a touch of chivalry shown when the Parliamentary commander sent to the castle to warn them that the well had been poisoned. On 9th November the king once again relieved the castle, collected his stores and treasure and then moved on again. Boys held out despite the fact that the castle was now partially in ruins; he re-stocked with supplies and still managed to carry out raids on the Roundheads. After the defeat of Charles at Newbury even Boys realised that the situation was hopeless; he surrendered the castle but not his arms, and he was allowed the honours of war, marching out of the castle with drums beating and colour flying. After the Civil War John Packer retook possession and built himself Donnington Castle House. In 1946 the castle was placed under the care of the Department of the Environment.

From a height of 400 feet the castle dominated the Bath road, and on the slopes of the hill the line of the 17th Century artillery fort can be seen. The castle enclosed a space measuring 110 feet by 69 feet, with high walls, four towers and a gatehouse. The corner towers are small and contained only a staircase. There are two square towers set at the centre of the north and south walls. Sir Richard probably had his apartments in the south-west corner of the courtyard whilst the chapel was probably sited in the north-east corner. The gatehouse is the only part of the castle which has survived to any degree; it is 65 feet high, comprising three storeys with the two flanking towers going up for a further two storeys. There was only one drawbridge and portcullis and a barbican, and the roof has some rather unusual vaulting.

Open to the public:

	Weekdays	*Sundays*
March–April	*9.30 a.m.–5.30 p.m.*	*2–5.30 p.m.*
May–Sept.	*9.30 a.m.–7 p.m.*	*2–7 p.m.*
Oct.	*9.30 a.m.–5.30 p.m.*	*2–5.30 p.m.*
Nov.–Feb.	*10 a.m.–4.30 p.m.*	*2–4.30 p.m.*

Dorchester Castle, *Dorchester, Dorsetshire. North of Sheep Lane, to west of Priory.*

The castle was part of a Roman camp; it was demolished in 1365 and a priory was erected. The site is now occupied by a prison. To the north-west of the town is Castle Mount with some earthworks, and in 1720 underground passages were discovered which linked the two sites.

Dorstone Castle, *Dorstone, Herefordshire. Less than a quarter of a mile to the south-west of Dorstone.*

An oval motte measuring 200 feet by 180 feet and rising to about 20 feet. There are indications of a bailey to the north-east with a ditch running along the south side.

Dover Castle, *Dover, Kent. On the east side of Dover.*

On the top of Dover's cliffs there are signs of occupation dating back to the Iron Age, and within the borders of an earthwork are found the traces of a Roman lighthouse and a Saxon church. The main castle dates from the period following the Norman invasion or perhaps just prior, since some areas were under strong Norman influence even during the reign of Edward the Confessor. All traces of the first Norman castle have gone and the present masonry edifice dates from the reign of Henry II (1154–1189), with most of the work dating from *circa* 1180, and it was continued during the reign of Richard I. A great keep was erected, together with a curtain wall, under the control of Maurice the Engineer—who received 8d a day, later raised to 1/-. He incorporated many flanking towers into the design of the curtain walls, fourteen around the inner bailey, together with two gates; in the north King's Gate, and in the south Palace Gate. Both gates had barbicans, but only the northern one survives.

Dover Castle's strength was put to the test when, in 1216, Prince Louis of France and his troops besieged it and Hubert de Burgh only just managed to hold them off. The northern gate was mined and after the fighting was over there were determined efforts to repair and strengthen this area. An outwork was built in front of the gate, which was blocked up, and further towers were erected to complete a most formidable defence. Henry III also had the curtain wall extended, and although that on the east has largely gone that on the west is still in good repair. He also had a hall put up in 1240, although this too has gone, and by 1256 the castle was essentially the same size as that seen today. In the 15th Century further work was carried out, and in Tudor times the defences were kept in good repair and strengthened for fear of a French or Spanish invasion. During the English Civil Wars the townspeople took the castle over in the name of Parliament, and consequently it was not slighted after the war. For a century the castle was left in peace but in 1745 it was felt that it should be brought up to date, and some quite savage "modernisation" was undertaken. The entire southern barbican was removed together with associated towers, the keep was strengthened to withstand heavy artillery, the eastern curtain wall was demolished, and most of those towers surviving were reduced in height.

Entrance to the castle is by Canon's Gate at the southern end of the curtain wall, with its mural towers, all erected by Henry III although modified in the 18th and 19th Centuries. The gateway, Peverell's Tower, is a composite construction of the reigns of John and Henry III. The wall from here to the northern point, the Norfolk Tower with its group of three strong bastions, is mainly of John's reign except for the brick section between Peverell Tower and the next mural one, Queen Mary's Tower, which is 18th Century. The main gateway, Constable's Gate, was let into the wall between 1221–27 and was exceedingly strong with five towers all united to form a hall and guard chambers, although even this group has suffered at the hands of the restorer. The inner bailey has its curtain wall with towers and barbicans and at the centre stands the keep. It is square (98 feet by 96 feet) and rises to 95 feet high. On the east face is a strong forebuilding protecting the entrance on the second floor. The first and second floors form self-contained apartments, that on the second probably being for the king. During the reign of Edward IV some extensive alterations were carried out. Spiral staircases lead up to the roof where there are corner turrets, and there are numerous mural chambers. To the south-east of the keep lies the pharos, the Roman lighthouse, an octagonal tower rising to a height of 80 feet and dating from the 1st Century A.D. Nearby is a church of the 10th or 11th Century.

During the siege of 1216 Hubert de Burgh constructed some underground earthworks and these were modified by 18th and 19th Century engineers and form an interesting part of the castle. During the Second World War Dover and the surrounding countryside were subjected to bombardment by German guns, but fortunately the castle did not suffer. The gun at Dover Castle, known as Queen Elizabeth's pocket pistol, is of an earlier vintage, dating from 1544.

Open to the public:

Keep	Weekdays	Sundays
March–April	9.30 a.m.–5.30 p.m.	2–5.30 p.m.
May–Sept.	9.30 a.m.–7 p.m.	9.30 a.m.–7 p.m.
Oct.	9.30 a.m.–5.30 p.m.	2–5.30 p.m.
Nov.–Feb.	10 a.m.–4.30 p.m.	2–4.30 p.m.

Grounds and Underground passages
Weekdays as above. Sundays 10 a.m. to sunset.

Dowsborough Castle, *Nether Stowey, Somerset.*

At the east of the village on Castle Hill, the moat and earthworks of a castle.

Drawdykes Castle, *Houghton, Cumberland. One mile south-east of Houghton.*

A pele-tower fitted, late in the 17th Century, with a three-storeyed front to convert it to a dignified house for John Aglionby.
On private land.

Drumburgh Castle, *Bowness-on-Solway, Cumberland. Three miles south-east of Bowness-on Solway.*

A portion of the original 16th Century castle wall was built into the present house, but an early castle certainly stood here, for a licence to crenellate was granted in 1307.
On private land.

Dudley Castle, *Dudley, Staffordshire.*

In the 11th Century the land was held by William Fitz-Ansculf, whose name appears in the Domesday book, and he built a castle there. In 1173 Gervase de Pagenel, who was then the owner, was one of the lords who revolted against Henry II (1154–1189), who promptly attacked and demolished the castle. However, in 1264 Roger de Somery was given a licence to crenellate—that is, to erect a fortified building. He fought in the Barons' War on the king's side, and was captured at the Battle of Lewes (1264). In 1300 the castle passed to Sir John de Somery who, by contemporary accounts, would appear to have been a real-life example of the "robber baron" of fiction. Some remodelling was carried out by the Duke of Northumberland during Tudor times under the direction of Sir William Sharington, who was a very keen advocate of the Italian style of building. In 1644 the castle was besieged by Parliament's forces, holding out for three weeks before it was surrendered. In May 1645 it was finally surrendered to the Roundhead General Sir William Brereton and, in accordance with the usual policy when dealing with any captured Royalist castle, it was slighted, that is the fortifications were rendered useless (1646). The main domestic buildings were largely unaffected by the slighting but in July 1750, for three days, a great fire raged throughout them causing very considerable damage. Tradition has it that the fire was a result of an accident caused by some coiners.

The castle stands on a hill over 100 feet high and has an oval bailey some 340 feet from north to south and 265 feet at its widest point; it is surrounded by a very deep ditch cut into the limestone. Beyond the ditch is another raised bank. The mound is at the south-west corner overlooking the town and, unlike many of these early castles, the wooden fortifications seem to have remained in use until the 14th Century. The gatehouse and barbican which still remain do include some Norman stonework and there were some stone buildings within the castle walls. During the period of Sir John de Somery's occupation of the castle his nefarious activities, amounting to outright brigandage, dictated a need for extra protection, and he built a large tower-house. He sited it at the top of the Norman motte and made it roughly oblong with drum shaped towers at the corners. The entrance was defended by a portcullis and the top of the wall was fitted with a parapet with battlements. He also had the bailey walled in and some new domestic buildings were erected along the eastern side, presumably to house some of Sir John de Somery's villainous soldiery. In addition there were a kitchen, a hall, a church and a great chamber.

There is an interesting and certainly rather unusual modern development at the castle, for the great earthworks have been adapted to house a zoo with an outstanding collection of animals.

Dudley Castle and Zoo open daily 10 a.m.–7 p.m.

Duffield Castle, *Duffield, Derbyshire.*

At the end of Castle Hill is the motte of a large Norman castle built by the Ferrers family, and originally supporting a keep almost as large as the White Tower of the Tower of London.

Dumwalloght Castle, *Cumrew, Cumberland.*

William de Dacre received a licence in 1307 to crenellate his manor house, and some traces survive.

Dunham Massey Castle, *Dunham Massey, Cheshire. North-west of the present house.*

There is little evidence of the castle which stood here and belonged to Hamon de Masci in the 11th Century, apart from the traces of a motte. *On private land.*

Dunstall Castle, *Earls Croome, Worcestershire. One mile north-east of church.*

A mock Norman Castle with two round towers, arches and a square tower.

Dunstanburgh Castle, *Dunstanburgh, Northumberland. One-and-a-half miles north of Craster.*

This is the largest castle in Northumberland, with the ruins covering no less than nine acres. It stands on a basalt cliff on the North Sea coast of the county, near the small fishing village of Craster. There is a long line of walls and towers and a keep, the gatehouse, on the left, of the usual round form although all the other towers are square. It was started in 1313 by Thomas Plantagenet, Earl of Lancaster, who then held the Barony of Embleton, and licence to crenellate was granted in 1316. Later alterations were made in 1372 and in 1383 when John of Gaunt, Duke of Lancaster, built up the gatehouse and made a new entry on the left of the castle, which then led directly into the courtyard. The keep or towerhouse was shut off by a small enclosed courtyard with its own separate gateway. The tower wall which runs along the edge of the cliff is built in 40-foot sections and is probably the work of local craftsmen. The modern approach is over the mouth of an old harbour from which the ditch ran, 80 feet wide and thirteen feet deep. The keep was 80 feet high and was originally the gatehouse, and a barbican was added to it later which was approximately 21 feet by 38 feet. There were four posterns on the outer bailey, two on the eastern sea wall, and the Egyncleugh Tower, which was at the east end of the south wall. There is an uncompleted moat at the front of the south wall.

Open to the public:

	Weekdays	Sundays
March–April	*9.30 a.m.–5.30 p.m.*	*2–5.30 p.m.*
May–Sept.	*9.30 a.m.–7 p.m.*	*2–7 p.m.*
Oct.	*9.30 a.m.–5.30 p.m.*	*2–5.30 p.m.*
Nov.–Feb.	*9.30 a.m.–4 p.m.*	*2–4 p.m.*

Dunster Castle, *Dunster, Somerset.*

Dunster Castle, scene of a famous siege in the English Civil War

Normans built the round towers, one of which remains with half its wall intact, and this is the only one of a dozen Norman castles in Somerset which was dismantled or destroyed by war. It was held for the Empress Matilda against Stephen by William de Mohun, who minted his own money even while surrounded by Stephen's men. It has belonged to only two families in all its history, for Elizabeth Luttrell bought it from the widow of the last Mohun in 1376. Part of it was built by Hugh Luttrell in 1421.

The castle was defended first for Parliament and then for the king during the Civil War. Luttrells were for Parliament, but the castle passed into the hands of the king and by the end of the Civil War was the only place in Somerset flying the Royal Standard. For 160 days it held out, and during this time it is said that the Roundhead commander, Blake, furious at the long resistance put up by Royalist Colonel Wyndham, threatened to put the Colonel's mother in the front line. In the 18th Century the castle was largely demolished, and has changed much; except for the Norman tower the oldest walls are now incorporated in the Tudor walls of the front. The oldest part of the structure

still in use is the 13th Century gateway leading up to the terrace. It has semi-circular flanking towers and an iron bound doorway. In this gateway is an ancient prison with an iron key plate which has spaces for eight keys. In the woodwork of the door is a bullet fired in the Civil War. In 1765 the 13th Century towers were fitted with battlements and different tops. In 1867 there were extensive alterations, but some fine early panelling and ceilings survived.

Open to the public: June—Wednesdays and Thursdays; July, August and September—Tuesdays, Wednesdays and Thursdays. Also Easter, Spring and Late Summer Bank Holiday Mondays. 10.15 a.m.–12.30 p.m., 2.15–4.30 p.m. October to May, Wednesdays only, 2.15–3.30 p.m.

Durham Castle, *Durham, County Durham. In the centre of the city.*

The castle was built on the hill above the river Weare. The original wooden structure, started in 1072, was strong enough to hold off a Danish attack in 1075. The gatehouse dates from the mid-12th Century, but was altered in the 16th Century. The four-storey keep is on a 44-foot-high mound and approximately 36 feet across its base. It has the entrance on the west side and was probably built around the mid-14th Century, a little later than the Great Hall, which was erected by Bishop Bek (1284–1311). In the 19th Century the castle was given over to the University.

Open to the public all the year—weekdays, first three weeks in April and July, August and September 10–12 a.m., 2–4.30 p.m. Mondays, Wednesdays and Saturdays remainder of the year 2–4 p.m. Admission 15p, Children 10p.

Eardisley Castle, *Eardisley, Herefordshire. West of the church.*

A mound, over 100 feet in diameter, is all that remains of a castle which belonged, at different times, to the De Bohun, Clifford and Baskerville families.

Eastnor Castle, *Eastnor, Herefordshire. Two miles east of Ledbury.*

Begun in 1812 by Sir Robert Smirke, it has round towers, a great hall 60 feet long and 65 feet high, and a gatehouse.
Open to the public Easter Monday, Spring Bank Holiday Sunday and Monday, and Late Summer Bank Holiday Monday 2.15–6 p.m. Also every Sunday June to September 2.15–6 p.m. Admission 20p, Children 10p.

East Retford Castle, *East Retford, Nottinghamshire. Two miles south-east at Castle Hill.*

A hill fortress extended during the English Civil War.

Eaton Bray Castle, *Eaton Bray, Bedfordshire.*

This was built by William de Cantelowe in 1221, but now only the motte and some masonry remains.

Eaton Socon Castle, *Eaton Socon, Huntingdonshire.*

Known as the Hillings: recent excavations have shown this to be the site of a castle with three clearly defined periods of building. The original was on a "D"-shaped site, and work was carried out in the 11th Century and again in the 12th Century. There is no trace of a motte.

Eccleshall Castle, *Eccleshall, Staffordshire. On the A519 from Newport to Newcastle-under-Lyme.*

In 1200 a licence to crenellate went to Bishop Muschamp, but the castle was later pulled down and rebuilt in 1310. The castle was badly damaged during the English Civil War and the remains used to build a farmhouse. Part of a tower and bridge still survive.

Eccleshall Castle, *Linton-by-Ross, Herefordshire. Three-and-a-half miles from village.*

Built in 1160/70 by Richard de Talbot, the castle has disappeared except for the motte, 120 feet in diameter.

Edlingham Castle, *Edlingham, Northumberland. Near the church.*

This tower-house was built, probably, towards the end of the 14th Century, and its first mention is in 1396. There was a bailey with the keep on the east and a gatehouse to the west. The keep was three storeys high with a vaulted basement. On the first floor was the hall, finely vaulted and with two good fireplaces. At the corners are diagonal buttresses.

Edmond Castle, *Hayton, Cumberland. Two-and-a-half miles south-west of Brampton, one mile north-west of Hayton.*

Built *circa* 1824–29 by Smirke in Tudor style with a battlemented top.
On private land.

Egremont Castle, *Egremont, Cumberland.*

The earliest motte stands outside the present castle and it held, at one time, a round tower. This castle was started by William de Meschines *circa* 1130; the wall and gatehouse date from this period and have a marked style of herringbone masonry. In the 14th Century the gatehouse was refaced. The hall block is largely ruined but the hall was on the top floor, probably in the 13th Century, and on the east side were other domestic buildings.
On private land.

Ellesmere Castle, *Ellesmere, Shropshire. Between Oswestry and Whitchurch.*

The site is occupied by a bowling green. It was a royal castle for many years but saw little action, even during the Civil Wars.

Elmham Castle, *Elmham, Norfolk. North of East Dereham and north of the village.*

In 1388 Bishop Spencer was granted a crenellation licence, and his manor house which stood inside an earlier earthworks was also surrounded by a moat. Few fragments remain.

Elmley Castle, *Elmley Castle, Worcestershire. South of the village.*

The late 11th Century castle is ascribed to Robert Le Despenser, but it fell into ruin and was largely rebuilt in the 14th Century. It again lapsed and was once more fortified in the 16th Century, but now only a few fragments mark the site.

Elsdon Castle, *Elsdon, Northumberland. North-east of the village.*

A very fine motte and bailey castle site with a ditch between bailey and mound—*circa* 1080.

Elvaston Castle, *Elvaston, Derbyshire.*

Extensively altered during the early 19th Century, it retains only one turret—on the right of the porch—from the old house, which was probably 17th Century.
On private land.

Ely Castle, *Ely, Cambridgeshire.*

A two-and-a-half acre motte and bailey castle, probably dating from the time of Henry I. The motte is about 40 feet high.

Essendine Castle, *Essendine, Rutland. Quarter of a mile south-east of the village.*

The remains of a motte and two baileys with a deep, wide moat.

Etal Castle, *Etal, Northumberland.*

A licence was given in 1341 to crenellate but in little less than a century (1438) it was ruined. In the 16th Century it was garrisoned by royal troops and it was captured by James IV, but apart from holding some Scottish prisoners at a later date it figured little in history, and by the end of the 16th Century it was again in disrepair. The site is roughly 180 feet by 170—with a gatehouse 36 feet square at the south-east corner with a long arch-way and guard rooms. The keep is opposite on the north-west corner and is four storeys high, 46 feet by 32 feet, with its entrance on the ground floor. Some small section of curtain wall remains.

Evenly Castle, *Evenly, Oxfordshire.*

Some fragments of a castle, possibly of the Norman period.

Ewhurst Castle, *Ewhurst, Surrey.*

Fragments of an Edwardian gatehouse with a guardroom at the side.

Ewyas Harold Castle, *Ewyas Harold, Herefordshire. Three hundred yards west of the church.*

A motte 75 feet in diameter and 40 feet high, and there are indications of a bailey to the north. It was built by William FitzOsbern in the 11th Century.

Eye Castle, *Eye, Suffolk.*

Only earthworks, a large oval with a tall motte, and a few masonry fragments survive on the north and south sides. The keep which once existed here was probably built by Robert de Malet in the 11th Century.

Eynsford Castle, *Eynsford, Kent. Just off Sevenoaks/ Dartford Road, A225.*

The land on which the castle stands was ecclesiastic land held, usually, by the Archbishop of Canterbury, and it is possible that a simple castle existed there as long ago as the Domesday survey. It was William de Eynsford I who, in about 1100, replaced the original wooden curtain with a strong stone one. This knight was unusual in that in 1135 he retired and became a monk of Christchurch. His son, William II, known as Gurham, built the stone hall which still exists on the site and he also increased the height of the curtain. The great hall and other buildings date from the third quarter of the 12th Century and were the work of William III (all the Lords of Eynsford were christened William right up until the time of the Reformation). This William was involved in a quarrel with Thomas à Becket over the appointment of a priest for Eynsford, and in some small way this quarrel, in which the king intervened, may have contributed to the troubles which eventually led to the death of Thomas à Becket. William V came near to ending the line, for he took an active part in opposing King John (1199–1216) and was amongst those who were besieged and captured in Rochester

Castle. John had threatened to hang the whole garrison, but in fact the knights were only held to ransom. Following the death of John, William V became an important official of King Henry III.

In 1261 the direct line ended when William VII died and the property was divided between the descendants of the sisters of William V. Around the middle of the 13th Century the hall suffered gravely from a fire but was reconstructed and even had some glass windows fitted. However, following the fire the period of occupation seems to have been fairly short. By the second half of the century there are indications that the castle was deserted and in 1264 the castle was seized because its owners had supported the barons against the king. Early in the 14th Century the castle was, for a while, inhabited again but there were disputes over the ownership. Nicholas de Criol, one claimant, apparently led his men into the castle and wrecked it, for excavation has shown that doors were ripped off, windows smashed and the whole place treated as a captured castle, to be sacked. The hall was patched up and used as a manorial courthouse but thereafter it does not appear to have been used for continuous habitation. From then on the story of the castle is one of conversions for other purposes. In 1783 it was used as hunting kennels, and the materials of which it was built used for other purposes. Gradually the walls and towers were demolished or fell down, and it was not until the beginning of this century that the first steps in its preservation were taken. The castle later passed to the Society for the Protection of Ancient Buildings who, in turn, passed it in 1948 to the Ministry of Public Works.

Eynsford had a bailey and at one end was a low platform surmounted by a tower and moat; this is the part that still survives. It was originally intended as a defensive position consisting of a watch tower which was situated more or less at the centre, with a strong wall around it. The curtain wall stands just 30 feet high, is six feet wide at the base and is constructed from flint rubble, much of which is laid so as to give a herringbone pattern. There are no towers or even arrow slits and it is quite plain. The original opening appears to have been to the east where, at the moment, there is a well which was dug during the 18th Century. When the hall was built the curtain was raised by an extra twelve feet. A bridge led to the main entrance and was originally of wood—there may well have been a drawbridge there. The supporting pillars of the bridge were changed for stone during the 13th Century. The gate tower, of which very little survives, was added at the same time that the wall was raised and there was a lookout post on the top of the wall. On the right of the entrance was the great hall; this was built in the first half of the 12th Century and severely damaged by the fire about 1250, subsequent to which there were some general repairs. Some Roman materials were incorporated into the walls.

The hall was a living area, with the main hall used for courts, etc., while the solar, which is at the northern end, would have formed the private chamber. Beneath the private chamber was an undercroft which might be used either for living quarters or as cellars. Of the great hall only the undercrofts have survived. Following the fire a kitchen was built on the eastern end of the undercroft of the hall, probably to replace the earlier great kitchen which is situated in the north-west corner. This kitchen probably dates from the late 12th Century, and remained in use until the castle was finally abandoned. The well was near the great kitchen. Excavations at the site of the hall have revealed pieces of glass which probably came from the windows of the hall and represent one of the earliest known uses of domestic glass in this country.

Open to the public:

	Weekdays	Sundays
March–April	*9.30 a.m.–5.30 p.m.*	*2–5.30 p.m.*
May–Sept.	*9.30 a.m.–7 p.m.*	*2–7 p.m.*
Oct.	*9.30 a.m.–5.30 p.m.*	*2–5.30 p.m.*
Nov.–Feb.	*10 a.m.–4.30 p.m.*	*2–4.30 p.m.*

Farleigh Hungerford Castle, *Somerset. Three-and-a-half miles west of Trowbridge, Wiltshire.*

Since a castle represented a position of strength and therefore was always a potential danger to the

Farleigh Hungerford Castle, originally built by the first known Speaker of the House of Commons

local lord or to the king, castle building was normally kept under control by the authorities. During periods of anarchy such as the reign of Stephen (1135–1154), when the central authority was very weak, men might build castles as they wished. Sir Thomas de Hungerford began to build this castle before he was, in fact, licensed to do so, but he was granted a pardon in 1383 for this breach of the regulations. Sir Thomas de Hungerford was a rich merchant and the chief steward of John of Gaunt's land south of the Trent. He was also the first recorded speaker of the House of Commons. His son, Sir Walter de Hungerford, was made Lord Hungerford in 1426, from which time the castle was known as Farleigh Hungerford instead of Farleigh Montfort as previously. Eventually it passed into the hands of Richard, Duke of Gloucester, who, on becoming Richard III, gave it to the Duke of Norfolk. The Duke was killed at the Battle of Bosworth Field; ironically, on the same battlefield Walter Hungerford, a descendant of the original owner, was knighted and, in 1486, he managed to regain possession of Farleigh Hungerford. The family suffered several personal tragedies, including a wife hanged at Tyburn and a husband executed for treason and unnatural vice! During the Civil War members of the family served on opposite sides, but eventually the castle was garrisoned by Parliament. In the late 17th Century the then-owner squandered a fortune and sold the castle, and by 1701 it was described as being in ruins. In 1891 it was again in the hands of the Hungerford family and in 1915 it was given over to the Commissioners of H.M. Works.

This castle was built in the 1370s and is very similar to those at Bolton and Bodiam (qqv), although there is some evidence to suggest that an earlier castle existed on this site. In 1342 there is a mention of a castle being burnt, and the layout of the building could be considered as indicating an earlier inhabited site. Certainly the natural features make the site very strong, for on one side is Dane's Dyke, a tributary of the river Frome, whilst on the east is the Frome itself. On the west an artificial storage pond was made and there is yet another ditch running across the site to the south. The main castle is square with cylindrical towers at each corner, and in the south wall is the gatehouse with its two rectangular towers with rounded fronts. Early in the 15th Century Sir Walter Hungerford, who had fought under Henry V and was for a while Treasurer of England, enlarged the castle and added the forecourt, with the main entrance being by way of the east gate which originally had a drawbridge. The extension is encircled by a wide, deep ditch and was defended by round towers with a postern on the north-west corner. The outer ward took in the local parish church of St. Leonard. Again the style of architecture and one or two other features suggest that when it was rebuilt by Sir Thomas it incorporated parts of an earlier church. As the castle now enclosed the old parish church which was now reserved for the Lord of the Castle, a new parish church was built. It was dedicated to St. Leonard and was consecrated in 1443. The former parish church has been modified and is now fitted out as a museum. It contains an effigy of Sir Thomas Hungerford.

Open to the public:

	Weekdays	Sundays
March–April	9.30 a.m.–5.30 p.m.	2–5.30 p.m.
May–Sept.	9.30 a.m.–7 p.m.	2–7 p.m.
Oct.	9.30 a.m.–5.30 p.m.	2–5.30 p.m.
Nov.–Feb.	10 a.m.–4.30 p.m.	2–4.30 p.m.

Farleton Castle, *Hornby, Lancashire. One mile south of Hornby, by the banks of the river Lune.*

Some fragmentary remains of a castle, owned at one time by the Harrington family, have survived.

Farnham Castle Keep, *Farnham, Surrey.*

Like Eynsford (qv), Farnham was an ecclesiastical estate which belonged to the medieval Bishops of Winchester. The town of Farnham does not appear in the Domesday book but grew up mainly during the 12th Century. As early as the 7th Century a charter states that land at Farnham was granted to the Bishop of Winchester but it was not until the time of Henry of Blois, Bishop of Winchester from 1129–1171, that any work began on the castle. He is also recorded as having built castles at Wolvesey and five other of his manors. The earliest castle was of the typical motte and bailey type, and the two wooden piers that survive in the hall may have been part of this original castle. However, the details of most of the buildings are very uncertain although the keep, on top of the 30-foot-high mound, is reasonably well documented.

In 1155 Henry II used the unauthorised visit by Henry of Blois to France as an excuse to pull down many of his castles. Farnham was probably one of those so treated, for it is known that the original keep had certainly gone by the 13th Century. Most of the stonework of the castle dates from the latter part of the 12th and the early part of the 13th Century. In 1216 Prince Louis of France, supporting the barons against King John, captured Guildford, Winchester and Farnham castles. In March Farnham was taken for the young King Henry III by the Earl of Pembroke, although the circumstances are unclear. The castle was in the charge of the constable and resident officials included a chaplain, a gatekeeper, a porter and probably a reeve, concerned with the running of the manor. For the great part of the year the castle was largely empty, being used only when the king or one of the bishops made a brief stay. It seems to have led a fairly peaceful existence apart from one mild flutter in 1265, when Simon de Montfort was known to be approaching the castle and some money was spent on preparing for a siege. There was a permanent store of weapons and armour kept in a special armoury and there are entries in the accounts for money paid out for oil to clean the weapons. By the late 14th or early 15th Century these entries cease so that, presumably, the weapons had long since vanished.

A great deal of building was carried out at Farnham by William of Wykenham who was Bishop from 1367 to 1404, but the very impressive brick tower was built by Bishop Waynflete (1447–1486). The accounts show that this was built in the five year period 1470–75. The bricks were made locally and replaced the local chalk which had been used on all previous occasions. Although built in the form of a tower it was primarily intended for domestic purposes and resembles a similar one at Tattershall (qv). From the 16th Century onwards the castle was used more and more as a dwelling place for the bishops but it was, at various times, leased out to other owners. The keep reflects these changes, for until the latter part of the 13th Century it was designed to serve as a final defensive position. By the end of the 13th Century a number of rooms including the Bishop's room were being used as living quarters, and in 1339 a small chapel was added. During the latter part of the Middle Ages further changes were made, again to afford more comfort as well as safety for the bishop.

When the English Civil War broke out in 1642 the castle was put in the charge of a Parliamentarian, George Wither, but he evacuated it and in November it was taken over by the Royalists. Since it is fairly close to London and situated in a predominantly Parliamentary area, it was very soon attacked. On 1st December 1642 Parliament's forces blew in the gate, and the Royalist commander surrendered. Parliament felt that they could not risk losing the castle again and orders were given for it to be slighted, but a garrison remained there throughout 1643–44. In January 1645 the Royalists made a daring raid and captured and held the castle for one day only. In July 1648 orders were given that it should be made untenable, and it was sold in 1649. With the restoration of Charles II the castle was restored to the Bishopric of Winchester and quite considerable sums of money were spent on alterations and restoration. The castle continued as a residence of the Bishops of Winchester until 1927, when the keep was made over to the Commissioners of H.M. Works. Some changes were made in the division of the diocese and part of the castle was altered to make a residence for the Bishops of Guildford, but they have not lived there since 1955.

The castle hill slopes steeply on the south but is almost flat on the north side, and a ditch and bank ran around where the present curtain wall stands. Part of the ditch still survives on the north and eastern sides. The wall was of late 12th or early 13th Century origin, built mostly of local chalk, but very little of the original work exists for it has been much refaced and rebuilt. Two or three square towers project from the walls, but they are really only extensions to the walls with no rear defence. The present entrance to the castle is through a brick gateway of the 17th Century, and then by way of the gatehouse which was preceded by a ditch and a drawbridge. The gatehouse is fairly simple, with two rectangular towers with rounded fronts. Inside the outer curtain wall, on the left, are some 18th Century stables now used as garages. To the north of the gatehouse stands the Bishop's palace with its great entry tower on the south side, with impressive looking—but false—machicolations. Contrary to the usual practice the curtain wall was not built on top of the mound but is rather around the base of the mound, rising up level with the top. On the outside of the curtain wall are four projecting turrets which are solid masonry up as far as the level of the mound, but there were originally rooms above this level. The entrance to the keep is modern, as are the steps which join the original entry, which was a three-flight stone staircase built against the east wall of the courtyard, leading up to the door. The drawbridge pit has now been filled in to form the top landing. The entry tower, like the others, was solid from the ground to the top of the mound but had rooms in the walls above this level. The doorway into the keep probably dates from the second half of the 12th Century; there are two holes for the draw bars of the drawbridge and above them is the portcullis slot. There is also a "murder hole" in the roof through which missiles could be launched against attackers. There is a short passageway leading in to the main area of the keep. In 1958 excavations were carried out here and at the centre of the keep were found the foundations of a tower 50 feet square with walls eighteen feet thick. The tower stood some 45 feet square and rose to some sixty or seventy feet above the top of the mound. At the centre was a well shaft thirteen feet square. To protect this interesting feature from the weather a concrete slab has been placed over it but steps lead down to an observation platform. The structure is interesting because it suggests that the original architects realised that the soft chalk of the original 12th Century mound was not strong enough to sustain the weight of a large stone keep. They therefore adopted this rather unusual method of sinking a foundation right down to original ground level.

At some time during the 13th Century the space between the sloping surface of the motte and the inside of the shell wall was filled in so that the whole of the mound was then level. The task was completed by the very early 14th Century. Between the entrance tower and the east turret the wall was slighted during the English Civil War. The east tower retains its original doorway although the steps leading to it are modern. The turret probably had two storeys and between these two towers the exit chutes for the latrines can be seen.

Open to the public:

	Weekdays	Sundays
March–April	*9.30 a.m.–5.30 p.m.*	*2–5.30 p.m.*
May–Sept.	*9.30 a.m.–7 p.m.*	*2–7 p.m.*
Oct.	*9.30 a.m.–5.30 p.m.*	*2–5.30 p.m.*
Nov.–Feb.	*10 a.m.–4.30 p.m.*	*2–4.30 p.m.*

Admission 5p, Children 2½p.

Farthingstone Castle, *Farthingstone, Northamptonshire. One mile north of the church.*

The earthworks, of a rather unusual style, of a large castle.

Featherstone Castle, *Haltwhistle, Northumberland. To the west of the village.*

This is a mixture of ancient and modern with some portions dating back to the 13th Century. In the 18th Century it was still fairly complete, with a rectangular curtain wall and a keep-like tower in one corner of the courtyard, which is square with two watch turrets. It belonged to the family of Featherstonehaugh.

Fillingham Castle, *Fillingham, Lincolnshire.*

Built in 1760, probably by Sir Cecil Wray, it is rectangular with circular corner towers and typical interior.
On private land.

Fillongley Castle, *Fillongley, Warwickshire.*

Castle Yard contains fragments of masonry, ditches and banks which mark the site of a Norman castle.

Folkingham Castle, *Folkingham, Lincolnshire.*

In Billingsborough Road, the remains of a moat and earthworks of a rectangular castle.

Ford Castle, *Ford, Northumberland.*

Licensed in 1338, William Herron fortified his manor house and built high, battlemented walls around a square courtyard. At each corner were square towers. At the centre of the south wall was the gatehouse and there were internal buildings along the north wall. In 1549 it was under attack by the Scots with French assistance but the besiegers were driven off. During the English Civil War it suffered at the hands of the Royalists. During the late 17th Century and throughout the 18th Century it was repaired and restored by various owners.
On local authority land.

Fotheringay Castle, *Fotheringay, Northamptonshire.*

The castle was probably started *circa* 1100 by the first Earl of Huntingdon, Simon de St. Liz, but it was extensively rebuilt by the Earl of Cambridge, the son of Edward III (1327–1377). The earthworks are probably 12th Century and the fragmentary masonry remains are 14th Century, but it was in considerable disrepair by the 18th Century. Its main claim to remembrance is the execution of Mary, Queen of Scots in 1587, in the hall. The scene has been graphically described and was full of incident, including the pathetic touch of her dog crouching for comfort in the skirts of the headless corpse. Only fragmentary remains of the castle can be seen today.
On private land.

Fouldry Castle, *Fouldry, Lancashire. A small island on the north shore of Morecambe Bay.*

A strong castle was erected here in the reign of Stephen and rebuilt in the 14th Century. It was an early example of the concentric castle, but much of the walls have gone and only some of the towers survive. There is a moat which was crossed by a drawbridge leading to a barbican on the west side, complete with its portcullis groove. The keep has its entrance on the north side, with portcullises and a passageway. It is square, about 60 feet long, but one side has fallen; it stood about 45 feet high, and at the corners were strong buttresses.

Fowey Castle, *Fowey, Cornwall.*

There was an embattled house known as "castle" and built by Thomas Treury, but it is now known as "Place House," with the entrance from the churchyard by way of a ruined gate. In 1734 there was still a square tower on each side of a narrow entrance; this housed an iron chain which crossed the estuary as a boom protection. To the west of the town is a circular earthworks.
Not open to the public.

Framlingham Castle, *Framlingham, Suffolk. Approximately four miles north-west of Wickham Market on the B1116.*

During the 12th Century there was a change of emphasis in castle design, more attention being given to the physical strength of each defence rather than the number of different defences. At Framlingham the curtain wall is fitted with a large number of square towers so designed that they could give covering fire along the bottom of the wall and, unlike some of the earlier wall towers, each of these has direct access to the courtyard. In the 12th Century Framlingham was the usual timber house, motte and bailey castle and belonged to Roger Bigod. The second son of the family, Hugh Bigod, was made Earl of Norfolk by Stephen and in 1173 he rebelled against Henry II. The king, returning from France, captured a number of rebel towns, and Framlingham surrendered. In 1175 it was completely levelled and the ditch filled

in, although the stone house was apparently left standing. The second Earl, the son of Hugh Bigod, Roger, rebuilt the walls and put up a chapel, probably at the turn of the century between 1190 and 1210. Roger also rebelled, this time against King John, who captured the castle in 1215. The castle stayed in the family of the Bigods until 1306 when it became Crown property, so remaining until 1312 when Edward II presented it to the Marshal of England, Thomas Brotherton. It passed then, via marriage, to the Mowbray family and Thomas, Lord Mowbray, who was a favourite of Richard II, was made the hereditary Earl Marshal of England, the first Duke of Norfolk. Henry IV took Framlingham when he came to the throne; the first Duke had been banished in 1399 and the new Earl Marshal, who had supported Richard II, was captured and beheaded at York in 1405. The Mowbray family died out and the Howard family inherited the castle in 1476. In 1513 Henry VIII created one of the Howards, Duke of Norfolk. Once again the family were in trouble with the king and the castle was taken over by the Crown. In 1553 Mary Tudor made her base here and gathered an army to attack the supporters of Lady Jane Grey; here she was proclaimed Queen of England, and in a very short time had disposed of the rebellion. In 1572 yet another member of the family went to the block because Elizabeth suspected that he was supporting Mary, Queen of Scots. James I gave the castle back to the Howard family but it stayed with them for a short time only and then passed to Sir Robert Hitcham. In 1636 Hitcham left the castle to Pembroke College, Cambridge, and much of the inside of it was destroyed to make a large poorhouse. This room is, at the present, used as a court house. In 1913 Pembroke college passed the castle to the guardianship of the then Ministry of Works.
Essentially the castle today consists of the wall only. It is entered by way of the bridge and gateway, at the top of which is sculpted the escutcheon of the second Duke of Norfolk. The main curtain wall is some 44 feet high, and its many towers were built between 1177 and 1215. The battlements were added by Thomas Howard, the second Duke of Norfolk. There is no separate keep, for the walls and towers were considered to be the main defences. The sides of the towers facing outwards are thick and strong whilst those walls on the inside, facing directly to the bailey, were almost certainly

of wood. The wall walk is reached by a spiral staircase housed in one of the towers. The rather attractive Tudor chimneys were added by members of the Howard family and, except on the eighth and ninth towers, are all dummies. On the west side is a small postern gate which leads down to the prison tower and the lower court.
Open to the public:

	Weekdays	Sundays
March–April	*9.30 a.m.–5.30 p.m.*	*2–5.30 p.m.*
May–Sept.	*9.30 a.m.–7 p.m.*	*9.30 a.m.– 7 p.m.*
Oct.	*9.30 a.m.–5.30 p.m.*	*2–5.30 p.m.*
Nov.–Feb.	*9.30 a.m.–4 p.m.*	*2–4 p.m.*

Frodsham Castle, *Frodsham, Cheshire. West end of the town.*

There are no visible traces of the Norman castle which stood here until at least 1727, but the ruins were pulled down to make way for Castle Park House which incorporated some of the Norman remains into the cellars.
On private land.

Giant's Castle, *Island of St. Mary, Scilly Isles.*

This is a prehistoric hill fort with three large trenches forming the main defences.

Gidleigh Castle, *Gidleigh, Devon. Near the Church of the Holy Trinity.*

The remains of a small Norman keep, some 22 feet by thirteen feet, which belonged at one time to the Proust family and was probably built by Sir William Prong, who died early in the 14th Century.

Gilling Castle, *Gilling, North Riding, Yorkshire.*

On a hill above the village. A conglomeration of 16th and 18th Century buildings based on the late 14th Century tower-house of Thomas of Etton. It is 80 feet square with the entrance on the west side, and to this has been added a Tudor manor house with an early 18th Century front. There are some fine ceilings, stained glass and panelling.
On private land.

Gleaston Castle, *Dalton in Furness, Lancashire. Two miles east of Furness Abbey, one-and-a-quarter miles west of Aldingham.*

This castle is quadrangular with the north end wider than the south; it has four corner turrets with connecting curtain walls, to form a bailey approximately 170 feet wide at the north and 120 feet at the south. The high walls are about nine feet thick, although the lime mortar was of poor quality and much has crumbled into little more than heaps. At the high, north-west corner stood the keep, 90 feet by 50 feet, and some sections about 30 feet high remain, indicating that it was probably of two storeys and had a cellar. In the west wall there is a postern gate and there was a semi-circular bastion, although this has largely collapsed. At the south-west end of the wall is another tower which is square and has a basement and three upper storeys—43 feet overall. It has a spiral staircase leading up the battlements, and there are some garderobes. To the south-east is another, larger tower connected by the curtain wall but most of the north tower and wall have gone.
The land went, after the Conquest, to Ernulph, who gave much of it to a Fleming named Michael. In the 16th Century it went to the Grey family and so was the home of the ill fated, short-reigned Queen Jane. The lands were forfeited to the Crown after her execution.
On private land.

Goodrich Castle, *Herefordshire. Half a mile north-east of Goodrich, three miles south-west of Ross.*

The Roman road probably came this way across the river Wye, although there is nothing definite known prior to 1101/2 when there is mention of "Godrics Castle". It seems likely that the original castle was built by a Godric Mappestone to guard the ford across the river. Eventually possession passed into the hands of the Talbots in the 14th Century, and it was a member of this family who was created Earl of Shrewsbury in the 15th Century. The castle left the Talbot family in 1616 when the 7th Earl died without male issue, and it then passed to Henry Gray, Earl of Kent. As with so many other castles Goodrich saw action during the English Civil War and in 1643 it was seized, together with Hereford, by the Earl of Stafford who declared for Parliament. It did not stay long in Parliament's hands and was soon taken over by the Royalists when Stafford withdrew. Two years later, in 1645, Parliament's troops again occupied Hereford and the Royalist garrison was besieged in Goodrich under the command of Sir Henry Lingon. Colonel Birch, the Parliamentary leader, tried a surprise attack but, apart from burning the stables, failed to achieve any result. After the surrender of the king in 1646 the Royalists were more heavily besieged, their water was cut off and they were forced to surrender. The castle was slighted but remained in the possession of the Earls of Kent until 1740, when it was sold to Admiral Thomas Griffin. In 1920 the then-owner, Mrs. Edmund Bosanquet, placed it in the care of the Commissioners of Works.

Of the original Godric's castle nothing remains, but it is thought likely that the rock-cut moat probably follows the line of defence. The earliest surviving piece is the square keep on the south side of the enclosure which was probably built around the middle of the 12th Century. Early in the 13th Century a square curtain wall with towers at the corners was built and of this the east curtain and the foundations of the south-west tower survive. The rest of the surviving curtain and angle towers, gatehouse and buildings belong to the period of restoration which took place at the end of the 13th Century. Very late in the 13th or very early in the 14th Century the narrow outer ward, together with the barbican, was built. The site is well chosen for the hill rises nearly 100 feet and the very steep cliff offers good natural defence. The road leading to the castle climbs the southern slope of the hill and passes along the outer side of the moat to the south side of the barbican. The moat is crossed by a wooden bridge, although originally there was a

The wall-walks of Framlingham Castle, with dummy Tudor chimneys on the towers

drawbridge there. The barbican is very well preserved and well designed and it is enclosed within a stone wall. From the barbican the gatehouse is reached by a sloping causeway and a bridge dating from the late 14th Century. The inner walls are carried across the bridge, the space between forming the pit of the drawbridge. The semi-circular sockets which held the pivot for the bridge can be seen slightly below the level of the pavement. Passing through the vaulted gatehall leads into the north-east corner of the tower which is completely surrounded with buildings. On the south side is the keep, and the kitchens lay on the western side. Beyond these was the great hall on the far western side and the lord's solar occupied the north-west section of the outer wall.

The keep is faced with ashlar and the present ground level entrance is not the original, which was on the first floor and reached by an attached staircase. The original doorway was blocked during the 14th or 15th Century and a window was cut through the wall. Around about 1300 the castle was rebuilt with a rectangular inner ward and towers at the corner. Three of them are circular and there is a wall walk which runs round approximately at the level of the second floor of the tower. The fourth corner, of course, is taken up with the gatehouse and the chapel. The south-west tower is also of three stages with a basement at the bottom which is reached by stairs leading into the hall.

Opposite, Goodrich Castle (originally "Godric's Castle"), guarding the ford of the river Wye, was held for nearly three centuries by the Talbot Earls of Shrewsbury

The earlier round tower was much smaller and the foundation can be seen on the floor. In the 15th Century one of the windows which lit the room was converted into the doorway of a circular staircase leading down to the stables. The second stage is on the same level as the hall and it is entered by a double doorway behind the screens and, no doubt, served as a buttery. The third stage has a well-lighted room and a fireplace. In the north wall there is a small passageway leading through to a garderobe.

The great hall measures some 65 feet by 27 feet and is lit by three windows on the west side. At the centre of the wall are the remains of a large fireplace, and the outer wall of the curtain is strengthened here by a rectangular buttress. On the north side of the hall is a small doorway of 14th Century date leading into a vestibule and then on to the solar and other private chambers. Above this vestibule is a small chapel, probably reserved for the lord's personal use. The western half of the northern wall is occupied by a two-storey solar. Below the solar is a large room reached by stairs from the vestibule at the north end. On the north side there is a small sallyport leading to the outer ward and protected by a double door and a portcullis. The gatehouse is closed at either end by a gate and portcullis and a narrow corridor fitted into the wall leads to a garderobe. The rest of this block is taken up with the chapel with a large unlighted cellar beneath it. The windows at the east and west of the chapel were put in during the 15th Century. The east wall which was of the original 13th Century construction, was later modified and heightened and a garderobe tower inserted at the same time. A long narrow building was also built against this wall; it originally had only one storey although a second one was added in the 15th Century. The south-east tower is basically the same as the south-west although there is, between the south-east tower and the keep, a building of two storeys, the lower part of which forms a dungeon. Most of the wall and the south-west and north-west bastions which formed the outer defence have disappeared but the space between the two bastions to the west was occupied by stables and a circular staircase built in the thickness of the south-west tower, was added as a direct means of access to the castle.

Open to the public:

	Weekdays	Sundays
March–April	9.30 a.m.–5.30 p.m.	2–5.30 p.m.
May–Sept.	9.30 a.m.–7 p.m.	9.30 a.m.–7 p.m.
Oct.	9.30 a.m.–5.30 p.m.	2–5.30 p.m.
Nov.–Feb.	9.30 a.m.–4 p.m.	2–4 p.m.

Greasley Castle, *Hucknall Torkard, Nottinghamshire. One mile south of Hucknall Torkard.*

A licence was given in 1340 to Nicholas, Lord Cantelupe, but apart from some minor masonry little survives.

Great Easton Castle, *Great Easton, Essex.*

In the grounds of Easton Hall there is a motte over 20 feet high with a wide ditch and traces of a bailey. *On private land.*

Great Hautbois Castle, *Hautbois, Norfolk.*

Slight traces of a castle for which a licence was granted in 1313 to Robert Baynard.

Great Swinburn Castle, *near Chollerton, Northumberland.*

The castle is traditionally said to have stood on the site of the present lawn of the house. Only two vaults were left when the castle was demolished in the 17th Century.

Great Torrington Castle, *Great Torrington, Devonshire.*

There are some small remains of a Norman castle with traces of a moat, although the greater part of the site is covered with a bowling green. The castle was apparently demolished in 1228 but rebuilt in 1340. On the south side of the lake is **Castle Hill House** built by Lord Rolle in the 1830s. It has a castellated wall with arrow slits. *On private land.*

Great Wymondley Castle, *Great Wymondley, Hertfordshire. South-west of the church.*

Another example of a Roman fort site being occupied at a later date by a motte and bailey castle, in this case in the south-west corner.

Greenlaugh Castle, *Garstang, Lancashire. One mile north-east of Garstang.*

A rather ruined tower, one of seven or eight erected under licence by Thomas Stanley, Earl of Derby in 1490. It was rectangular with corner towers. In the Civil War it was held for the king and withstood a siege for a while in 1644, but it was taken eventually, and slighted in 1649/50.

Gresham Castle, *near Cromer, Norfolk.*

A castle belonging to Sir Edmund Bacon, for which he received a licence to crenellate in 1319. It was 150 feet square with round towers, 36 feet in diameter, at the corners and a drawbridge in the centre of the north wall to cross the moat. No substantial remains survive.

Greys Court Castle, *Henley, Oxfordshire. Three miles west of Henley.*

A licence to crenellate was given in 1348 to John de Grey, but the castle has since been owned by many families. It stands on sloping ground covering an area of approximately one-and-a-half acres, but only the outer wall on the east side survives together with some of its tower, square and originally probably four storeys high. At the south-east corner is an octagonal turret sixteen feet in external diameter. Attached to this tower is a small building known as Bachelor's Hall. The well, near the south-west angle, is very deep, some 210 feet, and the mechanism, like that at Carisbrooke (qv), was worked by a donkey-powered rope. There is a mansion of the 17th Century on part of the site of the castle.

Open to the public: April 2nd to September 28th Mondays, Wednesdays 2.15–6 p.m. Admission to house 10p, Children half price.

Greystoke Castle, *Greystoke, Cumberland.*

William, Lord Greystoke, put up the pele-tower in 1353 but this is now at the back of the present building rather submerged by later additions. In 1675 Henry Charles Howard had a new façade erected and in 1789 the 11th Duke of Norfolk had further alterations carried out. In 1839 the famous architect Salvin supervised the erection of a mock-Elizabethan front and, following a fire in 1868, he

carried out repairs and further alterations especially to the interior.
On private land.

Grimsthorpe Castle, *Grimsthorpe, Lincolnshire.*

A 13th Century castle stood here, built by Gilbert de Gant, with four square corner towers of various sizes. There was also a gatehouse and a moat, and in the 16th Century there were some additions. In 1685 a new façade was added on the north and in the 18th Century Sir John Vanbrugh was involved in the rebuilding and designing. In the early 19th Century there was extensive remodelling, and the interiors are full of examples of fine decorative features of the 18th and 19th Centuries.
On private land.

Groby Castle, *Groby, Leicestershire. East of the church.*

A 20-foot mound, and probably there are some masonry remains built into the manor house walls. It seems that the castle was probably destroyed by Henry II.

Groveley Castle, *Little Langford, Wiltshire.*

Half-a-mile south-west of Little Langford, an Iron Age earthworks.

Guildford Castle, *Guildford, Surrey.*

In Quarry Street stands an arch which was part of the outer gate of this castle, which has now largely disappeared. The motte is 11th Century and it was surmounted in the 12th Century with a shell keep. The keep is a mere shell, 47 feet square and standing some 63 feet high, with the entrance on the west side on the first floor. To the south-west was an outer bailey. The castle became public property of the town in 1886.
Keep open to the public April to September, afternoons daily, admission 10p.

Hadleigh Castle, *Hadleigh, Essex. Half a mile south of the village of Hadleigh. One mile west of Leigh-on-Sea, Essex.*

In 1231 the powerful Baron Hubert de Burgh was given a licence to build this castle, but within a year he was in disgrace and Henry III had seized his lands. Although the castle was almost certainly unfinished Henry III realised the importance of its position overlooking the estuary of the Thames and decided to finish it. By 1350 the castle is recorded as having an old chapel as well as a new one, a Wardrobe, a King's and a Queen's chamber as well as a Great Hall. Although the castle was crown property it was granted on many occasions to a number of people for life tenancy, but in 1551 Edward VI sold it to Lord Riche. By the 17th Century it was already being described as ruinous, and it came under the care of the Ministry of Works in 1948.

The castle has a large bailey, some 350 feet from east to west, and 200 feet from north to south, which is surrounded on three sides by a ditch. There is no ditch on the south side since the slope of the ground is sufficient defence. Without doubt the most impressive remains of the 14th Century castle are the two towers which stand at the east end of the curtain wall. They were probably built around 1365 and project beyond the curtain wall so that the walls could be covered by flanking fire. They are three storeys high standing on deep plinths, with windows which are small and square with deep internal splays. The tower at the south-east corner has a fine fireplace and a group of three privy shafts which discharge through the plinth. The south wall has disappeared owing to a land slip but it is known that there was a "D"-shaped tower about half way along, as well as a range of buildings in the south-west corner. On the north

86

side is a very large "D"-shaped tower stepped forward again to cover the walls, whilst further along there was another very large, circular one, probably the one described in contemporary accounts as "the great tower". The entrance was protected by a barbican and on the west side a square tower at each angle with one buttress. The domestic buildings including the great hall were all concentrated at the western end of the bailey and ran from north to south.

Open to the public:

	Weekdays	Sundays
March–April	*9.30 a.m.–5.30 p.m.*	*2–5.30 p.m.*
May–Sept.	*9.30 a.m.–7 p.m.*	*9.30 a.m.– 7 p.m.*
Oct.	*9.30 a.m.–5.30 p.m.*	*2–5.30 p.m.*
Nov.–Feb.	*9.30 a.m.–4 p.m.*	*2–4 p.m.*

Hadlow Castle, *Hadlow, Kent. South of the church.*

An octagonal tower rises 170 feet high and was built in 1838/40 by Walter Barton May. By it is a corridor 120 feet long with a huge painted window of the Ascension. Of the original castle little remains.

Haggerston Castle, *Haggerston, Northumberland.*

One tower still stands of this castle which can be traced back to the early 14th Century. During the early 17th Century it suffered badly from a fire and was restored and repaired; but demolition was undertaken in the early 18th Century.

Hales Castle, *Woodlands, Somerset. Half a mile east of the village, standing above Longleat Park.*

A small earthwork, 120 feet in diameter, with a bank, which may have been a subsidiary part of Roddenbury Camp, an Iron Age encampment.

Halton Castle, *Halton, Cheshire. Behind Castle Hotel.*

William I gave this area, north-east of Chester, to Hugh Lupus, who subdivided it among eight

supporters; one, Nigel, became the first Baron of Halton. The castle stood on the cliff by the river above the town. It was roughly circular, with nine wall towers and a gatehouse flanked by two towers, but all has now gone except for some fragments of masonry. It stood until the 17th Century, when it declared for the king in 1643, but was taken a year later and demolished.

Haltwhistle Castle, *Haltwhistle, Northumberland. To the east of the town on Castle Hill.*

The remains of a motte and bailey castle.

Hamsterley Castle, *Hamsterley, County Durham.*

The scanty remains of a post-Roman camp.

Hanley Castle, *Hanley Castle, Worcestershire. South of the village.*

A royal castle of John (1199–1216) which housed the families of the Earls of Gloucester and Warwick, and is now remembered only by its moat.

Hanwell Castle, *Hanwell, Oxfordshire. Three miles north-west of Banbury.*

A tower which stood in the south-west corner of this rectangular structure still survives, but most of the castle was demolished in 1770. The main entrance was on the west front. The tower was adapted for use as a dairy.
On private land.

Harbottle Castle, *Harbottle, Northumberland.*

This was the site chosen by the Umfraville family for their centre of operations; here they erected a motte and bailey castle and, *circa* 1157, built the main castle. It stands on high ground and is partly enclosed by walls, one of which cuts off a bailey from an open space to the east. This bailey has the

motte at the north end with the minor remains of a shell keep, remarkable for its projecting towers, on top. In the 16th Century it was modified to serve as a solid foundation fort for artillery.
On private land.

Harby Brow Castle, *Allhallows, Cumberland. Near Aspatria on the north bank of the river Eden.*

A tower, 30 feet square and 60 feet high, which has been converted to a farm house.
On private land.

Hardknott Castle, *Boot, Cumberland. Nine miles north-east of Ravenglass, at the western end of Hardknott Pass.*

On a spur of land projecting from the mountain is this Roman fort covering approximately three acres. As usual it is square, with stone walls each pierced by a gate. Excavations have revealed the foundations of most of the internal buildings including a small bath block. To the north-east is a large parade ground.
Open to the public at any time, admission free.

Harewood Castle, *Harewood, West Riding, Yorkshire.*

Built originally in the 12th Century, the castle was much altered and restored, and in 1367 Sir William Aldburg was granted his licence to crenellate. It has passed through the hands of many owners. The form is rectangular with tall four-storey towers at the south-east and north-east corners, and originally also at the other corners. Entry was by way of a gate defended by a portcullis on the north wall. The portcullis chamber is connected to the Grand Hall, 55 feet by 29 feet which still has its stone benches, and above the hall is a solar.

Harlequin's Castle, *Burnham, Buckinghamshire.*

An enclosure of indeterminate date, also known as " Hardicanute's Castle ".

Harsley Castle, *East Harsley, North Riding, Yorkshire. One-and-a-quarter miles south-east of village.*

Some minor ruins on a site of four-and-a-half acres, with a 30-foot-wide ditch on three sides.

Hartlebury Castle, *Hartlebury, Worcestershire.*

In the mid-13th Century Bishop Walter Cantelupe erected a castle, and in 1268 Bishop Gifford was granted his crenellation licence. Further work was undertaken in the 15th Century but in 1646 its destruction was nearly complete. Some restoration was put in hand in the 17th and 18th Centuries. Of the earliest castle only the moat and remains of a tower in the north-west survive. At the centre is the 15th Century hall, much modified, whilst the wings are mostly late 17th Century.
Open to the public Easter to September, Sundays and Bank Holidays 2–6 p.m.

Hartley Castle, *Hartley, Westmorland.*

Part of a wall survives in the yard of a farm. The house is 17th Century and later. This land belonged to the Musgrove family but before that to the De Hardclays—of which the present name is a corruption. Andrew de Hardclay was created Earl of Carlisle by Edward II; he later sided with Robert Bruce, was declared a traitor, captured, and put to death by being hanged, drawn and quartered.
On private land.

Hartshill Castle, *Hartshill, Warwickshire.*

A motte and a fragment of 13th Century wall, as well as part of a Tudor house.

Hastings Castle, *Hastings, Sussex.*

Only the ruins of this castle survive, with the curtain wall on the north and east. It once belonged to Robert, Count of Eu. The church incorporates part of the building and the north wall is prior to 1094. Henry II was responsible for the keep, which was built in 1172, and the original entrance was by the chancel of the church.

Open to the public daily in summer, 10 a.m.–dusk. Admission 6p, Children 3p.

Hatherop Castle, *Hatherop, Gloucestershire.*

Basically a manor house of Tudor period but partly rebuilt around the mid-19th Century for Lord De Mauley. It is three-storeyed and incorporates a large, battlemented tower.
On private land.

Haughley Castle, *Haughley, Suffolk. North-west of Stowmarket and north of the church.*

Remains of a rectangular castle with surrounding moat and a motte, the entire area of approximately seven acres. It probably dates from the 12th Century.

Haughton Castle, *two miles from Humshaugh, Northumberland, on the right bank of the North Tyne.*

The castle has been owned by various important families including those of Widdrington, Swinburn and Pratt, and has been restored by the Cruddas family. References to it occur in the 16th Century, and in 1541 and 1587 it was raided by the Scots. It is a long, high, narrow building with square corner turrets and along the side walls are machicolated buttresses, a feature of French military architecture of the 12th and 13th Centuries, but very uncommon on British castles.
It seems to have been converted, in the late 14th century, to a castle, and heightened and lengthened. The hall was on the first floor. It was much altered in the 19th Century. The west wing was built by Salvin, and the staircase was put in in 1889.
On private land.

Hayes Castle, *Distington, Cumberland. Half a mile south of Distington.*

Only a fragment of wall survives.

Hayton Castle, *Clareborough, Nottinghamshire. One mile north-west of the village.*

Part of the moat exists of this castle of the de Hayton family, but 300 yards away is a 19th Century mansion.

Hayton Castle, *Hayton, Cumberland. South-east of Allonby.*

A rectangular house with windows dating from the 15th, 16th and 18th Centuries and on one side two very large buttresses. The architectural features suggest that it is probably a 16th Century structure much altered.
On private land.

Hazelwood Castle, *Hazelwood, West Riding, Yorkshire.*

Of the original castle only the chapel, of *circa* 1280, remains at the east end of the house, which is Georgian with castellation. There is also an 18th Century folly tower.
On private land.

Hedingham Castle, *Castle Hedingham, Essex. On B1058 off Colchester–Cambridge road (A604).*

As an example of a solid, square, Norman/Angevin type keep Castle Hedingham is superb. It was the seat of the De Vere family, the Earls of Oxford—a powerful family which has played a great part in the history of England, having fought, at various times, both for and against the king. The second Earl of Oxford, Robert, fought against King John and the castle was later occupied by French soldiers under the leadership of the Earl of Winchester. Robert's son, the third earl fought with Simon de Montfort against the king at Lewes in 1264, and the seventh Earl represented the family at Crécy. The ninth Earl married Edward III's granddaughter and was a great favourite of Richard II (1377–1399). A later Earl fought by the side of Warwick at the Battle of Barnet in 1471 and had the misfortune to be captured and held prisoner by the Yorkists for many years. He eventually managed to escape and was with Henry Tudor, later Henry VII, when he landed at Milford Haven and took part in the decisive Battle of Bosworth Field in 1485.

It was at this castle that the same Earl of Oxford suffered a very unfortunate experience. During the Wars of the Roses it had become common practice for the rich nobles to hire groups of retainers who formed, in effect, a private army. These they dressed in a simple uniform often bearing part of their coat of arms and, as such, this uniform was known as their livery. When Henry VII ascended the throne he realised that the existence of private armies presented a threat which was a danger to the country as a whole. He instituted the Statute of Livery which forbad the keeping of these private armies. He visited the Earl of Oxford at Hedingham Castle, and as he was leaving a large number of the Duke's retainers were drawn up to bid the king a ceremonial farewell. The king was impressed by the numbers and asked the Earl of Oxford if they were all his servants. When the Earl agreed that they were his retainers and wore his livery the king remarked that he had evidently broken the law and would see that the royal attorney spoke to him. As a result the Earl was fined 15,000 marks, an extremely large sum. After this period the power of the Oxfords waned, but not apparently their tempers; in 1604 the 17th Earl became so angry with Lord Burghley, who had inherited the Hedingham castle, that he had part of it demolished out of spite. The castle left the Oxford family in 1713.

Hedingham Castle was of the motte and bailey type, although the motte is natural rather than artificial. The bailey lay to the east, and in about 1140 on top of the very large motte (two acres) was built this enormous stone keep. It rises to a height of 110 feet to the battlements with twenty-foot-tall towers rising above them, and has a basement and three separate storeys. At the base the walls are twelve feet thick and it is likely that the enormous weight could only have been taken by a natural motte. On the ground floor the only openings cut in the wall are very small loopholes, and to make it difficult to mount a direct attack the main entrance is not on the ground floor but on the first floor. The entrance on the west side is approached by an outside staircase which means that attackers would find it difficult to gain momentum when attempting to break down the door. The main entrance was further protected by a portcullis and

a small barbican. Around the doorway is the characteristic "dog-tooth" or chevron decoration found on so many Norman buildings. The north-west turret houses a spiral staircase which gives access to each of the floors whilst on the second floor there is a passage built into the wall which runs right round the top of the castle. The first and second floors are spanned by a central arch 28 feet wide, which supports the floor timbers of the section above it. The roof is flat and was originally surrounded by battlements. Fireplaces, garderobes and closets are recessed into the various walls and at the base of the north-west tower is the castle well. Holes left in the outside masonry probably accommodated the wooden scaffolding used when building the castle and may well have been left to facilitate repairs should they be required. The outside is faced with square-cut stone and the four corner turrets project only slightly from the main wall. The centre of each wall is strengthened and supported by a buttress in the form of a pilaster. The bailey was fairly small but presumably contained the chapel, for there seems to be no accommodation inside the keep for such a building. Kitchens, stables and other domestic offices and buildings would also have been situated in the keep. In September 1918 a fire completely gutted the building and it was only sheer good luck that the walls themselves were not destroyed. The effects of the fire are still evident today from the rather rosy pink colouring on the inside of the wall. *Open to the public: Easter Monday 10 a.m.–6 p.m.; May to September, Tuesdays, Thursdays and Saturdays 2–6 p.m.; also Spring and Late Summer Bank Holiday Mondays 10 a.m.–6 p.m. Admission 12½p, Children 9p.*

Helmsley Castle, *Helmsley, North Riding, Yorkshire. Fifteen miles from Thirsk and Pickering on the A170.*

The castle stands on an outcrop of rock in the valley of the Rye, a fine strategic position, but there is little to suggest any building prior to that undertaken by Robert de Rood, Lord of Helmsley, from 1186 to 1227. The inner ward, keep, lower part of the curtain wall and angle towers all date from this period. The barbican was built on to the south face probably about the middle of the 13th Century and the south-east tower of the inner ward is thought to be of the same date. At the end of the 13th Century the west tower was modified and the keep was heightened. The chapel in the inner ward probably dates from the middle of the 13th Century. The great hall was probably built early in the 14th Century although the various kitchens were subsequently added at different dates. Towards the end of the 16th Century the third Earl of Rutland carried out some modification to the domestic buildings. The castle saw very little action until the English Civil Wars, when Sir Jordan Crosland held it for the king against Sir Thomas Fairfax. In 1644 he resisted a siege for three months but finally surrendered in November. It was owned then by the Duke of Buckingham, who returned to England in 1657 to marry Mary Fairfax, the daughter of the Parliamentary leader. When the second Duke died in 1688 Helmsley was sold to a London banker, Sir Charles Duncombe. He died in 1711 and the present owners, the Earls of Feversham, are descended from the sister of Sir Charles Duncombe whose husband assumed the family name of Duncombe.

The entrance to the castle was very strongly guarded by a barbican, mid-13th Century, the gateway flanked by drum towers with long side walls, and in front of this was a drawbridge. During the 14th Century the gatehouse was altered to improve accommodation on the first floor and from either end of the barbican walls ran along and across the inner ditch to join with the towers of the inner ward. At the south-east corner is the principal gatehouse, again with a drawbridge and portcullis. The inner ward measures approximately seventy yards by 100 yards and is encircled by a curtain wall with a circular tower at each of the other corners. There is also another entrance, flanked with semi-circular towers, in the north wall. The ward was surrounded by a wide, deep ditch cut into the rock, with a second, smaller, ditch enclosing that one. The lower sections of the curtain walls, gatehouse and angle towers remain but it is likely that the curtain walls were heightened at the end of the 13th or the beginning of the 14th Century. It may well be that the bailey was originally divided by a wall running from east to west between the keep and the west tower. Running along the south-east wall are the sites of the kitchen, pantry, buttery and by the west wall was the site of the old hall. The keep is not a large one but differs from most in having an apse at one side. When the keep was slighted the upper part was destroyed.

There was a single, large room on the first floor with a gabled roof but the arrangement of the upstairs room is not at all clear. At the beginning of the 14th Century the keep was heightened and the first floor was then divided in two with stone vaults inserted at each level. The chapel was consecrated in 1246 and lies to the west of the keep, and only the south and east walls remain. There was extensive remodelling of the rectangular west tower wall at the end of the 13th Century when garderobes were inserted and two windows cut. Later in the 16th Century a second remodelling was undertaken when some of these earlier windows were blocked, fireplaces were inserted in the east and west walls and new windows cut. The original door was blocked and a new one was cut on the east side at ground floor level, but now access is by means of an external staircase which is modern. At the north-west corner of the courtyard there are traces of some of the domestic buildings including part of an oven. The ditch was spanned

Helmsley Castle: the keep, from the south-west

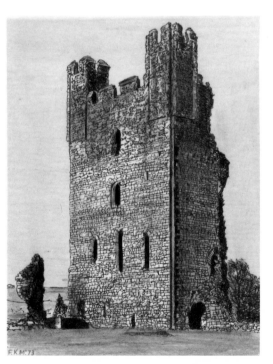

by a wooden bridge guarded by a small barbican of two drum towers and flanking walls.

Open to the public:

	Weekdays	Sundays
March–April	*9.30 a.m.–5.30 p.m.*	*2–5.30 p.m.*
May–Sept.	*9.30 a.m.–7 p.m.*	*2–7 p.m.*
Oct.	*9.30 a.m.–5.30 p.m.*	*2–5.30 p.m.*
Nov.–Feb.	*9.30 a.m.–4 p.m.*	*2–4 p.m.*

Hely or Hymel Castle, *Fineshade Abbey, Northamptonshire. South-west of the Abbey.*

The remains of a castle deserted early in the 13th Century.

Hembury Castle, *Hembury, Devonshire. One-and-a-half miles north of Buckfastleigh.*

This was an Iron Age camp and simply consists of an earthwork.

Hemyock Castle, *Hemyock, Devonshire. West of the church.*

It belonged to the Hidon family; only fragmentary remains survive although the gatehouse, with its two flanking towers and portcullis grooves, is still reasonably intact. There are the remains of a hall and traces of the moat. It was captured in 1642 by Parliamentary forces and was dismantled.

Hereford Castle, *Hereford, Herefordshire. On Castle Green.*

The first castle pre-dated the Conquest and was built by a nephew of Edward the Confessor *circa* 1048; it suffered under a Welsh attack in 1055. William FitzOsbern, Earl of Hereford, had it rebuilt as a motte and bailey castle with the bailey occupying the present Castle Green, with the Castle Pool being part of the moat.

Herstmonceux Castle, *Herstmonceux, Sussex.*

Sir Roger Fiennes was granted his licence to crenellate in 1440 but the major part was demolished in 1777, remaining in ruins until it was restored, or perhaps rebuilt, in 1913 and 1933. It has a wide moat crossed by a bridge which is partly original. Most was built of brick and the result is a castle like Bodiam (qv), but with polygonal towers rather than circular. In 1948 it housed the Royal Observatory.

Grounds open to the public.

Hertford Castle, *Hertford, Hertfordshire.*

A son of King Alfred the Great erected two mounds, one on each bank of the river Lea. That on the south formed the site for a Norman castle erected by William I. It was under siege by Prince Louis of France in 1216, but later was returned to the Crown. David, King of Scotland was imprisoned here for eleven years after his capture in 1346. King John of France was also a prisoner here after Poitiers (1346). A considerable section of wall survives, 30 feet high and seven feet thick, as well as part of a circular tower. The centre of the present building dates from Stuart times. There is a brick gatehouse with four octagonal turrets and, traditionally, there is a secret passage beneath the tower.

On local authority land.

Hever Castle, *near Edenbridge, Kent. Three miles south-east of Edenbridge off B2026.*

In 1384 Sir John de Cobham was given a licence to crenellate. In 1462 the castle was owned by Sir Geoffrey Bullen, Lord Mayor of London, and it was in these gardens that Henry VIII is supposed to have courted Anne Boleyn. The south front has at its centre a fine, three-storeyed gatehouse with square turrets at the corners and on the west side are some good chimneys and machicolations. In 1890 W. W. Astor came to England and in 1903 purchased the castle and poured money and 2,000 workmen into the job of restoring it, a task which took four years.

Open to the public (1973) from Easter Sunday, April 22nd to Wednesday October 17th on Wednesdays and Sundays and Bank Holidays. Gardens 1–7 p.m. (no admittance after 6 p.m.). Castle 2–7 p.m. (no admittance after 6.15 p.m.). Entrance gates close at 6 p.m. Admission: Gardens only, 20p (Children under twelve 10p); Castle, 30p (Children under twelve 15p). (Note: No admission to Castle without prior payment for admission to Gardens.)

Hexham Castle, *Hexham, Northumberland.*

There are considerable remains of this fine edifice, which was rectangular, with a gatehouse which became known as the Moot Hall; it has a long, vaulted chamber 30 feet by 20 feet, as well as a newel staircase and a guardroom. The keep was later used as a prison.

Heydour Castle, *Heydour, Lincolnshire.*

Some foundations and earthworks survive, but little else.

Highclerc Castle, *Highclerc, Hampshire.*

This is the largest house in Hampshire, but dates only from 18th and 19th Centuries. It has parks planned by the 18th Century landscape expert "Capability" Brown.

Highhead Castle, *Ivegill, Cumberland. One-and-a-half miles to the west of Ivegill.*

The façade of 1744–8 still stands although a fire of 1956 gutted the building, but on the north side is a 16th Century part still inhabited.
On private land.

High Wycombe Castle, *High Wycombe, Buckinghamshire. In Priory Avenue.*

A motte, approximately 30 feet high, surmounted by a folly.

Hinckley Castle, *Hinckley, Leicestershire. South of Castle Street.*

Only a mound survives of a castle destroyed *circa* 1175.

Holdgate Castle, *Holdgate, Shropshire.*

At the rear of the farmhouse stand the remains of a tower dating from the late 13th or early 14th Century.

Holt Castle, *Holt, Worcestershire.*

Of the castle only a three-storey tower of the 14th Century survives but behind this is a hall of the 15th Century which was remodelled with panelling in the 18th Century.
On private land.

Hop Castle, *Winterbourne, Berkshire. One-and-a-quarter miles north-north-west of the village.*

This is almost certainly the remains of a Georgian hunting lodge.

Hopton Castle, *Hopton, Shropshire.*

A Norman keep with a fine Norman doorway and windows added in the 14th Century.

Horeston or Horsley Castle, *six miles north of Derby, Derbyshire.*

The manor was held in the 11th Century by Ralph de Buron but by the 12th Century it was designated a royal castle. Excavations made late in the 19th Century discovered the base of a multiangular tower which was thought to be part of the keep.

Hornby Castle, *Hornby, Lancashire. Between the Lune and Wenning rivers, one mile from the junction.*

Originally this was a Roman fort. The Norman builder chose a high rock as his site and the foundations of two towers survive together with the keep, 36 feet across. The great tower was erected by Lord Mounteagle and bears his crest, with an eagle's claw. The baileys, upper and lower, extended as far as the town. It was owned during the 12th Century by Roger de Montbegon, and later

by Hubert de Burgh, a most important man at Henry II's court. Later still it passed to Sir Edward Stanley, who was made Lord Mounteagle in the 16th Century. It was to a member of this family that the letter was written which betrayed the gunpowder plot of Guy Fawkes. In 1849–52 a "castle" was built here for a financier, and this was modified in 1889 and again in the last 30 years.
On private land.

Hornby Castle, *Hornby, North Riding, Yorkshire.*

The home of the St. Quentin family in the 14th Century. It was altered by Lord Conyers in the 15th Century, and again in the 19th Century. It has been much reduced in size but the south side survives, with an archway leading into the courtyard with the keep, of late 15th or early 16th Century, on the right.
On private land.

Horsford Castle, *St. Faiths, Norfolk. Five miles north of Norwich.*

Walter de Cadamo built a castle here but it was in ruins and overgrown by the 16th Century. The moat is still visible; there are some earthworks and some remains of the keep encircled by a second moat.

Horton Castle, *near Chatton, Northumberland.*

Only minor fragments of a 15th Century castle exist in the present farm buildings, demolition taking place early in the 19th Century.
On private land.

Houghton Castle, *Houghton, Lancashire. Five-and-a-half miles west-south-west of Blackburn, between Derwent and Orr.*

Well situated, on top of a high crag, is a castle built in 1565 by Thomas Hoghton. The upper and lower courts are separated by a strong gatehouse which was blown up accidentally, when being used as a powder store in the Civil War.

Howgill Castle, *Milburn, Westmorland. Five miles from Appleby.*

The De Stutevilles held this castle from the De Meschines family during the reign of Henry I, but it changed hands several times. It stands by a stream on high ground and has a central block between two towers, 64 feet by 33 feet each, and with walls nine to ten feet thick. Each tower had a basement and was two storeys high with battlements at the top. The hall appears to have been destroyed at one time and rebuilt with much less substantial materials.

Huntingdon Castle, *Huntingdon, Huntingdonshire.*

Erected by William I, this castle remained in use only for a century or so; it stood by the River Ouse and the motte can be seen from the High Street standing some ten to fifteen feet high. The outer bailey extended to the west.

Huntington Castle, *Huntington, Herefordshire. Quarter of a mile north of the church.*

A motte 100 feet in diameter and 30 feet high, an oval inner bailey and a larger outer one, with some fragments of wall, probably 13th Century, and towers, indicate the site of a castle built, probably by William de Braose, in the 12th Century.

Hurst Castle, *Hampshire. Two-and-a-half miles south-east of Milford Church on a pebble spit. Usually approached by sea from Key Haven.*

This is another of the castles built by Henry VIII to defend the coast against possible continental invasion (cf Dartmouth). It was probably built between about 1539 and 1544 under the supervision of Thomas Bertie who, in 1550, became Captain of Hurst. The castle is in the form of a twelve-sided central tower surrounded by a curtain wall from which project three semi-circular bastions. It appears not to have been kept in good repair and between then and 1635 there are numerous references to the decayed state of the castle, the need for repairs and requests for further stores and equipment. In 1645 the castle was occupied by Parliament. Charles I was held prisoner there for a while just before his trial in November 1648. In 1649 the castle was surveyed and, possibly through fear of invasion from Prince Charles in Jersey, the garrison was increased and the castle restocked. Following the Restoration in 1660 it was decided that the castle should be dismantled, but this was not done, and in 1673/1675 repairs were still being carried out and a full garrison was in residence. There were 30 guns mounted in the tower, and garrisons have continued at the tower since this time. In 1682 it was alleged to be a hot-bed of smugglers, and in 1700 was being used as a castle. During the Napoleonic wars in the early 19th Century some alterations were made in order to resist the expected French invasion, and again it was possibly fear of the French which caused the authorities, in 1861, to set up two wing batteries on the east and west and to fill in the space between the tower and the central wall, together with other modifications completed by 1873. In 1933 the War Office handed over the care of the castle to the Office of Works but it saw another spell of military occupation during the Second World War.

The present entry is through the west wing, built in the 19th Century, and the Tudor entrance is on the left. Above the doorway is a blank plaque; on either side are the holes through which the original drawbridge chains passed, and above the gateway can be seen the slot which housed the portcullis. The central tower has two floors and above the doorway is the date *1585* and next to it a mason's mark. There is a second doorway which was heightened in 1889 to give greater protection to the magazine situated below, but this filling has now been removed. In the centre of the circular room is a brick pier which contains a staircase down to a chamber which lit the magazine. On the south-east side there is a small alcove which housed a garderobe. A modern external staircase leads up to the first floor but it was probably approached originally through the central staircase. There are three small rooms built into the thickness of the wall and as the windows are above the height of the curtain wall they are narrow and splayed internally. The roof has been much altered in the 19th Century and the parapet heightened, for originally the battlements were rounded like those on the north-west bastion and there was a tall, central cupola. The gun mountings are of 19th Century origin and the entrance which leads down to the basement is also 19th Century. The recesses in the wall housed the ammunition. Defaced inscriptions record that the tower was repaired and reformed in 1805. The ammunition hoist also dates from the 19th Century. The central tower is surrounded by a curtain wall with its three bastions. That on the north-west has been greatly altered and now has two storeys and a flat roof. The ground floor originally had four gun-ports and the one on the right retains its original smoke vent. A small room over the gateway still retains the portcullis complete with weights and chains, but the staircase leading to it is modern. A door leads from here to the first floor room of the north-west bastion which originally had two large windows. One of these was blocked up when the west wing was built and another window was opened out further north. The basement of the north-west bastion is almost completely filled with modern water tanks but there is an original staircase at the north end which leads down from the courtyard and gives access to a loopholed brick building jutting out at right angles from the curtain. This was known as the Caponiere and is of 19th Century origin; it gave covering fire along the length of the wall. The two other bastions consisted only of a basement, ground floor and a flat roof. The north-east bastion was masked by the east wing built in 1873 when an entrance was made through the bastion and the remainder of the ground floor and basement was used as a store for shells. At the end of the 19th Century the ground floor of the south bastion was strengthened by filling it with cement and the roof was then adapted for the heavier, modern guns. Originally the fort had accommodation for 24 guns at ground and moat level, and a list of 1628 records 27.

Open to the public:

	Weekdays	*Sundays*
March–April	*9.30 a.m.–5.30 p.m.*	*2–5.30 p.m.*
May–Sept.	*9.30 a.m.–7 p.m.*	*2–7 p.m.*
Oct.	*9.30 a.m.–5.30 p.m.*	*2–5.30 p.m.*
Nov.–Feb.	*10 a.m.–4.30 p.m.*	*2–4.30 p.m.*

Hutton John Castle, *Hutton John, Cumberland. In the south-east of Hutton John.*

An original pele-tower with a spiral staircase in the north-east corner. A range has been added at the side probably in the 17th Century, and was

modified in the 18th and 19th Centuries.
On private land.

Hylton Castle, *Hylton, County Durham. Two-and-a-half miles north-west of Sunderland.*

Only the tall five-storeyed gatehouse, 66 feet long and 36 feet wide, still stands. It has four machi-colated turrets at the west end, and on the east front there is a circular turret at each corner; there is a central, projecting tower. The earliest reference occurs in 1448 but it was probably built about 1400. In the late 17th Century another wing was added and there was extensive restoration in 1869.

Open to the public weekdays 10 a.m.–4 p.m., Sundays 2–4 p.m.

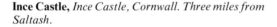

I J K

Ince Castle, *Ince Castle, Cornwall. Three miles from Saltash.*

This is essentially a manor house of the 16th Century with corner towers and a castellated gateway.
On private land.

Irthington Castle, *Irthington, Cumberland. Two-and-a-half miles from Brampton on the north side of the river.*

The Nook farmhouse marks the site of a Roman camp but when the Norman castle was built or destroyed is uncertain. It is said to have been about 100 feet by 75 feet with at least one tower at the south corner.
On private land.

Irton Castle, *Irton, Cumberland.*

By the river Irt; incorporated into a later building.
On private land.

Jordan's Castle, *Wellow, Nottinghamshire. Half a mile north-east of Wellow.*

A hill fortress with a wide ditch.

Keldy Castle, *near Pickering, North Riding, Yorkshire.*

One turret and some of the wall survives of what was probably an early 19th Century house.

Kelsborrow Castle, *Delamere, Cheshire.*

A semi-circular hill fort with a single ditch and bank, which is also known as Promontory Fort.

Kendal Castle, *Kendal, Westmorland. Half a mile east on the opposite side of the river.*

On a motte stands the ruin of a 12th Century keep, and on the north-east are the traces of a range of buildings of the 13th and 14th Centuries. Some of the curtain walls still survive and these probably date from the time when the castle was owned by Ivo de Taillebois, who acquired the land from his wife in the 11th Century.

Kenilworth Castle, *Kenilworth, Warwickshire. North-west edge of town on A46.*

Now largely an unoccupied ruin, this castle is remarkable for its size and the extent of its water defences. It was begun by Geoffrey de Clinton, a treasurer of Henry I (1100–1135) and the earliest buildings, circa 1120, were almost certainly of wood. During the reign of King John (1199–1216) the walls and towers were rebuilt in stone. The castle was later under the control of Simon de Montfort, who rebelled against Henry III and was killed at the battle of Evesham in 1265. Simon's supporters held the castle for six months against the king and defied every attack, until illness and starvation finally forced their surrender. Henry

made it part of the Duchy of Lancaster's holdings, and John of Gaunt spent much of his time there; he undertook some rebuilding, including the construction of a large hall. In 1563 Queen Elizabeth I (1558–1603) granted the castle to her favourite, Robert Dudley, Earl of Leicester. Dudley undertook considerable reconstruction, retaining the original fabric but modifying the Norman keep by having the narrow windows replaced with wider Tudor ones. Elizabeth visited the castle on several occasions and was entertained on a lavish scale. It continued in use as a place of residence until the 17th Century, when it was controlled by Parliamentary forces who decided to render it useless as a base and so blew up part of the massive keep as well as some of the walls and towers. Colonel

Scanty but romantically sited ruins of Kendal Castle, partly built by Ivo de Taillebois in the 11th Century

Hawkesworth, a Parliamentary officer who took over the castle, lived in the Gatehouse, which had also been modernised by the Earl of Leicester, and is still occupied today.

In 1937 the ruins, together with a grant for their upkeep, were given by Lord Kenilworth to the then Office of Works.

Although today only a ruin, Kenilworth still conveys a strong impression of a Norman castle, with a keep which has walls over seventeen feet thick in places. The old arrangement of an inner and outer bailey can still be seen, as well as traces of the original moat which encircled the keep, and John of Gaunt's hall. The lake was formed by damming two streams and is over one hundred acres in area. The Norman dam was breached by Parliament's men.

Edward II was imprisoned within the walls of Kenilworth, and traditionally it was here that Henry V received the insulting French gift of tennis balls prior to his Agincourt campaign.

The novelist, Sir Walter Scott, used the castle as the background for many of his characters and events.

Open to the public all the year, weekdays 9.30 a.m.–7 p.m. Sundays 2 p.m.–7 p.m. (Summer 9.30 a.m.–7 p.m.). Closes 5.30 p.m. March, April, October; November to February 9.30 a.m.–4 p.m. Sundays 2 p.m.–4p.m. Admission (1972) 7½p, children and OAPs half price.

Kielder Castle, *Kielder, Northumberland. Quarter of a mile east of Kielder, on a hill above North Tyne and Kielder Burn.*

Built in 1772/5 by the Duke of Northumberland and strengthened in the 19th Century.

Kildale Castle, *Kildale, North Riding, Yorkshire.*

To the west of the church are the remains of a motte and bailey castle with the railway cutting through the site.

Kilpeck Castle, *Kilpeck, Herefordshire. West of the church.*

There are some masonry remains of a shell keep retaining a fireplace on the north side. The castle is probably of 12th Century origin and there are indications of several outer enclosures.

Kilton Castle, *Kilton, North Riding, Yorkshire. One-and-a-half miles south-west of Loftus.*

Tucked away in some woods, a long, narrow site set by a cliff edge with a surviving small tower and some walls.

Kimbolton Castle, *Kimbolton, Huntingdonshire. Eight miles north-west of St. Neots on the A45.*

An earlier castle was rebuilt in the early 16th Century and again early in the 17th Century, when it was arranged around a central courtyard. It was yet again altered late in the 17th Century, and then the Earl of Manchester approached the famous architect Vanbrugh and asked him to redesign it. This was done, and during the first two decades of the 18th Century a magnificent house was erected in typical Classical style, with painted interior walls and ceilings.

Open to the public Spring Bank Holiday Sunday and Monday; Late Summer Bank Holiday Monday and July 22nd to August 26th Thursdays and Sundays, 2 p.m.–6 p.m. Admission 10p, Children 5p.

Kinderton Castle, *Middlewick, Cheshire. On the river Dore at Middlewick.*

Owned by Gilbert de Vanables in the 11th Century; all has disappeared except for part of the moat with a motte in the south-west of the bailey.

Kineton Castle, *Kineton, Warwickshire. Near the station.*

A large motte, over 120 feet in diameter, and some fragments of a wall.

King Charles' Castle, *Tresco, Scilly Isles.*

This stands 200 yards north-west of Cromwell's Castle (qv) and much of its original materials were taken to build Cromwell's Castle. The original fort was probably built during the reign of Edward VI, although extra defences were added during the period of the English Civil War. *The ruins are freely accessible.*

King John's Castle, *Tewkesbury, Gloucestershire. In Myrtle Road, quarter of a mile north of the town.*

In fact this was probably part of the Tewkesbury Abbey, with a staggered, three-storey tower.

Kingsbury Castle, *St. Michaels, Hertfordshire. South-west of St. Albans.*

Early earthworks, most of which were levelled in the 10th Century although a part remained until the mid-12th Century. Indications can still be seen by the slope of the gardens of houses in Fishpool Street and Dagnell Street.

King's Castle, *Wells, Somerset.*

An Iron Age Camp with six banks, roughly triangular in outline, is situated behind the golf course.

King's Castle, *Wiveliscombe, Somerset.*

On Castle Hill, north of the town, is an earthwork, probably of the Iron Age.

Kingsland Castle, *Kingsland, Herefordshire.*

A mound 180 feet in diameter and fifteen feet high, with two baileys.

King's Sutton Castle, *King's Sutton, Oxfordshire.*

Four miles south-east of Banbury, some traces of ancient earthworks.

King's Weir (Kingswear) Castle, *Dartmouth, Devonshire. Located on the opposite side of the river bank to Dartmouth Castle.*

This really forms a complementary outwork to Dartmouth Castle (qv); it was begun in 1491 and building continued at least until 1501/2. It is very similar to the square tower built at Dartmouth, as are its gun-ports. The castle became obsolete in the late 16th Century when the guns of the Dartmouth Castle were considered sufficiently powerful to guard the estuary. It was at this point that the chain which normally barred the harbour was secured. It was abandoned and fell into ruin.

Kinnersley Castle, *Kinnersley, Herefordshire. Behind the church.*

A fine Elizabethan house, five storeys high and embattled, dating from the time of Roger Vaughan *circa* 1585–1601. A castle of the De La Bere family stood here in the 14th Century.

Kirby Lonsdale Castle, *Kirby Lonsdale, Westmorland. North of the vicarage on the west side of the river Lune.*

The remains of a motte and bailey castle.

Kirby Ravensworth Castle, *Kirby Ravensworth, North Riding, Yorkshire. Five miles north-west of Richmond.*

This castle had eight chief towers but only fragments survive. It belonged to the FitzHugh family.

Kirkby Fleetham Castle, *Kirkby Fleetham, North Riding, Yorkshire.*

West of the Post Office are the moat and walls of a castle for which licence was granted in 1314.

Kirkby Malzeard Castle, *Kirkby Malzeard, West Riding, Yorkshire. West of Ripon.*

This was built by Roger de Mowbray and surrendered to Henry II, who ordered its demolition. The site is oval and covers about half an acre; the foundations are traceable but nothing more.

Kirkby Muxloe Castle, *Kirby Muxloe, Leicester-shire. Four miles west of Leicester.*

The present castle was begun by Sir William Hastings, who also built Ashby-de-la-Zouch. A strongly fortified manor house with towers, gate-house and drawbridge occupied the site and in 1474 Hastings was granted his licence to crenellate three houses, including Kirby. Work began in 1480, but in 1483 Hastings died and the conversion was not completed. In 1911 the then-owner gave the site to the Commissioners of Works who tidied and repaired the area, completing the task in 1913. A moat surrounds the rectangular castle which had square corner and central towers, with the gate-house in the centre of the north-west wall. The manor house which previously occupied the site was partly demolished in 1480 but the 14th Century hall and living quarters were retained. An oak bridge, fragments of which still survive, crossed the moat to the gatehouse which is of brick, with patterns inset. The gatehouse is rec-tangular with corner turrets containing stairs or garderobes. From the gatehouse ranges of two-storeyed buildings extend on either side but these are largely in ruins now. The west tower, 25 feet square and three storeys high, is in good order, with gunports on the ground floor; these are early examples and this may explain their very poor siting for any guns fitted would, in some cases, be firing directly at the wall of the castle! There is evidence that the other corner towers were of similar design.

> *Open to the public weekdays only :*
> *March–April   9.30 a.m.–5.30 p.m.*
> *May–Sept.   9.30 a.m.–7 p.m.*
> *Oct.   9.30 a.m.–5.30 p.m.*
> *Nov.–Feb.   9.30 a.m.–4 p.m.*

Kirkoswald Castle, *Kirkoswald, Cumberland.*

On the north a single tower stands complete with its spiral staircase, this was probably to the north-east of the hall. The castle was oblong with two towers on the south side, one of which survives as does the gatehouse on the west. The moat is still very apparent.

Knaresborough Castle, *Knaresborough, West Riding, Yorkshire.*

Begun, probably, by Serlo de Burg, who received the land from William I, Sir Hugh de Morville, one of the four knights who killed Thomas à Becket, spent some time here. Richard II was imprisoned here.

Standing by the river Nidd are the remains of this two bailey castle, built between 1310 and 1340. There are some remains of the curtain wall, 40 feet high, next to the keep and with semi-circular towers. The keep stood at the northern point of the castle and measured 64 feet by 52 feet, with a chamfered north corner and comprising a base-ment, ground floor and two upper storeys. Direct access from the bailey into the basement was by means of steps. In a tower in the south-east corner was a spiral staircase giving access to the upper floors. The first floor may well have been occupied by the hall but there is an unusual feature in that there are two large doors; the one at the south leads to the inner bailey and the one at the east goes to the outer bailey. It seems likely that there was some form of drawbridge and there is a plat-form in front of the south door that seems to support this idea. There are signs of additions to the keep in the 14th Century. A strong gatehouse linked the two baileys.

Open to the public daily Easter to October 10 a.m.–5.30 p.m.

Knepp Castle, *Shipley, Sussex. Between Shipley and West Grinstead.*

This house was built in 1809 by Nash and has the appearance of a castle, with its four turrets and circular towers. In 1904 it suffered a disastrous fire but was rebuilt.

On private land.

Knepp (Old) Castle, *Shipley, Sussex. Off the Worthing Road, three-quarters of a mile south of the house called Knepp Castle.*

The fragmentary remains of a small motte (30 feet high) and keep may be seen. It was one of the castles belonging to the de Braose family. It is said to have been destroyed by King John to prevent the French seizing it, and during the English Civil War it was finally demolished.

Knook Castle, *Upton Lovell, Wiltshire. On Knook Down.*

An early earthworks with a single bank and ditch and an entrance on the south-east.

Knockyn Castle, *Knockin, Shropshire. Six miles south-east from Oswestry.*

Founded by Guy Le Strange in the 11th Century, it was demolished during the reign of John but repaired and later used as a source of material for local building. Traces of the keep still survive.

Kenilworth Castle, a strongly defended Norman hold partially "civilised" during its ownership by Robert Dudley, Earl of Leicester

Kyloe Castle, *Kyloe, Northumberland.*

Some masonry remains have been incorporated into the farm buildings.

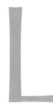

Lambton Castle, *Lambton Castle, County Durham.*

The original castle was demolished in the 18th Century to be replaced by Lambton Hall, which was enlarged and castellated in 1833. It was

damaged in 1854 and altered in 1875, and later housed a school.
On private land.

Lammerside Castle, *Lammerside, Westmorland.*

One-and-a-quarter miles north-west on the opposite bank of the river there are the remains of an oblong pele-tower of the 14th Century, with an internal cross wall.

Lancaster Castle, *Castle Hill, Lancaster, Lancashire.*

On a hill was the Roman fortress of Longoricum, and there are still traces of the fosse on the north side of the hill. Roger de Poictou received the land from William I, and built a tower in 1094. The castle was taken over by Stephen, and later King John held court here. In the 13th Century Henry III gave the land and castle to his son, Edmund "Crouchback", and created him Earl of Lancaster. It saw action in the Civil War, being under siege on several occasions, and there are still traces of earthworks of this period on the south-west side. The main surviving feature is the gatehouse which stands 66 feet high and was built by John of Gaunt using much of the earlier Norman materials. There are two octagonal flanking towers with machicolations and a portcullis. Some of the keep survives; it was 80 feet square with ten-foot-thick walls, and dates back to Roger of Poictou, although it was altered by John of Gaunt and again in the reign of Elizabeth. The south-west turret is known as John of Gaunt's Chair. In the basement is the chapel, and there are cells two floors below the ground. On the south side a tower, Dungeon Tower, used as a prison, was removed in 1812. The castle measures 380 feet by 350 feet but much of the bailey has been altered. On the west side is the Shire Hall built in 1802.
The site is partially occupied by a courthouse. Open to the public April 20th–28th, May 26th–June 2nd, and throughout August. Tours every 30 minutes.

Langley Castle, *Hexham, Northumberland, One-and-a-half miles south-west of Haydon Bridge on A686 to Alston.*

This was built *circa* 1350 as a strong tower-house, which was rectangular with corner towers projecting well forward. The entrance was on the first floor guarded by a portcullis, and the tower on the south-west corner was occupied by the latrines and garderobes with "group" seats. By the 16th Century it was largely in ruins and would have stayed so had it not been taken over in 1890 by Cadwallader Bates, who restored and embattled it.
Banqueting rooms: not open to general public.

Laughton-en-le-Morthen Castle, *Laughton-en-le-Morthen, West Riding, Yorkshire.*

Remains of a motte and bailey castle, near the church.

Launceston Castle, *Launceston, Cornwall. Near the centre of the town.*

Launceston was, until 1840, the county town of Cornwall, and the castle belonged originally to Robert of Mortain, Earl of Cornwall. It was built at a fairly late date, probably between 1227 and 1272, for the builder is thought to be Richard, Earl of Cornwall, who was Lord of Launceston for this period. He remodelled the inner defences to form a strong tower rising from a circular shell keep, protected by a lower wall which has now gone. On the death of Richard's son Edmund in 1300 the castle went to the Crown and was held for a while by Piers Gaveston, and in 1337 it was granted to Edward, first Duke of Cornwall. It was very neglected; a survey of that date stated that the walls were ruinous, the hall had two cellars which needed reroofing, and there was mention of a kitchen, a small upstairs hall, a chamber and a little chapel. The necessary repairs were completed by 1345. The great hall was re-roofed with slate, a new chamber was built with stone walls and much of the curtain wall was repaired as well as the high tower. It was held for the king in 1646 but was captured by Parliament and slighted.
By 1650 the hall and chapel had quite disappeared and only one old tower remained in reasonable repair; it was used by the County of Cornwall as a jail. This state of affairs continued until 1840, when the castle area was laid out as a public garden. In 1951 it was placed under the care of the Ministry of Works.

Open to the public:

	Weekdays	*Sundays*
March–April	*9.30 a.m.–5.30 p.m.*	*2–5.30 p.m.*
May–Sept.	*9.30 a.m.–7 p.m.*	*2–7 p.m.*
Oct.	*9.30 a.m.–5.30 p.m.*	*2–5.30 p.m.*
Nov.–Feb.	*10 a.m.–4.30 p.m.*	*2–4.30 p.m.*

Laxton Castle, *Laxton, Nottinghamshire.*

A large motte surmounted by a second, smaller motte; a few fragments of masonry but little else of the castle of the Alselin family.

Leasowe Castle, *Wallasey, Cheshire. Two miles west of Wallasey.*

Now a railwaymen's convalescent home, but it was built in 1593 by the Earl of Derby and altered in 1818 to incorporate a castellated front.
On private land.

Leconfield Castle, *Leconfield, East Riding, Yorkshire. Two-and-a-half miles north of Beverley and south-west of the village.*

Site of a Percy castle licensed in 1308, with a moat enclosing an area of approximately four acres.

Leeds Castle, *Leeds, Kent. Off the A20.*

The manor was owned by Hugh de Crevecour in the early 12th Century and it remained in this family until the mid-13th Century, but in 1272 it became a royal castle. Edward I (1272–1307) gave it to Eleanor, the queen, and for long it was part of the queen's dower. In the early 16th Century some rebuilding took place, and in 1552 it went to Sir Anthony St. Leger. It passed through several hands until, in 1821, the then-owner Fiennes Wykeham-Martin set to work to rebuild it—perhaps "re-create" is a better description. Much of its picturesque appearance today is due to his embellishments.
The castle stands in a lake with the entrance at the south end by way of an elaborate barbican, with a mill, which dates back at least to the 13th Century, attached. Only that part of the barbican guarding the approach from Maidstone survives, with its portcullis groove. Next comes a gatehouse with some Tudor windows and earlier machicolations. This building was modified during the period of Edward I's reign and at the same time a wall with fine D-shaped turrets was added, but only the foundations of four now survive; that at the north-east is still in very good repair. Of the original main building only a cellar remains, and the rest of the "medieval" pile is 19th Century. To the east is the Maiden's Tower which dates from the Tudor period with 19th Century battlements. Separate is the Gloriette, reached by way of a bridge (19th Century) at the north end of which is a tall tower containing a dated 15th Century bell. The Gloriette is D-shaped and of two storeys with Tudor windows, although the tower is of Edward I's reign. Much of the interior has been remodelled at various times.

Leeds Castle, *Leeds, West Riding, Yorkshire.*

Probably built soon after the Conquest by a

Cell door in the dungeons of Lancaster Castle

member of the Paganel family, on a site bounded by Millhill, Bishopsgate and part of Boar Lane. Little seems to have happened to it apart from a siege by Stephen and a short spell as a prison for Richard II.

A sham castle is also to be found in Leeds, at the north end of Waterloo Lake in Roundhay Park.

Leicester Castle, *Leicester, Leicestershire.*

The first castle was started during the 11th Century; it stood by the river Soar and had two baileys. The inner bailey is entered by way of a gateway north of the church or by the Turret Gateway (1422–3). The gateway leads to an extension of the castle known as the Newarke. The motte, 30 feet high, still stands and to the northwest is Castle Yard. On the east is a gatehouse of mid-15th Century, whilst Magazine Gateway dates from *circa* 1410. The castle saw fighting during the English Civil Wars.

Lewes Castle, *Lewes, Sussex.*

When a Norman king left England to campaign in Normandy or elsewhere it was the custom to appoint two justiciars to control the kingdom during his absence. William of Warenne was given this appointment in 1074, and this is some indication of his importance. William had been granted lands in Sussex and at Lewes, on the river Ouse, he built himself a castle. It differed from the standard Norman castle in having two mottes, one overlooking the town and containing the keep while the other overlooked the river. Both mounds were built up of large lumps of quarried chalk. By the end of the 11th Century the wooden palisades on the motte and around the bailey were replaced by strong walls built mainly of flint rubble. The walls show the herringbone pattern, so often found in Norman architecture, whereby the first course was of flat stones, the next course was placed sloping to the left, the next to the right and the pattern repeated. The smaller motte at the north east corner of the bailey, known as Brack Mount, was presumably of less importance since it seems never to have been altered. Entrance to the castle from the town was through a square gatehouse and there were at least two other square towers.

Limestone was transported all the way across the channel from Caen in Normandy to face these buildings.

Despite the importance of the site Lewes saw little action until 1264. In May of that year Simon de Montfort, who did so much to found the machinery of British democracy, fought and defeated Henry III just outside the town of Lewes. Some fighting must have also taken place within the town, although there are no contemporary records of any damage sustained by the castle. Shortly after this two extra towers were added to the shell keep; they are of flint, as there is an abundance of this material on the Sussex downs. Both towers are pierced with numerous arrow slits. During the first half of the 14th Century a strong barbican was added to the castle and much of this still survives today, although there has been some restoration. The barbican had tall turrets with loopholes of the cruciform shape which could accommodate both long bows and crossbows, and the top has a very fine machicolated parapet. After its brief spell of military glory the castle suffered rather ignominiously at the hands of the burghers and from that date onwards little heed seems to have been paid to it as a military structure.

By the early part of the 17th Century it was being slowly demolished to obtain the raw materials for other buildings. In 1774 what little was left of the castle was leased to a local wood-merchant who converted the keep into a summer house. Today the doorway leading into the western tower and the round staircase in the eastern tower are the results of his efforts. Later the castle was acquired by the Sussex Archeological Society, who still own and maintain it today.

Open to the public all the year: Weekdays 10 a.m.–1 p.m.; Sundays 2–5.30 p.m.; Easter to September 2–5.30 p.m. Admission (1972) 10p, Children 5p.

Lewisham Castle, *Aldbourne, Wiltshire.*

South of Stock Lane, traces of a 13th Century motte and bailey castle.

Leybourne Castle, *Leybourne, Kent.*

There are considerable remains of a small castle which was held, at one time, by the Leybourne

family. A gatehouse survives which has one most unusual feature: there is a long slot above the gateway some three feet long and six inches wide, connected to a series of chutes, so that defenders might pour boiling water or other unpleasant liquids down over attackers outside the gate. There are also some ruins of a chapel. The remains of the building have been incorporated into a modern home. There is a Tudor gatehouse with linenfold gates.
On private land.

Liddell Castle, *Kirkandraw, Cumberland. Half a mile north-east of Kirkandraw.*

An earthwork with a high mound marking the castle which was allegedly destroyed by Edward III. There are signs of two baileys, and the motte is in the east corner.

Lilbourne Castle, *Lilbourne, Northamptonshire.*

A Roman camp—Tripontium—was here, as well as a castle of Stephen's time (1135–54) but only some minor fragments and mounds survive. Half a mile to the west there is another motte with a moat.

Lincoln Castle, *Lincoln, Lincolnshire.*

Like Pevensey and Porchester (qqv) this castle occupies part of a Roman camp site. The castle was begun in 1068 and many houses were demolished to accommodate its six acres. There were great ditches to the north, east and west; the walls were of early Norman stonework, and on the west was a gatehouse with a projecting barbican. The main entrance was from the cathedral side with a great Gatehouse, Norman with 14th Century additions. The inside of the castle was taken over in the 18th Century for the erection of a prison—now it is a Record Office. Numerous towers —Lucy, Observatory, Cobb Ham and others— survive along the walls.

John of Gaunt's gatehouse at Lancaster Castle; earlier Norman masonry was used in its construction

Open to the public daily April to September, 10 a.m.–4 p.m., October to March, 2–4 p.m.

Lindisfarne Castle, *Holy Island, Northumberland. Five miles east of Beal across the sands.*

This began life as a 16th Century artillery fort which fell into ruins, but in 1902 it was acquired by Edward Hudson who commissioned Sir Edwin Lutyens to repair, restore and modify it.
It was captured in 1715 for the Old Pretender by the captain of a ship favourable to his cause. It continued in use as a station of the Royal Artillery Coast Brigade during the latter part of the 19th Century.
Open to the public April 1st to June 2nd and then June 25th to September 30th—daily (except Tuesdays) 1–5 p.m. June 3rd to 24th Wednesdays only 1–5 p.m. Admission 20p, Children 10p.

Linstock Castle, *Houghton, Cumberland. One-and-a-half miles south-east of Houghton.*

Originally the residence, in the 12th and 13th Centuries, of the Bishops of Carlisle, but later simply a pele-tower to which was added a range of buildings.

Liskeard Castle, *Liskeard, Cornwall. North of the town, in a field called Castle Park.*

These fragmentary ruins are all that is left of a castle built by Robert de Mortain and which, by 1540, was described as ruins.
On private land.

Longford Castle, *Britford, Wiltshire. Just off the A338.*

The castle dates from 1591 when it was built by Sir Thomas Gorges in a park which covers some 250 acres. It originally had five round towers (two of these survive) on a triangular plan, but during the building Gorges ran out of money. His wife begged the gift of the hull of a ship of the Spanish Armada, wrecked when her husband had been in

charge of Hurst Castle (qv). The treasure it contained was used to complete the building, and there the family lived for many years. It passed to Lord Coleraine who held it for the king until it surrendered in 1645. It escaped slighting but has been much restored and altered. In 1870/8 the façade was rebuilt by Anthony Salvin. The Long Gallery houses a collection of pictures and antiquities, such as the Imperial Steel Chain made in Augsburg in 1577, captured by King Gustavus Adolphus, and purchased by the Earl of Radnor in the late 18th Century.
On private land.

Longtown Castle, *Longtown, Herefordshire. Above the river Monnow, on the south end of a tongue of land.*

An oblong enclosure of about three acres. At the north-west corner was the motte surmounted by a circular keep. The bailey was divided by a wall with a gatehouse, probably of 12th–13th Century origin. The keep still has three projections, semi-circular, one with a spiral staircase. There are substantial fragments of the walls. The castle was built by William FitzOsbern and later passed to the De Lacy family.

Lowther Castle, *Lowther, Westmorland.*

The original structure dated from the 17th Century. It was badly damaged by fire in 1720 and was rebuilt in 1806/11 by Smirke, with a very long front complete with turrets and battlements.
On private land.

Ludersgate Castle, *Ludersgate, Wiltshire. West of the town.*

A royal castle built, certainly before 1141, on a site of a Roman camp. Only part of the keep and some earthworks still stand.

Ludlow Castle, *Ludlow, Shropshire.*

In the same way that strong castles were needed to guard against the warlike Scots, others were needed to protect England against the warlike Welsh. The border areas between these countries were known as the Marches and Ludlow was one of the 32 castles erected to overawe and contain the Welsh. It seems likely that a castle was built here about 1080 by Roger de Lacey. He chose well, for the fortress is perched on the cliff overlooking the rivers Teme and Corve. Unfortunately Roger de Lacey rebelled against William Rufus and was exiled, and the castle passed into the hands of the Crown. Ludlow was granted to Payn FitzJohn by Henry I but he was killed fighting the Welsh in 1136 and was followed by Sir Joyce de Dinan, who built a chapel in the middle ward and extended the castle. In 1138 Gervase de Paganel, supporting Queen Matilda in the struggle for the crown of England, captured Ludlow and Stephen besieged the castle. During the siege Stephen rescued Prince Henry of Scotland, who was being pulled from his horse by a grappling iron thrown from a window of the castle. When Sir Joyce died in 1166 the castle was taken over by Hugh de Lacey, who had captured it a few years before in Joyce's absence, with the help of one of the ladies in the castle who let down a rope from the battlements. From 1181–1190 the castle was back under royal control.

In about 1310 Roger Mortimer became the first Earl of March, but he became a threat to the young King Edward III and was captured at Nottingham in 1330 and hung at Tyburn for treason. During the Wars of the Roses Ludlow belonged to Richard, Duke of York. The Battle of Ludford Bridge was fought on the River Teme when Henry VI moved in to attack the castle. Richard attacked the Lancastrians early in the morning before they were ready, but Sir Andrew Trollope deserted him and took his troops over to the king's side. York was forced to flee to Ireland, and Ludlow was sacked; the Lancastrians were in control until 1460 when they lost the Battle of Northampton. From 1472 to '83 the young Prince of Wales and his brother lived in the castle before they went to London, where they met their mysterious death in the Tower of London and became known as the "Princes in the Tower".

The gatehouse is dated 1581, and the keep was also repaired at this time and used as a prison. A local court set up by Edward IV, with jurisdiction over the whole of Wales and called the Court of the Marches, was abolished in 1689 but between these two dates it was based at Ludlow. Originally the main entrance was through the keep via a drawbridge.

There was some fighting around Ludlow during the Civil War but it was not seriously damaged, although held by the Royalists. In 1642 the Earl of Essex led 20,000 men in an attack on Ludlow but it held out, and did so again on later occasions. Some dismantling took place in 1651. The castle was left desolate, and during the reign of George I the lead was taken off the roof on the main building, so that the inside suffered greatly.

The town of Ludlow was almost certainly planned and laid out at the time the castle was built and the town in many ways followed the Roman pattern with a regular set of intersecting streets. The original castle is set at the north-west corner and is separated from the outer ward by a deep ditch. The back of the castle is protected by the steep, rocky banks.

Open to the public daily April to September 10.30 a.m. to 1 p.m. and 2–4.30 p.m. Weekdays only in October to March, the same hours.

Lullingstone Castle, *Lullingstone, Kent.*

A gatehouse of the 16th Century in red brick, three storeys, rectangular with wood framed windows and battlements. A two-storeyed house nearby is also named Castle.

Open to the public May to September, weekdays 9.30 a.m.–7 p.m., Sundays 2–7 p.m. October to April closing 4 p.m.

Lulworth Castle, *East Lulworth, Dorsetshire. Near the church.*

This was the home of the Newburgh family until the 16th Century. The existing house was started in 1600 and completed about 1650. It was garrisoned during the Civil War by both sides, and suffered much damage. In 1830 it was used by Charles X, who was driven out of France by a revolution. It has tall, round, five-storeyed towers at each corner of a four-storeyed central building.

Opposite, Lewes Castle, originally built by the Conqueror's "justicar", William de Warenne

Lumley Castle, *Chester-le-Street, County Durham. One mile to the south of Chester-le-Street.*

Two licences are recorded in 1389 and 1392 as being issued to Sir Robert Lomley. There is a courtyard about 80 feet square and at each corner is a large, square tower with octagonal, machicolated turrets. On the west side a broad staircase leads up to the Great Hall, 60 feet by 30 feet, with a minstrel's gallery at one end. On the east is a very fine gatehouse, turreted and machicolated. Internally there has been considerable remodelling. About one mile away there are indications of an earlier castle.
The land is now owned by a restaurant.

Luton Castle, *Luton, Bedfordshire. Near Copt Hill.*

This belonged first to the de Someries—it was also known as Someries Castle—and then to the Wenlock family. It was one of the first buildings to be built of brick, and dates from the mid-15th Century. The gatehouse, with its polygonal projections, survives, as does a chapel and a section of wall.

Lydford Castle, *Lydford, Devonshire.*

Some fortifications existed at this spot certainly as early as the 10th Century and possibly as early as the 8th Century. There is reason to think that a Norman castle may well have been erected here soon after the Conquest; certainly it was garrisoned in 1198/99, and repairs were carried out early in the 13th Century. In 1216 it was passed by King John to William Brewer, but when he died it reverted to the Crown. It was still royal property in 1238 but in 1239 it was granted by Henry III to his brother Richard, Earl of Cornwall and since 1337 it has been part of the possessions of the Duchy of Cornwall. In 1546 the building was said to be in a very poor state of repair and by the very early 18th Century only the roofless shell of the keep was standing. It was repaired soon afterwards

and was used as a court and prison until the beginning of the 19th Century, when these functions were taken over by Princetown. In 1833 it was again in a derelict state and in 1922 the Duchy of Cornwall placed it under the care of the Commissioners of H.M. Works.

Cornwall was one of the few British centres for the production of tin and the local courts which dealt with the tin miners were known as Stannary Courts, from the Latin name for tin. Lydford gained a somewhat unsavoury reputation for harsh punishment, certainly as early as the 13th Century. The Court of Stannary was held in the upper room of the castle which also contained the prison. Some protection is afforded to the castle by the natural features of the site which is bounded by the river Lyd and a small tributary. An earthwork, some ten feet high, crosses the isthmus and there may also have been an outer ditch although this has now disappeared and the bank was probably surmounted by a palisade. It seems likely that the first Norman castle was built at the tip of the promontory west of the church, probably in a small triangular enclosure, with a high earth bank and a rock-cut ditch. It seems likely that the strong-house to be used as a prison was built in about 1195 as a tower, some 52 feet square, with walls more than ten feet thick and two storeys high. It fell into disrepair and was drastically rebuilt early in the 14th Century, then the top storey was removed and two new storeys were added. At the same time a ditch was dug around the tower and the soil excavated from the ditch piled round the base. In the 16th or 17th Century the ground floor was filled in with rubble and the cross wall thickened.

The keep is entered through a pointed arch door which leads directly into a small chamber in the thickness of the wall. On the right a staircase gives access to the second floor. On the inner side of the opening a modern steel gallery has been built at first floor level and until 1958 this ground floor was cobbled over twelve feet of rubble filling. The cross wall was rebuilt in the 16th or 17th Century and pierced by two openings. The stairs on the right of the entrance lead to the west angle of the keep and open into the principal chamber. On the right is a door leading into a garderobe set within the thickness of the wall. A spiral steel staircase leads to the ground floor and on the left is one of the few original windows complete with its later

blocking, done at the same time as the two storeys were added at the top. In the corner is a large well eight feet in diameter and certainly over 30 feet deep although this too has been filled in with rubble. The large chamber on the second floor was almost certainly intended as a hall whilst the other rooms were divided, no doubt by wooden partitions.
Open to the public at any time, admission free.

Lydney Castle, *Lydney, Gloucestershire. One mile west of Lydney in Deer Park to the south-east of the Roman Temple.*

A 12th Century castle stood here, but now only the foundations are to be seen of the motte and bailey site.

Lympne Castle, *Lympne, Kent. Near Hythe.*

A castellated house, also known as Stutfall Castle. This was part of a Roman fort but a Norman castle erected here was largely destroyed by a landslide. The whole site was restored in 1905.
Open to the public: April to October, Wednesdays and Sundays also Bank Holiday weekends. July to September, daily 10.30 a.m.–1 p.m. and 2.30–6 p.m. Open on other days when possible and to parties by appointment. Admission 15p, Children 5p.

Lyng Castle, *Lyng, Norfolk. Five miles north-east of Dereham.*

There are only very slight traces of the castle, which was licensed in 1344 by John de Norwich.

Lyonshall Castle, *Lyonshall, Herefordshire. North-east of the church.*

Remains of a 13th Century castle, quadrangular in shape, with moats, which has belonged to the families of De Lacey, Carey and Devereux.

Macclesfield Castle, *Macclesfield, Cheshire.*

South of the church on a path called Black Wall Gate, leading from the town to the river, stands a wall which was part of the palace of Humphrey, Duke of Lancaster. Also near the Congleton Road, at Castle Field, was a motte.

Mackworth Castle, *Mackworth, Derbyshire.*

Part of the gatehouse, dating from the very late 16th Century, still stands complete with battlements and gargoyles.

Maiden Castle, *Brough, Westmorland. Five miles south-east of Brough.*

This small fort with thick walls of stone dates from about 2nd to 4th Century A.D.

Maiden Castle, *Broxton, Cheshire.*

An Iron Age fort of one-and-a-half acres with two ramparts on the south and east and an entrance on the east side.

Maiden Castle, *near Dorchester, Dorset. Two-and-a-half miles south-west of Dorchester.*

One of the most famous of all European earth fortresses, this has been occupied intermittently for thousands of years. Situated on top of a hill, it measures some 1,000 yards in length and is surrounded by three high banks with their corresponding ditches. The earliest occupants of Maiden Castle were people of the late Stone Age; their camp was very much smaller and is no longer visible on the surface but numerous relics of this occupation have been unearthed including a unique doll or idol. The village was occupied until sometime around 2000 B.C. when, for some unknown reason, it was deserted. The next people to take over the site were remarkable for their industry and application. They built a mound, between two trenches, which runs in an almost straight line—there is a slight curve at one end—for nearly six hundred yards. On its way it crosses the original ditch and mound erected by the Stone Age people and it seems to have been used purely for burial purposes. One grave has so far been located; this was at the eastern end and was of a 30-year-old man whose body had been hacked to pieces after death, which might suggest some ritual cannibal activities. The burial is dated to around 2000 to 1500 B.C. Shortly after this the site was again deserted for some unknown reason.

The next inhabitants of Maiden Castle appeared early in the Iron Age, for by around 300 B.C. people were again living there. These inhabitants built some fortifications located by the earth works at the eastern entrance and consisting of a wall nine feet wide and seven or eight feet high. A wooden palisade crowned it and about seven feet behind was a "V"-shaped ditch. As the timber weathered over the years some of it was replaced by dry stone walling of thin slabs of limestone. Behind these earthen walls lived a fair-sized community with numerous timber huts and streets. A large number of circular pits about eleven feet deep were dug, and these were probably for storing grain. The large number suggests that as they were finished with they were filled up with the rubbish of the village. The settlement prospered and grew until it covered some 45 acres. The entrance to the Iron Age village was on the eastern side and it is perhaps some indication of the volume and importance of traffic that there were two entrances. The village expanded to the west and the new entrance more or less repeated the pattern of the eastern one. Both entrances had some timber work and the sum result was to produce a maze-like entrance which prevented easy access to the town for an attacker. Some time in the 1st Century B.C. the earlier single rampart was reinforced with multiple banks, with the idea of keeping attackers well away. A very strong case has been made out to suggest that this innovation was due to the adoption of a new

weapon, the sling. This extension of the ramparts made it difficult for the slinger to approach the target and so reduced his effective range. The main gateway was strengthened by high walls of large limestone blocks.

In A.D. 43 the Emperor Claudius invaded Britain, and the south-east of England soon fell to the invaders. The Romans then penetrated and pacified the rest of the country by first reducing the organised centres of opposition. Under their commander Vespasian, later to be Emperor, the Second Augustan Legion was allotted this task in the south-west. Eventually they reached Maiden Castle, where an early reconnaissance was doubtless made, and the Romans realised that the only practical way in was through one of the gates. The western gate was the more heavily defended, for there were no less than seven ramparts. Whether a probing raid to test the defences was made is not known, but the main attack was delivered at the slightly less formidable eastern gate. After drawing up the legion in battle order Vespasian began a bombardment by the Roman artillery—which consisted of a large number of very heavy, powerful crossbow devices mounted on portable frames. These *ballistae* could be operated with speed, and showers of bolts or arrows were launched against the defenders. Numerous arrowheads have been discovered, including one embedded in the vertebra of one of the defenders. Presumably under cover of the confusion caused by the arrows, the Roman legion now advanced and fought its way from rampart to rampart. Some huts built in the innermost part of the gateway were set ablaze and amidst the smoke and confusion the defenders were cut down by the highly efficient Roman legionaries. Once the town had been taken steps were taken to render the castle defenceless, and therefore useless. No doubt some of the inhabitants were taken as hostages by the Romans, whilst those left buried their dead; and excavations have brought to light many skeletons whose bones bear signs of sword cuts. The inhabitants were probably left in peace, but the development of the Roman town of Dorchester and, possibly, other factors, caused them to abandon the site, and by about A.D. 70 the settlement was once again deserted. For three hundred years it seems to have remained empty, until in about A.D. 380 a small, square temple was built at the eastern end. Accompanying it was a small, two-roomed cottage which was probably

built as a dwelling place for the priest, and some modification of the earthworks were also carried out by the builders. It is not known to which god it was dedicated, but its worship continued for a century or more. By the 6th Century the temple had disappeared, and the only sign of occupation at this period is one burial.
Open to the public at any time, admission free.

Maiden's Bower Castle, *Topcliffe, North Riding, Yorkshire. One mile south-east of Topcliffe.*

This was built in 1071 by William Percy and strengthened in 1174. It is a motte and bailey site with two baileys and a well preserved, deep ditch.

Malpas Castle, *Malpas, Cheshire. Near the church.*

The motte is approximately 120 feet in diameter and part of the outer ditch survives. It was built by the first Earl of Chester.

Manchester Castle, *Manchester, Lancashire.*

According to Leland, writing in 1536, the remains of Old "Mancastel" were even then being destroyed and the materials were used for bridge building. It was situated almost "two flyte shots" outside the town on the same side of Irwell.

Marlborough Castle, *Marlborough, Wiltshire.*

A castle here was started by William I. Here King John was married and from here Henry III summoned Parliament. For a time it belonged to the Seymour family but it was largely remodelled by John Webb, trained by the famous Inigo Jones. Both the diarists Pepys and Evelyn visited the castle, as did Charles II. The castle became an inn, remaining so for some time, serving as a luxury coaching inn until 1843 when it became the centre of the then-new Marlborough College. Now only a motte, some 60 feet high, survives.

Maxstoke Castle, *Maxstoke, Warwickshire. Three miles from Maxstoke on A47 from Birmingham.*

A licence was given in 1346; the castle was built by William de Clinton, Earl of Huntingdon, and was modified in 1440 by the 1st Duke of Buckingham. It was rectangular with four corner towers and a large gatehouse in the north wall. Against the walls were various buildings of which only the beam holes survive. The towers were all embattled and polygonal. The chapel was probably on the west wall and the great hall to the south of it, but in 1820 a number of rooms were built against the wall and there were also some 17th Century additions and modifications. The whole building is surrounded by a large moat.
On private land.

Melandra Castle, *Melandra Castle, Derbyshire. Three-quarters of a mile north-west of Glossop.*

Originally this was a simple Roman fort but it was later strengthened by the addition of stone facings. The four walls are pierced by four gates and the entire camp covers about two acres, measuring nearly 400 feet by 370 feet.

Melbourne Castle, *Melbourne, Derbyshire.*

Robert of Holland received a licence to crenellate in 1311 and this was, until the 18th Century, an impressive edifice, but all has now disappeared except for a piece of wall.

Membury Castle, *Membury, Devon.*

Iron Age single-rampart earthworks, covering about two/three acres, with an entrance at the north-east end which is designed to lead the unwary into a blind alley.

Merdon Castle, *Merdon, Hampshire. North corner of Hursley Park.*

A castle with a double moat, built by Bishop Henry de Blois in 1138 but demolished by Henry II. Traces of masonry from the keep and the walls still remain.

Mere Castle, *Mere, Wiltshire.*

It was built in 1253 by Richard, Earl of Cornwall, and was rectangular, 390 feet by 102 feet, with rectangular corner towers and two round towers on the east side. Little now remains.

Mereworth Castle, *Mereworth, Kent.*

Despite its name this is a house built in 1723 by the 7th Earl of Westmorland. It is a very fine example of Palladian architecture, with columns, pediments and a central dome.
On private land.

Mettingham Castle, *Mettingham, Suffolk. Two miles south-east of the town and one mile south of the church of Mettingham.*

Here are the ruins of a fortified house of the 14th Century, built by Sir John de Norwich and licensed in 1342. The site occupied approximately five acres with a moat which encircled and also bisected the site, and the castle itself occupied the northern section. Part of the curtain wall survives as does the gatehouse with its two square, flanking towers.

Middle Castle, *Baschurch, Shropshire. Two-and-a-half miles from the village between Chester and Shrewsbury.*

This castle was fortified in 1308 by John, Lord le Strange and it remained in this family for centuries. It was small and square with a central courtyard and an exterior moat, and to the east another piece of land was enclosed within a moat. On the north-east side was a gatehouse complete with drawbridge and on the south side was a large room, probably the kitchen. It was mostly only two storeys high except for a tall tower in the north-east corner of the inner court. It fell into ruins in the late 16th Century.

The huge ramparts of Maiden Castle, stormed by the Romans during the early stages of the Claudian invasion

Middleham Castle, *Middleham, North Riding, Yorkshire. Two miles south of Leyburn.*

In 1069 Alan the Red, a relative of the Duke of Brittany, was granted this land, and much later it formed part of the lands of Richard Neville, Earl of Warwick—the "King Maker", who died in the Battle of Barnet in 1471. Along with his other lands it passed to the Crown and was given subsequently to Richard, Duke of Gloucester, later Richard III. Following his defeat at the Battle of Bosworth Field the castle became the property of Henry VII and remained as a Crown castle until 1604, when James I gave it to Sir Henry Lindley. It stayed in this family and passed through the hands of various other owners until 1925, when it was taken over by the Commissioners of H.M. Works.

The earliest castle on this site was some 500 yards south-west of the present masonry building and, presumably, was built by Alan the Red. It was a simple earthwork; the keep which exists today was not begun until about 1170 by Robert FitzRalph. There were originally two courtyards, although one has been built over by the town. The central rectangular keep was surrounded by a wall, most of which dates from the latter part of the 13th Century. The wall was four feet six inches thick and probably stood about 24 feet high with parapet and walk. The outside is further strengthened by a number of pilasters and is pierced by a number of splayed windows. On the south-west corner was the Princes' Tower, a rounded bastion, whilst that on the south-east was rectangular. The north-east tower was modified in the 14th Century to form a gatehouse. The main entrance was on the north-east side and had a drawbridge and a three-storey gatehouse. The passageway in was protected at the bailey end by a portcullis. The first floor was approached by means of an intra-mural staircase and was occupied by two rooms with a further two in the storey above. There were corner turrets and battlements which were apparently decorated with sculptured figures of armed men. The central keep measured 105 feet by 78 feet, making it one of the largest in the country, and the walls vary between ten and twelve feet thick. The entrance was on the first floor with a flight of stairs on the east face of the keep, which terminated in a forebuilding and a porch. A central wall bisects the keep, with the great hall on the eastern side of the first floor;

originally it had a wooden roof, and at the end were screens covering the door into the hall. A spiral staircase built into the south-east corner of the keep leads down to the kitchen and cellars or up to the battlements. Since no fireplace exists it may be assumed that there was an open fireplace in the centre of the now missing floor. The usual domestic offices, a pantry and buttery, were at the southern end and were divided off with partitions, while the larders, cellars and kitchens were on the ground floor below. In the north-west corner of the ground floor is the castle well. Garderobes were installed in a small turret on the south of the keep and there was a double garderobe turret on the west. Two features mentioned in a 16th Century survey, a pigeon house and a bell turret, have disappeared. At some time, probably in the 15th Century, doors were cut through the south and west wall of the great chambers and these led, by way of a wooden bridge, to rooms which were then part of the curtain wall.

To the east of the keep is a chapel, late 13th Century, of three storeys. The first and second served as basement and vestries and perhaps as a dwelling-place for the priest. The chapel is so much in ruins that it is difficult to reconstruct the details. There are foundations of a square tower in the curtain wall at the north-west corner; nothing else has survived but it probably contained a gateway to a bridge over the ditch. The eastern curtain is now largely in ruins but a small portion of the southern end retains the original wall walk and parapets. A two-storey tower dating from the late 13th Century, at the south-east corner of the castle, has two windows in the upper storey and to the west is a one-storeyed building of about the same date. About the same time that these towers were built garderobes were added at the north-east and south-west corners of the south-east tower. On the south-west the round tower was originally a bastion, but this was raised by two storeys. Richard of Gloucester's eldest son Edward was traditionally born in this tower, hence its name "the Prince's Tower", but in the 16th Century it was simply known as the Round Tower. On the west side of the castle there is a three-storeyed tower occupied entirely by garderobes. The north-west tower was added in the 14th Century and enlarged and made higher in the 15th Century. In 1538 it is described as having a "square house" within it.
There was a moat surrounding the castle and this

was in turn surrounded by a wall which was said to be 252 yards long, but apart from some odd foundations on the north-west the wall has now disappeared. Around the curtain wall of an outer ward, now also gone, were numerous small out-buildings which, by the 16th Century, were in ruins.

Open to the public:

	Weekdays	*Sundays*
March–April	*9.30 a.m.–5.30 p.m.*	*2–5.30 p.m.*
May–Sept.	*9.30 a.m.–7 p.m.*	*2–7 p.m.*
Oct.	*9.30 a.m.–5.30 p.m.*	*2–5.30 p.m.*
Nov.–Feb.	*9.30 a.m.–4 p.m.*	*2–4 p.m.*

Middleton Castle, *Middleton, Norfolk. Three miles south-east of King's Lynn.*

The gatehouse of the castle belonging to the Scales family still stands after restoration by Sir Lewis Jarvis in the late 19th Century. It is 51 feet by 27 feet and 54 feet high, built of small red bricks during the reign of Henry VI. There are four turrets, three octagonal and one square with a staircase; the archway leads through into a court-yard some 250 feet by 140 feet where there were originally domestic buildings, and around the site there is a moat. Near Middleton Hall is a motte which may have supported an earlier castle.
On private land.

Middleton Stoney Castle, *Middleton Stoney, Ox-fordshire. Three miles from Bicester; east end of the church.*

Some masonry remains of a castle belonging to the Longespee family of Salisbury.

Midford Castle, *Combe Down, Somerset.*

A small, three-storeyed house built for Disney Roebuck with the 19th Century addition of a castellated gatehouse.
On private land.

Mileham Castle, *Mileham, Norfolk. Three hundred yards from the church.*

A motte and bailey castle at The Hall Yards. There are some traces of the keep on the motte.

Millom Castle, *Millom, Cumberland. Near Duddon Sands.*

Licence to crenellate was given to Sir John Huddlestone in 1335, and the castle remained in the family for centuries. Huddlestones served at Agincourt and at Edgehill. In 1648 the castle was besieged by the Roundheads. There are con-siderable remains. On the east side there is an entrance which leads through to the courtyard in which are the remains of the original gatehouse. On the north are the kitchens whilst to the south is the solar. The Great Hall is on the west side next to the ruins of the great tower. The building was converted for use as a farmhouse in the 19th Century.
On private land.

Miserden Castle, *Miserden, Gloucestershire. Half a mile north-east of Chine.*

The motte and bailey, with remains of a 13th Century gateway, of a castle built for the Musard family in the late 11th Century. It appears to have been abandoned late in the 13th Century.

Mitford Castle, *Mitford, Northumberland.*

Protected on two sides by rivers and on the third side by a moat, the castle sits on top of a small hill of sandstone. It was originally an ordinary motte and bailey castle and in the early 13th Century a small five-sided keep, unique in England, was built inside the earlier shell keep which then be-came, in effect, a bailey wall. Only a couple of vaulted chambers of the basement survive. To the south was the outer bailey with its curtain walls, in which was built a 13th Century chapel or church of some kind. The castle was abandoned early in the 14th Century and was in ruins by the 16th Century.

Moccas Castle, *Moccas, Herefordshire.*

Three-quarters of a mile south-west of the village, on what was very swampy ground, is the site of a castle licensed in 1296. It was small, covering just over two acres.

Moreton Corbet Castle, *Moreton Corbet, Shropshire.*

On a site roughly triangular in shape, with a keep of the very early 13th Century which has a fine fireplace on the first floor. In 1579 the gateway at the northern apex of the site was altered by Sir Andrew Corbet, and there are Elizabethan additions on the south side.
On private ground.

Morpeth Castle, *Morpeth, Northumberland.*

In the 15th Century a gate tower was erected on the much earlier Norman motte and bailey castle. This tower was machicolated and had corner turrets, and there are remains of this tower together with some of the curtain wall behind it. In the English Civil War it was held by Parliament and for 21 days resisted a siege by the Marquis of Montrose. Not far away on Ha Hill there are more remains of Norman masonry.

Mortimer's Castle, *Much Marcle, Herefordshire. North of the church.*

A motte and bailey castle with a motte 150 feet in diameter and 20 feet high. On the east was an inner bailey; there was an outer one to the east and north, with another enclosed area to the north-east.

Mounsey Castle, *Dulverton, Somerset. On the B3222.*

Trees cover the flattened top of this hill near a river and obscure the small earthwork of an Iron Age fort (cf Brewers Castle).

Mow Cop Castle, *Mow Cop, Cheshire.*

Folly built by Randle Wilbraham in 1754–1760, in the form of a ruined tower on a dramatic 1,100-foot crag.

Mulgrave Castle, *Mulgrave, North Riding, Yorkshire.*

Three-quarters of a mile south-west of the new Mulgrave Castle are the overgrown remains of a 13th Century gatehouse with semi-circular towers. The curtain wall is partly 13th Century and later. There is a rectangular keep, with four semi-circular towers of *circa* 1300 with some 16th Century windows inserted. The new castle was built for the Duchess of Buckingham in the 18th Century.

Muncaster Castle, *Muncaster, Cumberland. Three-quarters of a mile south-east of Ravenglass village on A595. North of the river Esk.*

Following his defeat at the Battle of Hexham in 1464, Henry VI took refuge here and, in gratitude, made a present of a glass vessel. This became known as the Luck of Muncaster, and was carefully preserved for centuries. Part of the original tower is incorporated into the present house, which was built in 1862/6 by Anthony Salvin. There are some very fine rooms with some good Tudor fireplaces and 18th Century features.
Open to the public: grounds and bird garden, Easter Saturday to end of September daily 1 p.m.–6 p.m. Admission 20p, Children 10p. Castle: Easter Saturday to end of September Wednesdays, Thursdays, Saturdays, Sundays and Bank Holidays 2 p.m.–5 p.m. Admission 15p extra, Children 8p.

Musbury Castle, *Musbury, Devonshire.*

Situated on a high hill, a prehistoric earthwork.

Nafferton Castle, *Ovingham, Northumberland. One-and-a-half miles north-west of the village. North of A69.*

Erected early in the 13th Century, this castle had no "planning permission" and was not completed or, if it was, later partly demolished.

Naworth Castle, *Brampton, Cumberland.*

In 1336 a crenellation licence was granted to Ranulph de Dacre, Sheriff of Cumberland, but the remains here probably date from 1385. The shape is that of an irregular quadrangle with a deep ditch on three sides, whilst the fourth side had a moat complete with drawbridge and a strong gatehouse. It was granted originally to Hubert de Vallibus (or Vaux) by Henry II, and remained in this family. The castle stands on a triangular piece of land by the river Irthing, and on the south front is the entrance leading into the courtyard. The outer defence has a deep ditch crossed by a drawbridge. On the east are the chief quarters and on the north is the Great Hall entered by way of a flight of stairs from the yard. It measures 70 feet by 21 feet; there are dining rooms and kitchens and a chapel on the west front. The Hall and Gatehouse leading into the outerward were built by Lord Thomas Dacre, although during his lifetime the castle was described as being ruinous and unoccupied. In the late 16th Century and early 17th Century a certain amount of repair and restoration was carried out by Lord William Howard. On 10th May 1844 a serious fire destroyed much of the castle, but not Belted Will's Tower in the north-east. This is the tower built by Lord William, who was a hard man on wrongdoers; he was made Warden of the Marches, and is said to have hanged malefactors on oak trees near the castle.
On private land.

Neroche Castle, *Neroche Castle, Somerset.*

This may well be an example of the Normans utilising a prehistoric fort as a site in which to build their castle. The motte is at the north and is large, as are the ditches surrounding the site, but little else can be traced.

Netley Castle, *Netley, Hampshire. Two hundred yards west from the Abbey.*

Another of Henry VIII's coastal castles, built in 1542 and garrisoned until 1627. In 1851 it was extended and a Gothic-type tower was added, and there were later modifications.
On private land.

Newark Castle, *Newark on Trent, Nottinghamshire.*

There were several fortifications erected prior to the main castle which was built by Alexander, Bishop of Lincoln in 1123. It was soon taken over by Stephen, and then saw action during the reigns of John and Henry III. During the English Civil War Newark was strongly for the king; in 1643 it beat off an attack by Roundheads and in February 1644 it was again under siege, but Prince Rupert brought troops from Chester to the rescue. In 1645 Parliament was back again and the king, on his way to relieve Newark in June, suffered the great defeat at Naseby. The king and survivors reached the safety of Newark; he left later for Oxford and the town was again closely invested, but when the king was taken by the Scots in 1646 Newark surrendered. The castle was slighted in May 1646.
The castle was roughly rectangular, three and four storeys high with square corner towers and a gatehouse at the north end, together with a barbican and a drawbridge over the moat. In the early 13th Century it was largely rebuilt using red sandstone. The north-west hexagonal tower is 13th Century work and at the foot of the north-west tower is a circular Norman postern gate. The gatehouse,

45 feet by 30 feet, is three storeys high with walls nine feet thick, and on the north wall are two very strong buttresses, one on each side of the Norman towers. There are remains of a south-west tower, rectangular, 24 feet by fifteen feet, traditionally the place of King John's death.

Open to the public at all reasonable times; parties of six and more are conducted round the site, on application to the Curator, Newark Museum, Appleton Gate.

Newbiggin Castle, *Newbiggin, Westmorland.*

The land was granted to Laurence de New-binninge and the castle was probably erected during the reign of Edward I. The present house

Newark Castle has seen much action; during the Civil War this Royalist stronghold was repeatedly attacked

dates from 1533 when Christopher Crackenthorpe had it built, complete with battlements.
On private land.

Newcastle upon Tyne Castle, *Newcastle upon Tyne, Northumberland.*

The Romans established a town here as it was convenient for Hadrian's Wall; it was known as Pons Aelius. The present castle stands, more or less, on the same site as the Roman camp. The present castle was first begun by Robert "Curthose", the eldest son of William the Conqueror, who acquired his name because of his allegedly shorter than normal legs. He had been to Newcastle on his return from Scotland in 1080, and there began the building of the Castle. Like all Norman castles of the period it was originally of

the motte and bailey type. Most of the earthworks have disappeared but it is thought that the original motte was at the east end of the bailey where the present Half-Moon Battery stands. The earliest wooden palisades and buildings were gradually replaced by stone and there are fragments of the original wall, including a postern gate on the south side, still standing.

It was apparently during the reign of John that the shell keep, with numerous turrets and buttresses, was built. The castle passed into the hands of Robert Mowbray, Earl of Northumberland, from whom William the Red captured it in 1095. Early in the reign of King Stephen the castle was taken over by King David of Scotland and it was not until 1157 that Henry II regained possession. It was Henry who, between 1168 and 1174, spent well over £1,100 on erecting the very fine rectangular keep with a bailey wall around it. Work was delayed in 1173/4 when William the Lion of Scotland was carrying out a number of raids in the area. The name of the man in charge of building was Maurice and a man with the same name was responsible for some building at Dover Castle. It is thought highly likely that Newcastle and Dover are the work of the same man, for certainly there are many points of resemblance. When Richard I was on the throne the castle was, for a while, entrusted to the Bishop of Durham but later the king took it back again. King John authorised money to be spent on the castle and ditches, and in 1213 he paid compensation to some townspeople who were deemed to have suffered from new work on the castle. Henry III ordered extensive repairs to be carried out including some to the 13th Century hall, probably built during the reign of John, which stood against the eastern curtain wall until it was demolished in 1809. It was also during the reign of King Henry III that the new gateway on the north-west corner of the castle was built. This was intended to replace the great gate built in the 12th Century. The new gate, called the Black Gate, was built in 1247–50 and cost the enormous sum of £500. In 1296 the threat of further Scottish attacks caused the authorities to carry out another survey of the castle and what they found did not please them, for it was in a poor state of repair. Money was spent in building a brattiche over the chapel and the walls were given extra protection by hanging wooden shields from the battlements. One thousand small jars were purchased—these

were to be filled with lime and thrown at the enemy to burn the eyes and skin. As is so often the case, once the danger was past no action was taken; by 1334 the Sheriff complained that there was not one room in the castle in which a man could shelter nor one gate that could be shut, and he begged that something should be done. Orders also had to be issued to stop the townsfolk from tipping their rubbish into the moat. Even with the repairs that were undertaken it seems that a lot was left undone, for in 1357/8 the prisons known as the Great Pit and Herron Pit had to be repaired when part of the loft collapsed and nearly killed the prisoners. Later on, in the same prison, the latrine had to be altered, for some of the prisoners had used it as a way of escape. The last repairs recorded took place in 1458.

The keep stands on a broad, spreading plinth and there are tall buttresses and corner turrets. Three are quite usual whilst the fourth, on the north-west corner, is multi-angular instead of square; it is thought that this may well have formed a platform to house a small catapult. The middle of the west front has a larger buttress than normal because this housed the shafts running down from the latrines. At the east front of the keep is a quite elaborate forework which originally had three towers, although only two remain. On the right is a long slot which held the draw bar which dropped into place to bolt the gate shut. Near the entrance there is a small niche; this would be filled with oil and a wick would be floated in it to provide some very meagre illumination. At the top of the stairs there is a landing and on the left side another short flight of stairs leads up to the main door of the keep. As with the majority of Norman castles, the entrance to the keep was on the second floor. The main door leads directly into the King's Hall, which is quite brightly lit for a castle. There is a fireplace on the west wall and at the northern end a door leads into a small room in which there is a well. Buckets were kept in a recess on each side of the well and two small holes led the water down pipes to a cellar in the tower which served as a cistern. The well is nearly 100 feet deep and still contains about 50 feet of water. Opposite the entrance is a small garderobe whilst on the south a door leads into the King's Chamber, again a fairly large room hollowed into the thickness of the wall. It has a large fireplace and four windows, and at the far end of the chamber is a small privy.

On the north side there is a vaulted prison fitted in the north-west tower of the keep; the door was shut by means of a draw bar slotted on the outside. On the opposite corner, the south-east, a door leads to a main spiral staircase and this runs for the full height of the tower. The first floor, known as the Queen's Hall, is very similar to the one above only in this case the Queen's Chamber is at the north, the opposite end from the King's Chamber on the floor above. This meant that the wall on either side was left reasonably strong, whereas if both chambers were set in the same side of the wall there would be an inherent weakness since the wall would be thin. The ground floor, or basement is also reached by the spiral staircase and made a fine, cool storage place. In the south-west corner is yet another prison, with its own separate privy. The postern which opens at ground level on the west side of the keep was a later insertion and there is a second one in the south wall. The pillar at the centre of the basement is the one through which the pipes lead down from the well. In the east wall a flight of stairs leads into the thickness of the south wall, which turns through the bays of the two windows into the south-west turret. It then becomes a staircase which rises for a little way into the west wall and stops. Whether this was intentional and there was a change of plan, or the money ran out, is not known. A vaulted gallery runs all the way round through the four walls of the tower in the upper part of the King's Hall and there are loopholes cut into the wall. In the north-east corner a passage leads to a second spiral staircase which leads up to the battlements. The room at the top of the castle was probably used by the garrison troops. The roof, flag tower and battlements are modern reproductions. The chapel of the keep was actually beneath the forebuilding. The keep measures some 62 by 56 feet.

Keep Museum open to the public April to September, weekdays (except Mondays) 10 a.m.–5 p.m.; October to March 10 a.m.–4 p.m.

Newnham on Severn Castle, *Newnham on Severn, Gloucestershire.*

West of the church are some earthworks, probably of a castle built by Edward I.

Norham Castle, *Norham, Northumberland. Eight miles south-west of Berwick, seven miles north-east of Coldstream.*

Norham Castle was the most important castle in this part of the palatinate of Durham, for it commands one of the fords over the Tweed and so was of prime importance in guarding the Scottish border. Usually it was commanded by a Constable appointed by the Bishop of Durham although, if the See were vacant, this honour devolved upon the king. On the north and west the site is protected by a steep cliff forming part of the River Tweed's southern bank. On the east it is protected by a deep gully. In 1121 the Bishop Ranulph Flambard ordered the castle to be built; it was almost certainly of the motte and bailey type, but little is known about the castle until 1136 when David of Scotland invaded Northumberland. He besieged and captured Norham and other castles but they were later restored by treaty. In 1138 David again crossed the border, causing tremendous damage, and again captured Norham despite its brave defence by nine knights. On this occasion the fortifications were totally destroyed but in 1138 the great Battle of the Standard resulted in the total defeat of the Scots and peace was signed in 1139. North Durham, which contained Norham, was restored to the Bishop. In 1157 Henry II ordered the rebuilding in stone of the castles of Newcastle, Bamburgh, and Wark-upon-Tweed, and at the same time Hugh of Puiset, the Bishop of Durham, built a stone keep and fortified the castle at Norham. His architect, Richard of Wolviston, from Durham, undertook the supervision. Part of the keep, part of the gates and some of the walls of the outer and inner baileys survive today. The work was apparently finished by 1174, for by then the Bishop's loyalty was in doubt and he was forced to give the castle to the king, in whose hands it remained until 1197 when it was restored to the then Bishop, Phillip Poictou. Some eleven years later it was once again a royal castle and it was not until 1217 that it was again restored to the Bishop, who was at that time Richard of the Marsh. The castle was kept in good condition and a considerable amount of money was spent on it.

In 1215 Alexander II of Scotland invaded Northumberland and besieged Norham. For 40 days the Constable, Sir Robert Clifford, held out until Alexander accepted defeat and raised the siege.

When Robert the Bruce became leader of the Scots he mounted many raids into Northumberland, and the castle was, for a time, placed under royal control in order to cope with these attacks. Early in 1318 Bishop Lewis Beaumont appointed Sir Thomas Grey of Heton as Constable and Sheriff of Norhamshire. The Scots under the Bruce laid siege to the castle, and the siege was to last very nearly a year. At one time the Scots captured the inner bailey but the defenders retook it after three days and the castle held out. It repeated the same impressive feat a year later, when it held out again for seven months. In September 1322 it was yet again besieged but once more held off the attackers. Five years later in 1327 the Scots again attacked, and this time their siege was successful— they finally took Norham by storm. In March 1328, however, peace was signed, and Norham Castle was returned to the Bishop of Durham.

For a century Norham fades from the pages of history except for mundane entries such as the costs of repairs. However, when the Wars of the Roses broke out in the mid-15th Century, Norham once again figured in the fighting. In 1463 a Lancastrian army of English, French and Scots led by King Henry and Queen Margaret attacked and besieged Norham, but for eighteen days the castle held out until it was relieved by the Earl of Warwick. Its gallant record was somewhat marred in 1464 when it changed sides and declared for Lancaster. However, when the Lancastrians were defeated at Hedgeley Moor and Hexham, Norham quietly surrendered. Some repairs were made and the castle was kept well stocked. It was fortunate for Henry VII that this had been done, for in August 1497 James IV of Scotland crossed the border and attacked Norham. The siege lasted for just over a fortnight and although the Scots made use of artillery the garrison, encouraged by Bishop Fox, resisted all attacks. The fortifications were repaired and some new buildings added during the early 16th Century. In 1513 Henry VIII invaded France and her old ally Scotland crossed the Tweed, and by the latter part of August Norham was again under siege. On this occasion some large Scottish cannon, including "Mons Meg" which today stands in Edinburgh Castle, were bombarding the walls. The bombardment was very effective, with the outer walls being destroyed in two days and the outer bailey taken by storm. The strong defences of the inner bailey held up the attackers

for a while, but ammunition ran short and on 29th August the castle surrendered. The Scottish defeat at Flodden Field, in September 1513, halted the Scottish invasion and soon Norham was back in English hands. These heavy sieges had all left their mark and by now only the keep and part of the west wall were standing; but from 1513 to 1515, under the direction of William Franklyng, a great deal of repair work was carried out and in 1523 some gunners were sent from Portsmouth to strengthen the garrison. From the middle of the 16th Century neglect became the castle's lot, and reports speak of it falling into ruin. Little more of note happened there until 1923 when Mr. C. Romanes placed the castle in the hands of the Commissioners of H.M. Works.

Two gates lead into the outer ward; that known as the West Gate is in the north-west corner of the outer ward and faces the small town. It was built during the 12th Century, altered greatly during the 13th Century and then, in the 14th Century, it was walled up. Very early in the 15th Century the gate was reopened and much of the surviving masonry dates from this period. There is a stone causeway with a gap which was closed by a drawbridge, whose end sank into a pit which can still be seen under the present bridge. In 1408 the gate tower was demolished except for some of the lower masonry which still survives. A new gate was built with an outer portcullis and a doorway opening inwards. During the fighting of 1497 and 1513 the gateway was very badly damaged but it was restored in 1520. In 1554 it was again walled up except for a small postern gate. South of the gate are the remains of a building which served as an outhouse and workshop. Some of the wall probably dates from 1509, and this 16th Century masonry ends at the foundations of a turret beyond which are the remains of the earlier wall. At the foot of the slope of the motte was the chapel with the lower undercroft which was, in the early 16th Century, converted to a stable. The entrance to the inner ward is by way of a modern wooden bridge which stands on the site of the earlier drawbridge. On the left of the gateway are the remains of the Bishop's Hall which was 60 feet by 30 feet and now stands as it was rebuilt in the 16th Century. Immediately on the left is the site of the kitchens and other domestic offices. At the far end of the hall was the Great Chamber, again another large room, 23 feet by 49 feet. From the great hall a

The museum of antiquities in the hall of the keep at Newcastle Castle

spiral staircase led down to the various chambers and cellars built against the east wall of the ward. Most of this work dates from the 16th Century although some parts of the earlier work were incorporated.

The keep is in the south-east corner and measures 60 feet by 84 feet, rising to a height of 90 feet. It was first built as a three-storey building and the marks of the original roof can be seen on the eastern wall. Between 1322 and 1325 a great deal of reconstruction of the keep was carried out; it was rebuilt from the second storey upwards and the west front was completely refaced. The original roof was removed and two extra floors inserted above the second storey. During the attack of 1513 the keep was burnt and only its southern half was reroofed. The ground floor is divided into two unequal parts by a wall five feet thick. That on the south is again divided by a cross wall. In keeping with normal practice the original entrance was on the first floor and access to the basement and upper floors was by means of a staircase built into the wall. On the southern side of the keep is Clapham's Tower, projecting well forward from the curtain wall. It was built in 1513 and is fitted with gun ports, positioned so as to give command of the outer ward. On the outer wall there are the remains of

Sandur's Tower which is semi-circular and was added, probably in the 13th Century, and rebuilt, with a triangular shape to house artillery, during the early part of the 16th Century. The southern wall has a number of turrets of various shapes projecting forward and about half way along there was originally a gate known as the Sheep Gate which was approached by means of a drawbridge crossing the wide outer moat. The lower section, which is all that now remains of the gate tower, dates from the early 13th Century; the upper part, which was used by the Constable, was added later. Outside the south gate, across the road, are the remains of the earthworks forming the outer bailey moat.

Open to the public:

	Weekdays	Sundays
March–April	9.30 a.m.–5.30 p.m.	2–5.30 p.m.
May–Sept.	9.30 a.m.–7 p.m.	2–7 p.m.
Oct.	9.30 a.m.–5.30 p.m.	2–5.30 p.m.
Nov.–Feb.	9.30 a.m.–4 p.m.	2–4 p.m.

Norris Castle, *East Cowes, Isle of Wight, Hampshire.*

Built by James Wyatt in 1799 for Lord Henry Seymour.

Northallerton Castle, *Northallerton, North Riding, Yorkshire. Two hundred yards west of the church.*

A motte and bailey site with a 60-foot ditch on the south and west and a stone gatehouse leading into the bailey from the east.

Northampton Castle, *Northampton, Northamptonshire. By Castle Station and Gold Street.*

Hardly anything survives of what was an important castle, for here the lords gathered to swear allegiance to Matilda against Stephen in 1130/31, and Henry II held a meeting to condemn Thomas à Becket. By the 14th Century the castle was in disrepair and in 1662 it was largely demolished. The entrance was to the north with a barbican in the present Castle Lane. The last substantial remains, including the motte, suffered when the railway arrived at Northampton in the 19th Century.

Northborough Castle, *Northborough, Northampton-shire. Seven miles from Peterborough.*

It is thought that the castle was built *circa* 1350, but only part of the gatehouse and hall still stand. The gatehouse, with a guardroom above, had no portcullis and faced the hall, 50 feet away, which measures 36 feet by 26 feet.

Norwich Castle, *Norwich, Norfolk. In Castle Street.*

In the 11th Century Norwich was one of the largest towns in England, but its exposed position on the flat Norfolk plains and its proximity to the sea required that it should be well defended, and William I ordered a castle to be built there at a very early date. It was built on a ridge of rising ground and altogether some 98 properties had to be destroyed to accommodate the motte and bailey, but practically all traces of this castle have disappeared. The first constable was Ralph de Guader who became involved in a rebellion against William I and was forced to flee when the revolt was put down. Norwich seems to have been associated with revolts, for in 1087 Roger Bigod took the castle in another rising, this time against William II, who later gave it to the Earl of Devon, Richard de Redvers. The keep was built by Henry I on top of the motte, and although little of it is original it represents a type of keep built between the period of the two Williams and Henry II. In the middle of the 12th Century the castle became the property of William, Count of Mortain, who was Stephen's only surviving son, but it was confiscated a few years later by Henry II. Various repairs were carried out. Henry Bigod, Earl of Norfolk, and his Flemish mercenaries occupied the city and captured the castle in 1136.

In 1215 John gave orders that the men of Norwich were to help in fortifying the castle against the barons but this did not stop it falling into the hands of King Louis's troops, and a garrison was left there.

The wooden palisade was apparently not replaced by a stone wall until 1268/9, at a cost of £500. Under Henry III the castle served as a prison but little else of note appears to have happened there until the 16th Century. In 1549 Jack Kett led a rebellion of peasants and small farmers against Lord Somerset, who was then the Protector. The Earl of Warwick hastily summoned some German mercenaries and at the Battle of Mousehold Heath the peasants were, not surprisingly, defeated by the professionals. Kett was captured, taken to Norwich and hanged from the castle battlements.

The exterior was restored in 1834/9, but the job was poorly done, and in 1884 it was purchased by the town council as a museum. Of the original castle little remains except the keep, 96 feet by 92 feet and 76 feet high, and even this has been so much altered both inside and out that, apart from its shape, it hardly resembles the original castle. The entrance is on the east side through Bigod's Tower, with its three flights of stairs leading up to the third storey in which was the Great Hall. In the basement the walls are honeycombed with tunnels.

Open to the public 10 a.m.–5 p.m. weekdays (5.30 p.m. in July and August) and Sundays 2.30 p.m. to 5 p.m.

Nottingham Castle, *Nottingham, Nottinghamshire.*

A mound and fort stood here in the 10th Century; William I had a castle built here early in his reign, and for most of its span the castle was owned by the Crown. It was captured by John in 1191 and recaptured by Richard I in 1194; and in 1212 the walls were decorated with the bodies of 24 Welsh hostages. In 1603 it was granted to Francis, Earl of Rutland, and much of it was pulled down, but sufficient remained for it to be used when in 1642 Charles I raised his standard here—only to have it blown down by the wind. It was very soon afterwards taken by the Roundheads. Much of the castle was demolished after the Civil War and in 1679 the Marquess of Newcastle built a fine Italian villa on the site—but this was burnt down by a mob in 1831.

The castle stood on top of a sandstone cliff and had a rectangular enclosure with three large corner towers and a Norman keep. During John's reign (1199–1216) another outer enclosure was added, with a strong curtain wall with towers and a moat. Tradition has it that it was by a secret passage leading into the castle that entry was made to capture Mortimer, the lover of Edward III's mother Isabella, who was sent to London, tried and executed. This passage, known as Mortimer's Hole, is at the south-east of the castle. The Gate-

house still survives as well as some of the wall.
*Open to the public weekdays 10 a.m.–6.45 p.m.
(5.45 on Fridays) in summer, and 10 a.m.–dusk in
winter. Sundays 2–4.45 p.m.*

Nunney Castle, *Nunney, Somerset. Three miles
south-east of Frome.*

The licence for this castle was granted on 28th
November 1373 to Sir John De La Mare, but the
family had owned the land since the early 13th
Century. Like Bodiam (qv) Nunney was built at a
time when England was under threat of French
invasion. It saw no action until the Civil War
when, in September 1645, Colonel Richard Prater
held it for the king. The Roundheads besieged it;
cannon-fire damaged the wall, and after two days
the castle surrendered. In 1910 the breached north
wall collapsed, and in 1926 the owner handed the
castle over to the then-Ministry of Works.
The castle is surrounded by a moat which came,
originally, to the foot of the walls and was, in turn,
covered on three sides by a twelve-foot-high wall.
The main body of the castle is a rectangular block
with large, circular towers at the corners in close
approximation to the style of castle popular in
France at this period. The walls were 54 feet high,
and the entrance was by a gateway four feet wide
and guarded by a drawbridge. A machicolated
parapet ran all around the top of the wall and
towers.
On the ground floor was the kitchen and some
storerooms, while the first floor was probably occupied by servants' quarters and the second floor
was taken up by the Great Hall. On the top floor
were the private apartments. The towers were
floored at the same level as the main building and
contained the garderobes.
Open to the public:

	Weekdays	Sundays
March–April	*9.30 a.m.–5.30 p.m.*	*2–5.30 p.m.*
May–Sept.	*9.30 a.m.–7 p.m.*	*2–7 p.m.*
Oct.	*9.30 a.m.–5.30 p.m.*	*2–5.30 p.m.*
Nov.–Feb.	*10 a.m.–4.30 p.m.*	*2–4.30 p.m.*

Oakham Castle, *Oakham, Rutland. At the north
end of the town.*

The late 12th Century hall survives and the site
was surrounded by a stone wall prior to the 13th
Century, but there does not appear to have been a
keep. The hall is 65 feet by 44 feet, and originally
the entrance was at the east end.

Odell Castle, *Odell, Bedfordshire.*

Few traces of the original motte and bailey castle
survive and the stone buildings were already in
ruins during the 16th Century. Later buildings
have, more or less, erased all but the faintest
traces.

Odiham Castle, *North Warnborough, Hampshire.
Half a mile west of the village on the left bank of
Whitewater Stream.*

The fragmentary remains of the castle include part
of the octagonal keep of 1207–12, measuring more
than 22 feet high and originally rising to over 60
feet. Much of the west wall, which contained the
staircase has collapsed. It was besieged by the
French in 1216, and surrendered after two weeks.
Simon de Montfort, the baron whose efforts led
to the foundation of Parliament, owned it for a
while. David Bruce, King of Scotland, was imprisoned here for a while in the mid-14th Century.

Offton Castle, *Offton, Suffolk. Four miles south of
Needham Market.*

A square site has a surrounding moat and to the
south are indications of a bailey.

Ogle Castle, *Ogle, Northumberland. North-north-west of Milbourne.*

Built in the 14th Century, licensed in 1341, this towerhouse was defended by a double moat with drawbridge. It was added to in the 15th and 16th Centuries, but little remains today.
On private land.

Okehampton Castle, *Okehampton, Devonshire. One mile south-west of Okehampton.*

Following William of Normandy's victory at Hastings the greater part of the country submitted, but in the north and south-west there were rebellions. Both were equally ruthlessly suppressed. William appointed Baldwin FitzGilbert Sheriff of Devonshire, and he chose the present site for his

castle which stands on a spur of land extending into the valley of the West Okement river. It is surrounded by a ditch and bank about 100 yards west of the mound which itself was probably built up from materials quarried from the ditch. In its early days it would have been little more than an earthwork with a wooden palisade, but by the end of the 13th Century the castle was apparently rebuilt, probably by the first Courtenay Earl, Hugh the second (1292–1341). By this time the defensive aspects of the site were far less important and the emphasis was far more on domestic architecture. In 1525 the owner of the castle, Earl Henry, was made Marquess of Exeter. He played a prominent part in the internal politics of Henry VIII's reign and in 1537 he was accused by Thomas Cromwell

Nunney Castle, built late in the 14th Century on ancestral lands of the De La Mare family

of taking part in a plot with the Pole family. He was tried, found guilty, and beheaded in January 1538; it was ordered that the castle should be dismantled, and since then it has remained in ruins. Although ruined and uninhabited it still had certain parliamentary qualifications attached to it and was at one time owned by Robert Clive of India. In 1917 a trust was set up to preserve and maintain it and in 1967 it was made over to the Ministry of Public Buildings and Works.

The motte stands at the southern part and as the bailey slopes northwards down to the tail of the spur of land it gives the whole castle a long, narrow shape. Entry to the castle was by way of a barbican joined by two long walls to a gatehouse of two storeys, but little remains of any of these buildings. On the right hand side of the gatehouse was the guardroom, and from this stairs led to the hall which would have been covered with a wooden roof. From the hall there were two other rooms of which the upper was probably a smaller solar. Beyond a passage which led to the north-west postern gate was a kitchen which was, in turn, linked to the hall by a passage. The room houses two ovens built into the base of the mound. On the other side of the bailey there is what appears to be another smaller kitchen again fitted with ovens. Next to this kitchen was the chapel and there were lodgings for the priest between the chapel and the curtain wall. Running along the curtain wall, from the chapel towards the gatehouse, are three sets of lodgings used, no doubt, by the various officials and soldiers of the castle. Each has two windows, a fireplace and a garderobe. Beneath the rooms were cellars used for storage or perhaps as quarters for the servants. Beneath the garderobe is a vaulted cess-pit which is situated between the two lodgings at the southern end.

The rectangular keep stands on the top of the mount and was built at two different periods; on the northern edge is a square tower and to this, in the 14th Century, was added an extension in the form of a rectangular block. The turret in the north-east corner leads to the upper floor and each of the rooms had a fireplace and garderobe built within the thickness of the wall. The slate lined outlets for the garderobe chutes can be clearly seen from the outside.

Open to the public:

	Weekdays	*Sundays*
March–April	9.30 a.m.–5.30 p.m.	2–5.30 p.m.
May–Sept.	9.30 a.m.–7 p.m.	9.30 a.m.–7 p.m.
Oct.	9.30 a.m.–5.30 p.m.	2–5.30 p.m.
Nov.–Feb.	10 a.m.–4.30 p.m.	2–4.30 p.m.

Oldberry Castle, *Dulverton, Somerset.*

Prehistoric earthworks in Burridge Woods.

Old Bolingbroke Castle, *Old Bolingbroke, Lincolnshire. South of the church.*

Only the motte and some traces of masonry survive of William de Roumane, Earl of Lincoln's castle. Originally a simple wood structure, it had masonry added at a later date. It was enlarged in the 14th and 15th Centuries but suffered the common fate of slighting following the English Civil Wars (1643/4). The last standing remains collapsed in 1815.

Oldburrow Castle, *Lynton, Devonshire. Four miles east of the village.*

Well over 1,000 feet above sea level, this was the ideal site for a Roman signal station. It consists of a large outer earthwork some 280 feet in diameter surrounded by a shallow ditch, and on the north and south-west are two openings, the south-west one being the original. At the centre of the enclosure is a small mound some ten feet in diameter and fifteen inches high, which presumably covers the foundations of the signal tower.

Oldbury Castle, *Oldbury, Wiltshire.*

Three-quarters of a mile south-east of the village, an Iron Age hill fort.

Old Castle, *Almeley, Herefordshire. Two-thirds of a mile north of the church.*

A 30-foot-high mound which was part of a motte and bailey castle; there may well have been a Roman fort on the same site.

Old Castle, *Malpas, Cheshire. South-east of Malpas on the Welsh border, by the side of a stream.*

A number of mounds together with very fragmentary remains which mark the site of the castle and a battle fought during the English Civil War in 1644.

Old Castle, *Putley, Herefordshire. Half a mile north-east.*

A house of *circa* 1700, heavily restored.

Old Sarum Castle, *Old Sarum, Salisbury, Wiltshire. One-and-a-quarter miles north of Salisbury.*

Old Sarum town site is situated on a steep-sided mound encircled by a deep ditch which has two entrances. It is possible that the site was originally an Iron Age hill fort. Although four Roman roads converge on the site the proof of Roman occupation is meagre, but it was known by the Romans as Sorbiodunum. To the Saxons it was Searisbyrig, and from the time of Aethelred II until early in the reign of Henry II there was a mint here. In the Domesday book the town is referred to as Sarisberie. Between 1075 and 1078 the Bishopric of Sherborne was transferred to Old Sarum, and about this period the outer fortification were increased to roughly their present size. At the centre of the town was the motte, and four ramparts divided the town into quarters. These ditches did not quite reach the wall but a small passageway was left to allow access from one quarter to the other. The eastern part of the town formed the outer bailey whilst the smaller, north-western section contained the cathedral church, which was consecrated in 1092. Within the castle was built the palace of Bishop Roger who died in 1139. Despite some friction between the church and state, matters continued more or less amicably until 1139, but in that year King Stephen seized the bishop's castles. From then on the friction grew worse and soon the Pope was getting complaints from the clergy of Old Sarum. They claimed that the military were constantly interfering with the ecclesiastic arrangements; that accommodation was a problem, and that the town itself was unhealthy and uncomfortable. As a result the foundations of the present cathedral church of Salisbury were laid in 1220 and in 1226 the old church was abandoned. When the clergy and all their dependants left, the town soon declined and in 1331 Edward III gave permission for the Dean and Chapter to demolish the old church and houses and use the materials to repair the church of New Sarum. The castle remained in use certainly until the latter part of the 14th Century, since there is on record a command by Edward III for it to be garrisoned. By the middle of the 15th Century it is described as having fallen into decay and by the latter part of the 15th Century the town was deserted. Empty though it might be, until 1832 the town of Old Sarum was still entitled to be represented in Parliament by two members—an example of a "rotten borough" widely quoted by political reformers. The site was transferred to the Ministry of Public Works in 1892.

The original Iron Age earthworks were modified during the long period of occupation but the major alterations occurred when the Normans took over the site. They erected a curtain wall some twelve feet thick and then levelled the inside of the site. The present entrance is through a gap in the east rampart where stood originally the east gate. A road leads from the outer gate to that of the inner bailey, crossing the inner ditch by a wooden bridge, and remains indicate that this was originally crossed by a drawbridge. The gatehouse standing on the north-west side of the inner bailey had two drum towers, and the hole for the draw bar of the gate can still be seen on the left hand side. There are also the remains of two vaulted guard towers. The entrance passage is some 55 feet long and was probably built during the latter half of the 12th Century. The inner bailey is roughly 300 feet in diameter, encircled by a massive curtain wall with external buttresses at intervals. There is a wall walk which connects to the gatehouse and there are several postern and other towers.

Situated within the bailey were numerous domestic buildings and just inside the gate are the remains of ovens indicating that this was probably the site of the bakehouse. The well was situated in the middle of the courtyard and is about five feet in diameter although it widens out a little lower down. The site also contains the remains of the old palace and cathedral.

Open to the public:

	Weekdays	Sundays
March–April	9.30 a.m.–5.30 p.m.	2–5.30 p.m.
May–Sept.	9.30 a.m.–7 p.m.	9.30 a.m.–7 p.m.
Oct.	9.30 a.m.–5.30 p.m.	2–5.30 p.m.
Nov.–Sept.	10 a.m.–4.30 p.m.	2–4.30 p.m.

Old Swinford Castle, *Old Swinford, Worcestershire.*

An early 19th Century castellated building.

Old Wardour Castle, *Wardour Park, Wiltshire. One-and-a-half miles south-west of Tisbury.*

The manor or village of Wardour dates back to the late 9th Century when King Alfred is recorded as visiting there, and in the Domesday book it is listed as belonging to Wilton Abbey House of Benedictine Nuns. In 1393 John, the 5th Lord Loval of Titchmarsh, was given licence to crenellate. The ownership was disputed at various times and subject to legal action, but in 1605 the owner was made Baron Arundell of Wardour and from that time the castle and lands have descended with the Barony. The last Lord Arundell died in 1944 and the property then passed on to the female line. In 1936 the castle was placed in the hands of the Ministry of Public Buildings and Works.

The family were one of the leading Catholic families in the country and continued to practise their religion throughout the persecutions and denunciations of the Reformation. In April 1643 the castle was besieged for Parliament by Sir Edward Hungerford; with a force of 1,300 men he felt confident that he could tackle the 25 Royalist soldiers and women defending the castle. On 2nd May he called upon them to surrender, but the wife of Lord Arundell, aged 60, declined to co-operate. For several days cannon battered at the castle with little success, and then plans were made to carry it by mining. The mines were discharged, and a further threat of severe damage and assault finally persuaded the garrison to surrender on 8th May. The defenders were taken to Shaftesbury and the building and contents were severely damaged by the Parliament men. The castle was placed under the command of Edmund Ludlow, but Wiltshire was strongly Royalist and the Parliamentary commander soon found himself, in turn, under threat. He refused to surrender the castle and made preparations to resist a siege. First the Royalists managed to infiltrate a saboteur in the form of a kitchen boy, who succeeded in destroying one of the garrison's cannons, but that was all. In December of that year the castle was under close siege. An earthwork was built on a hill commanding the castle gate and attempts were made to persuade Ludlow to surrender. The gateway and portcullis were blown up by the attackers and the Parliamentary garrison began to suffer from shortness of supplies. By the end of January there were a number of breaches in the wall, and about three weeks after this Sir Ralph Hopton sent reinforcement to the besiegers. Mining and countermining were carried out, and in March 1644 another appeal for surrender was made. On 14th March a mine was sprung; ten doors and two of the six turrets were blown in and part of the first floor room in which Ludlow was lodged was very badly damaged. Some of the garrison's supplies were also destroyed. The attackers attempted to storm the castle, but were driven back. On 16th March there was another truce and Ludlow asked to be allowed to march out under arms, a request which was refused. However, the defenders were very short of supplies and there was considerable discontent; on 18th March Ludlow left the castle and met the Royalists, and they agreed to try and get the terms he wanted. Ludlow returned to the castle and ordered his 75 men to surrender. In fact the Royalists' promises were not all kept, and two soldiers were executed while the others were taken to Oxford—although Ludlow himself was quite well treated. There was little attempt to put the castle back into repair after the Civil War, and when the family returned at the Restoration they built a small house on the south side of the bailey wall. In the 18th Century the castle ruins were surrounded by a formal garden.

The bailey is very large with a thin curtain wall which dates from the 16th Century but probably follows the line of the earlier one. The entrance is through an 18th Century gateway on the north and it is quite possible that there was a gatehouse originally on the west wall. The Gothic banqueting house possibly occupies the site. On the left of the gateway behind some trees is a terrace with a grotto which was built in 1792 by Joshua Lane, who was noted for this kind of work. Further to the west are the remains, probably, of the banqueting house which was built in 1687. Also within the bailey is a three-seated closet dating from the 18th Century complete with a carved panel. The remains of the keep, or tower, are of interest for they are those of a tower-house, a compromise between defence and comfort. It is hexagonal with two projecting towers guarding the entrance and there is a central, hexagonal courtyard. The original entrance was fitted with a portcullis, and an inscription above the doorway records the recovery of the property and the restoration of the Arundels, with the Arundel coat of arms above. The ground floor is raised about three feet above the outside level and the entrance passage was originally vaulted with an early type of fan vaulting. The rear end retains the original doorway. The portcullis slot can be seen in the moulding on the jamb. In the centre of the courtyard is the well, and an extra water supply was also piped into the castle. An inventory of 1605 lists thirty-five rooms in the castle. The left hand side of the entrance was the porter's lodge complete with its own little garderobe. On the other side was a store room. There were four storeys of lodgings, sets of two rooms with the bedchamber usually having a garderobe leading off from it. Access was by mural stair. The first floor was well equipped, with a fine hall with a screened passage at the far end. Running off from the hall was the lord's chapel and at the other end were buttery and service rooms with a kitchen attached.

Open to the public:

	Weekdays	*Sundays*
March–April	*9.30 a.m.–5.30 p.m.*	*2–5.30 p.m.*
May–Sept.	*9.30 a.m.–7 p.m.*	*2–7 p.m.*
Oct.	*9.30 a.m.–5.30 p.m.*	*2–5.30 p.m.*
Nov.–Feb.	*10 a.m.–4.30 p.m.*	*2–4.30 p.m.*

Orcop Castle, *Orcop, Herefordshire. One-eighth mile north-west.*

A moated farm in the valley with a motte over 200 feet in diameter and 20 feet high, with indications of a bailey to the north.

Orford Castle, *Orford, Suffolk. Six miles southwest of Tunstall along B1078, or half a mile northwest of Orford Quay along B1084 from Woodbridge.*

When Henry II came to the throne in 1154 one of the most powerful barons was Hugh Bigod, the Earl of Norfolk, whose castles rather dominated East Anglia. It was probably because of this that Henry decided to build a castle at Orford near the coast of Norfolk, and the resulting castle was one which is unique among British strongholds. Work on the castle began in 1165/6 and it was completed by the year 1172/3, at a total cost of over £1,400. It appears that the first two years were occupied in building the keep, since this was the strongest and most important part of the castle. The subsequent five years were spent in erecting a curtain wall, flanking towers and other buildings. No sooner had the castle been completed than a rebellion against the king, led by his own sons, broke out. One of the supporters of the rebels was Hugh Bigod, who had by then reached the astonishing age—for that period—of 80 years. The rebellion was crushed and Bigod lost much of his power. Orford Castle thus became even more important in ensuring the king's control of the country. As a royal castle it remained true to the king, unlike some, but in 1217 the castle was actually taken over by Prince Louis, the French leader of the rebellious knights. Little damage seems to have been done and the castle very shortly passed back into royal control. Whenever there was an alarm Orford was placed in a state of preparedness and for this reason small amounts were spent on repair and maintenance of the castle throughout its active career; there are frequent references to it in the royal accounts. In 1308 there is mention of a garrison of ten crossbowmen and archers being maintained there for the period January to March. In March 1336 Edward III granted the castle to Robert de Ufford and from thence forward it remained in private hands right up to 1930, when Sir Arthur Churchman presented it to the Orford town trust. In 1962 it was placed under the protection of the Ministry of Public Buildings and Works.

Originally Orford Castle consisted of the keep set in the bailey surrounded by a curtain wall; of all the buildings only the keep has survived. The last standing section of the curtain wall collapsed in 1841. Evidence would suggest that Orford Castle was a very advanced form of military architecture for the period, for it is known to have had a number of square towers spaced along the wall. These were an important innovation for that time since they meant that the defenders were now able to discharge their arrows against any troops who had gained the wall.

The keep consists of a tall tower, circular in section, which had three additional towers set equidistant around the outside. In fact the external wall is not exactly circular but polygonal, although the inside rooms are completely circular. It stands on a splayed plinth and rose 90 feet above ground level to the top of its turrets. The walls were ten feet thick and the whole thing is built mostly from local stone. The inside is divided into three main storeys and the smaller rooms (such as garderobes) and staircases are set within the turrets. The entrance to the keep was on the south-west at first floor level, with a forebuilding to protect it which rises about half way up the main tower. The original roof of the tower was conical whilst those of the gatehouse and turrets were flat. The steps are modern although they probably follow the line of the original ones. Inside the doorway are the grooves which housed the portcullis, situated in the room above. Beneath the entrance vestibule is a basement entered by means of a wooden ladder and which was almost certainly used as a prison. A passage leads to what was once a garderobe recess but this has been broken through and modified to allow access to a lower chamber which was probably the cess pit but was later adapted for use as a cell. Off from the vestibule is the great hall which is an impressive, circular room with a stone bench running around the walls. There is a big fireplace and the room is well lit by three windows. In the south-west tower is the kitchen which has a double fireplace and a sink and drain. Another passage on the far side of the kitchen leads to a double garderobe, whilst the window recess on the left of the fireplace opens on to a staircase leading up to another chamber in the north turret, probably used by the constable. The main staircase is in the southern tower; five-and-a-half feet wide, it leads down to the main basement where there is the well, some 32 feet deep. The same staircase goes to a mezzanine halfway between the first and second floors. A passage leading off to the left from the main staircase runs through to a chamber which was probably for the chaplain, and the chapel was behind the staircase in the large southern tower. Further up the staircase is a passage which leads off to the left on to the chapel roof and the second storey of the keep which was probably used by the important visitors to the castle. This has a great circular hall with extra chambers running off from it and a large fireplace. A short passage from the window on the left of the entrance leads to another kitchen built into the west turret which, in turn, leads through to a single garderobe. The staircase continues upwards to the flat roof of the great tower although this is a modern replacement. On the west turret the grooves which once took the wooden shutters, used to close the gaps in the battlements, can be seen. From the top of the tower it can be seen that the earthworks extended south-west for about 180 yards and probably even further. The keep itself stands on a platform encircled by a ditch with a rampart beyond this which probably formed a complete circle around the keep, although part is now missing. Outside the rampart is a second ditch with part of its own rampart well preserved. Yet a third ditch separated this rampart from another platform still further to the south-west.

Open to the public:

	Weekdays	*Sundays*
March–April	*9.30 a.m.–5.30 p.m.*	*2–5.30 p.m.*
May–Sept.	*9.30 a.m.–7 p.m.*	*9.30 a.m.–*
		7 p.m.
Oct.	*9.30 a.m.–5.30 p.m.*	*2–5.30 p.m.*
Nov.–Feb.	*9.30 a.m.–4 p.m.*	*2–4 p.m.*

Oswestry Castle, *Oswestry, Shropshire. Behind Bailey Head.*

A shell keep stood on top of the surviving mound but there are very few pieces of standing masonry.

Ouston Ferry Castle, *Ouston Ferry, Lincolnshire. South of the church.*

An earlier castle was apparently demolished in 1095 and was then re-occupied in 1174. The motte seems to have been slighted.

Oversley Castle, *Ragley Hall, Warwickshire.*

The house is early 20th Century and the castle to which it is attached, is early 19th Century. *On private land.*

Oxford Castle, *Oxford, Oxfordshire. West of the city.*

In 1071/73 Robert d'Oilgi was busy building a castle to hold down a town which had resisted William, its new king. Deep ditches were dug and the river Isis diverted to fill them, and a high motte was thrown up. The main approach was by way of the present Castle Street and over a long bridge, through a strong gatehouse to a courtyard. There were several towers including a large, square bastion called St. George's Tower which still stands; and on top of the 60-foot motte was a shell keep, in the shape of a decagon. The surviving tower is 30 feet square at the base and tapers to 22 feet square at the top; above the roof the parapets rose another thirteen feet and were fitted with two large openings, probably to accommodate catapults. Excavations uncovered a small chamber twelve feet square, set in the motte, which housed the well 54 feet deep. In 1649 much of the old castle was destroyed and in the 18th Century the tower was used as a prison.

Orford, the important castle by which Henry II dominated the East Anglian barons

Peak Castle, *Peak, Derbyshire.*

Situated at the top of a very high cliff, this castle was rectangular and quite small. On the north side were two small towers, and a keep with eight feet thick walls; measuring 38 feet by 32 feet, it was three storeys high. There was a drawbridge leading to the keep entrance.

Peckforton Castle, *Beeston, Cambridgeshire.*

Built in 1844–50 by Salvin for the first Lord Tolle-mache, but far more than a folly since it is, more or less, a replica of a medieval castle complete with gatehouses and a Great Hall.
On private land.

Pembridge Castle, *Welsh Newton, Herefordshire. Four miles north-west of Monmouth off A466.*

A good example of a small Welsh border castle. In the north-west angle is a round tower dating from *circa* 1200 and on the east side were some other buildings, now gone. In the 17th Century a hall was built utilising parts of the 13th Century curtain wall. The gatehouse has the usual semi-circular flanking towers although part of these have been restored. The chapel is by the north tower and dates from the 16th Century.
Open to the public May to September, Thursdays 10 a.m.–7 p.m. Admission 5p.

Pendennis Castle, *Pendennis Point, Cornwall. One mile south-east of Falmouth.*

This is another fort like that at St. Mawes (qv) which it faces across the estuary. It was built by Henry VIII when it was feared that France might invade Britain. Unlike St. Mawes, Pendennis did achieve some glory for it resisted a six-month-long siege during the English Civil War. The town of Falmouth owes its existence largely to one of the Governors of the Castle, Sir Peter Killigrew, for it was due to his intervention that a charter of incorporation under the name of Falmouth was granted in 1661. The siege of the castle took place in 1646. On March 13th St. Mawes surrendered to Parliament with hardly a struggle, and on the 18th Sir Thomas Fairfax reached Pendennis and called upon the governor, Colonel Arundell, an old man of 70, to deliver up the fortress. The demand for surrender was refused, as was another delivered a month later, but the castle was cut off on the landward by Colonel Fortescue and Hammon, whilst on the seaward side a blockade was set up. On July 26th the situation was so desperate that Arundell sent a message to Prince Charles that they could not hold out much longer. At the end of the month there was an attempt to break out and seize supplies which was beaten back, a number of casualties being suffered. At last, on August 17th, realising that no further purpose could be served, Colonel Arundell surrendered; but as a

Pendennis Castle; the entrance gateway

mark of appreciation by his enemies, he was allowed to march out with the full honours of war. The survivors of the castle numbered about 900 men and 24 officers. During the Civil War and afterwards Pendennis Castle served as a prison for a number of distinguished people, and the last to spend their time there were some French captured at the Battle of Corunna in 1809. Like several other castles, in the 1914/18 War it was reconstituted to serve as part of the coastal defences, and again in 1939.

The original castle built by Henry VIII in 1545 consists of a circular tower surrounded by a curtain wall. The three-storey central round tower has an additional domestic block for the governor on the north-east side. Running around this is the curtain wall whilst the principal entrance to the keep was protected by a drawbridge and portcullis. Over the door are the Royal Arms carved into the stone. The doorway leads on to the ground floor of the domestic block where a spiral staircase went up to the Governor's lodgings on the first floor. Above the entrance is the room from which the drawbridge and portcullis were worked and the two slots through which the chains passed can be seen; on either side of the slits are narrow channels through which ran the ropes to the portcullis, which still exists. It was finally raised in the latter part of the 19th Century when the drawbridge was replaced by the present, permanent bridge. This floor also contained living quarters and it is here that Charles II, as Prince of Wales, is supposed to have spent three weeks as a fugitive in 1646. The two main floors of the round tower are devoted to guns which fired through ports, and the rooms were subdivided to provide accommodation for the garrison. Large calibre guns were mounted on the roof, while the basement served as a kitchen. The gunports are splayed so that the gun could be turned through a considerable angle. The guns themselves were of iron or brass and fitted on to wooden carriages; they fired cast iron or stone balls. The largest appears to be one which could fire a five-and-a-half inch diameter ball, but since most of the balls which were excavated are larger it seems likely that bigger cannon were used.

The curtain wall is approached from the ground floor; the block house on the rocks below is called Dennis Fort or Little Dennis and was demolished in 1654, although the shell is still visible. The large, outer enclosure was added by Elizabeth I who, in

1598, strengthened the defences in face of the rumour that Spain was once again preparing to attack England with another Armada. When the Spaniards raided Penzance in 1595 it was actually said that Pendennis Castle was unfit to repel any attack, and a large labour force was put in to restore it. The work probably took some eighteen months. The outer gateway was finished later, probably about 1611. During the 18th and 19th Centuries further improvements were made. The angular line of the outer wall is typical of forts of this period, which were designed primarily to house artillery.

Open to the public:

	Weekdays	*Sundays*
March–April	*9.30 a.m.–5.30 p.m.*	*2–5.30 p.m.*
May–Sept.	*9.30 a.m.–7 p.m.*	*9.30 a.m.– 7 p.m.*
Oct.	*9.30 a.m.–5.30 p.m.*	*2–5.30 p.m.*
Nov.–Feb.	*10 a.m.–4.30 p.m.*	*2–4.30 p.m.*

Admission 10p, Children and OAPs 5p.

Pendragon Castle, *Mallerstang, Westmorland. Three-quarters of a mile north of the village.*

On a mound stand the remains of a late Norman pele-tower which dates from the time of Edward I. It was built by Roger de Clifford and was burnt by the Scots, but later repaired and restored by Anne Clifford, Countess of Pembroke, *circa* 1661. Much was later demolished by Thomas, Earl of Thanet, in 1685, but some masonry remains.

Pengersick Castle, *Germoe, Cornwall. South of the Parish of St. Breage.*

Not a great deal is known of this castle but it probably dates from the reign of Henry VIII and belonged to a Godolphin family. There is a square tower of three storeys. It was at one time in the ownership of the Duke of Leeds but has been much converted and turned into a house.
On private land.

Penrith Castle, *Penrith, Cumberland. On Railway Street.*

The castle was probably built late in the 14th Century, for a licence was granted in 1397/99, and

it has had many owners since. It was in the form of a parallelogram with a deep ditch encircling it and an entrance on the town side, by way of a gatehouse and drawbridge. It was already falling into decay during the 16th Century, for a survey of this period mentions two towers, the Red Tower and the White (or Bishop Strickland's Tower), as well as domestic offices, as being in good repair whilst the Gatehouse and gates were in ruins. It suffered even more in 1648 when it was captured by Parliament and partly demolished, the building materials being sold for the benefit of the Commonwealth.

Pentillie Castle, *Pillaton, Cornwall.*

Remains of a small tower standing beside the house which is known as The Castle, designed by William Wilkins and finished in 1810.
On private land.

Penwortham Castle, *Penwortham, Lancashire. On Castle Hill, north of the Church.*

A motte and bailey castle which belonged to Warren de Busli or Bussel, but landslips have effaced it. In 1856 traces of a wooden structure were excavated.

Penyard Castle, *Weston-under-Penyard, Herefordshire. One mile south-west of the village.*

The collapsed remains of a 14th Century castle.

Pevensey Castle, *Pevensey, Sussex. In the villages of Westham and Pevensey on the A259 from Eastbourne to Bexhill.*

During the latter part of the 3rd Century Britain suffered from raids by various sea-going peoples from Europe, especially the Saxons. To combat these pirates the Roman high command created a string of forts spaced along the coast from Hampshire to Norfolk. One of the forts erected early in the 4th Century was that at Pevensey; the Romans called it Anderidos or Anderita. This part of the coast was known as the Saxon Shore and an overall commander, the Count of the Saxon Shore, was appointed. When in the 5th Century the last Roman troops vanished from Britain most of these castles were abandoned but some, like Pevensey in Sussex, Portchester in Hampshire, Walton Castle and Burgh Castle both in Suffolk, retained their importance throughout the medieval period. In all of these a Norman castle occupied part of the Roman fort.

The original Roman fort was built on a peninsula of dry ground which rose above the surrounding marsh, and later a causeway was built across the ditch, perhaps as late as the 5th Century. Pevensey was raided by the Saxons in 491 and according to a national diary of the times, the Anglo-Saxon Chronicle, a large number of Britons were massacred.

It was not far from Pevensey that William the Conqueror first landed in 1066. After the Battle of Hastings, when the spoils were shared out, the country around Pevensey went to the Conqueror's half-brother Robert, Count of Mortain. In 1088 it saw action when Odo, Bishop of Bayeux held the castle against the king and it had to be taken by siege. In 1101 William, Count of Mortain rebelled unsuccessfully against Henry I and, as a result, the family lost Pevensey. It saw battle again in 1147 when Gilbert, Earl of Pembroke held it against Stephen, but shortage of food forced its surrender. In 1264 some of Henry III's troops, who had been defeated by the barons at the Battle of Lewes, took refuge in the castle which was immediately surrounded by troops commanded by the son of Simon de Montfort. The castle held out successfully and the besiegers were forced to lift the siege.

During the medieval period it became traditional that Pevensey was always granted to the Queen of England, until 1372 when it was given to John of Gaunt. In 1399 Pevensey was again under siege, this time by the troops of Richard II. Sir John Pelham, the Constable, was with the army of Henry, Duke of Lancaster, who was claiming the throne of England. In his absence his wife was left to defend the castle and this she did most successfully; when Henry IV was crowned Sir John was granted the castle. It was at Pevensey that prisoners such as James I, King of the Scots, and Queen Joan of Navarre were held.

Neglect of the Roman walls began to have its effect; there are many references to them falling down and by the 13th Century they seem to have been largely derelict. By the early 15th Century the keep was also in a ruinous condition, a rather surprising fact when it is remembered that at this period the castle was successfully withstanding a long siege. For the greater part of its service Pevensey Castle was a royal stronghold and consequently the accounts for its repair appear in the records of the Exchequer. By the Tudor period the castle was uninhabited, and a report of 1573 stated that it was practically impossible to repair. However matters altered in 1587 when it was known that King Phillip of Spain was threatening an invasion. A report said that the castle should be repaired and also mentions two guns; one of these is now in the Tower of London, whilst the second, the Pevensey Gun, bearing a Tudor Rose and the cypher *E.R.*, lays where it fell not far from some contemporary earth emplacements. The Spanish Armada was defeated, and there was no invasion; consequently the services of Pevensey were not called upon and once again it was allowed to moulder away. In 1925 the Duke of Devonshire presented it to the Office of Works but Pevensey was not to be forgotten yet. In 1940, when there was an imminent threat of a German invasion of Britain, the castle was restored for use as an observation and command post and as such was used by regular troops and the Home Guard until 1944. The towers of the medieval castle were fitted up as living accommodation and "pill-boxes" holding machine-guns were erected on the keep as well as on some of the Roman bastions and the Roman walls. All the new defences were camouflaged so as to blend in with the rest of the castle. In 1945 it once again came under the care of the Ancient Monuments Section of the present Department of the Environment, but wisely, the modifications were left untouched as a valuable chapter in the history of Pevensey Castle.

Almost every Roman fort was rectangular but Pevensey is unusual in that the space of little under ten acres is enclosed within an irregular oval wall. The main entrance was in the south-west, the only direction from which the fort could be approached by land. In front of the entrance there was a ditch, eighteen feet wide, dug across the isthmus. Part of this ditch is now exposed to the right of the entrance. There was probably a wooden bridge across this ditch and the main entrance was probably a rectangular gatehouse set back between

two solid, round-fronted towers some 30 feet apart. (The western bastion still survives up to parapet level.) The entrance was nine feet wide and flanked by two oblong guard rooms. Another gate at the east was simpler, being a ten-foot archway without gatehouse or flanking bastions, and probably led only to the harbour. The present archway is a modern reconstruction. On the north-western wall there was a small Roman postern gate some seven feet wide and angled so as to reduce the chances of direct frontal attack. The walls are about ten feet thick and composed of sandstone rubble and flint. They were built in sections which were then joined together. Part of the north-west wall has collapsed, and among the fallen pieces are two concealed machine-gun posts. Most of the wall on the south side has collapsed but elsewhere it still stands to a height of 25 feet and some of the parapet still exists. Built along the wall are a number of round faced bastions. There were originally at least fifteen, although only ten survive, and they are spaced in such a way that each section of wall in between can be flanked by any two towers. The north-west bastion has another "pill-box" designed to look like part of the ruins and to the rear of the bastion

Pevensey Castle, the ancient coastal fortress where Roman, Norman and Second World War defences may be seen on the same site

there is another tower which also dates from 1940.

When Robert of Mortain decided to use the Roman fort he had to undertake certain repairs. The Roman ditch had probably long been silted up and Robert dug a new one (not now visible) which is actually slightly further out. He also carried out repairs and alterations to the walls and strengthened the gate. However, the main feature of Robert's work was the cutting off of one corner of the Roman fort to form the inner bailey of his castle. He dug a deep ditch and erected some wooden fencing but by the end of the 11th Century, or early in the 12th, the wooden keep was gradually converted to masonry. If not completed before 1101 it must have been the work of his successor Richer de Aquila. Inside it is roughly rectangular, 55 feet by 30 feet, but externally the towers and bastions are most irregular, being rectangular with semi-circular ends. Altogether there were five of these towers of which three survive. In the north one is that very important feature of any castle, the well. As was usual the original entrance to the keep was on the first floor, probably between the two bastions on the west, and there are no openings at all at ground level. The original keep possibly rose to a height of some 80 feet. Towards the end of the 12th Century another building, 25 feet by 20 feet, was added to its south-west angle but its purpose is not known; possibly it was a forebuilding to guard the entrance. One of the 1,940 strong points was erected on the ruins of this and it blends in quite well, as does another among the fragments of another bastion.

The present gatehouse leading to the inner bailey was probably begun around 1220 but has been altered over the intervening period. In the 15th Century the wooden bridge was replaced by a stone causeway with a drawbridge. Now only the passageway and shells of the towers survive but in both towers the basement chamber is complete. The basement in the southern tower is approached by a staircase but the other can only be reached by a trapdoor, and both were almost certainly used as prison cells. The one with the trapdoor in the roof was probably reserved for lowly prisoners. The curtain wall, with its three round-fronted towers, surrounding the inner bailey dates from the middle of the 13th Century and was probably built by Peter of Savoy who became Lord of Pevensey in 1246. The 11th Century bank was removed to make room for these walls and the soil was spread over part of the outer bailey, raising the ground level by more than five feet. The 13th Century walls have lost their battlements but otherwise are in reasonably good repair. The ground floors are on a level with the courtyard and were directly approached—probably through a lobby from which there is a garderobe—and the first floors were reached through the wall walks of the curtain wall.

The upper rooms have fireplaces and the interiors of all these towers were adapted in 1940 as quarters for troops. Brick partitions and wooden floors were inserted, windows were glazed and roofs put on. Most of the original domestic structures were probably built of wood, and in 1302 there is mention of a wooden chapel. There was also a wooden hall, probably set against the north curtain wall where there are two large fireplaces and holes for the corbels which carried the chimney hoods. Between the gateway and the keep is

the well which is lined down to a depth of 51 feet. The total depth is unknown since it has never been cleared. A second well, found in the western section of the outer bailey, was lined with wood and is almost certainly of Roman origin.

Open to the public:

	Weekdays	Sundays
March–April	9.30 a.m.–5.30 p.m.	2–5.30 p.m.
May–Sept.	9.30 a.m.–7 p.m.	2–7 p.m.
Oct.	9.30 a.m.–5.30 p.m.	2–5.30 p.m.
Nov.–Feb.	10 a.m.–4.30 p.m.	2–4.30 p.m.

Peveril Castle, *Castleton, Derbyshire.*

Since parts of Derbyshire were rich in minerals, particularly lead, they were highly valued by the Crown; and therefore William the Conqueror gave the land into the care of William Peverel, a very trustworthy man. By the time of Domesday in 1086 there was a castle on the site, but few traces have been discovered. The northern curtain wall was almost certainly erected either by William Peverel or his son and dates from the late 11th Century. The wall is unusual in that it did not replace an earlier wooden one but was the original structure, probably because there was a plentiful supply of local stone. The keep was erected in 1176 and probably occupied the site of the original gateway, and a new one was made close to its north-west face. In 1251 repairs were carried out to the keep and there is mention of a turret although it is difficult to identify to what this refers. The castle passed through the hands of various owners including John of Gaunt, who seems to have owned most of the castles in Britain at one time or another, and excavations at the site have revealed no pottery of a later date than the 14th Century. Certainly by the 17th Century the castle was in ruins, and in 1932 the Duchy of Lancaster placed the ruins in the care of the Office of Works.

Modern steps lead to the gateway of which part of one pier and the beginning of an arch remain. Until the 12th Century it seems likely that this was indeed the main entrance to the castle. The large courtyard slopes steeply but there is a small area of flat ground which originally held a few buildings. In the north-west corner are the remains of a new hall, probably built in the middle of the 13th Century, but it is independent of the curtain wall. Amongst these surviving pieces may be seen the traces of both a central fireplace and a wall fireplace. At the west was the dais on which the lord's table stood, while the kitchen, buttery and pantry were at the eastern end. Most of the west curtain wall dates from the early 12th Century. The remains of the keep lack any indication that there were fixed fireplaces, so the only heat may have been in the form of metal braziers. The remains probably indicate the full height and the faces have buttress work typical of the 12th Century. The entrance was, as usual, on the first floor and reached by an external wooden staircase. The first floor, which was the main one, has two large windows and there are passages built into the walls at the north and south corners; the southern one contains a small garderobe. Near the south-east corner of the walls are the remains of two very large buildings, and possibly this was the hall built about 1177 and replaced by the new one on the north-west corner. To the east of this presumed hall foundation is a very thick wall of the 11th Century, but its use is unknown. Further out are the remains of the original chapel.

Open to the public:

	Weekdays	*Sundays*
March–April	*9.30 a.m.–5.30 p.m.*	*9.30 a.m.– 5.30 p.m.*
May–Sept.	*9.30 a.m.–7 p.m.*	*9.30 a.m.– 7 p.m.*
Oct.	*9.30 a.m.–5.30 p.m.*	*9.30 a.m.– 5.30 p.m.*
Nov.–Feb.	*9.30 a.m.–4 p.m.*	*9.30 a.m.– 4 p.m.*

Pickering Castle, *Pickering, North Riding, Yorkshire. Seven miles north of Malton, sixteen miles west of Scarborough.*

Pickering Castle stands on a limestone bluff at the edge of the North Yorkshire moors and is at a natural crossing point of the east to west path along the northern edge of the valley. There was a settlement here in the days before the Conquest, and in 1086 the Domesday book records that the manor of Pickering, previously held by Earl Morcar, was then in the possession of the king. When the castle was first built is uncertain but there was one in existence very early in the 12th Century. Six hundred yards to the west of the castle is a small promontory known as Beacon Hill which has on the top a Norman motte with some

traces of earthworks. It may be that this was the earlier site of the present castle, but it could be a siege work raised during the troubled reign of Stephen. Records of work on Pickering appear during the latter part of Henry II's reign and generally they are fairly small, suggesting that the castle was in a reasonably good state of repair, although there is some evidence to suggest that it sustained damage during Stephen's reign.

The builders used the rock on which the castle was built as the material for construction, as well as local timber, and Pickering is a little unusual in that the wooden defences continued in use until the 14th Century. Because it was set in ideal hunting country Pickering was visited, at one time or another, by most of the medieval monarchs. In 1267 the Honour and castle of Pickering were granted to the younger son of Henry III, Edmund "Crouchback", when he was made Earl of Lancaster. However, in 1322 the castle returned to royal hands when the son of "Crouchback" was executed for treason. In 1322 after a successful attack by Edward II on some rebellious Scottish lords, Robert the Bruce invaded Northern England. Ripon was burnt and the countryside was ravaged, but Pickering was saved because the local inhabitants agreed to pay the Scottish king a levy and also to give hostages. In October of that year the Scots withdrew, but orders in December and January show that further trouble was expected. The constable of the tower was ordered to acquire a heavy crossbow with 100 bolts, eight ordinary crossbows with 1,000 bolts, and 40 lances. Edward II also ordered that extensive rebuilding should take place at Pickering, and orders were given for the wooden defences to be replaced by a stone wall and a gateway with a drawbridge, Most of the building work was actually carried out in 1324/26, and there are records of payment of wages to waggoners, stonemasons and other craftsmen. In 1326 the castle was handed over to Henry, the younger brother of Earl Thomas of Lancaster. When Bolingbroke landed on his successful attempt to topple King Richard II he went first to Pickering Castle and spent two days there, and it is said that Richard was held prisoner at Pickering for a short period before he was taken to Pontefract (qv), where he is generally supposed to have been murdered.

During the latter part of the 15th Century Pickering saw further action, but it was largely of a domestic nature concerned with a quarrel over the true ownership. By the 16th Century much of the castle was in decay, the drawbridges were gone, the towers needed extensive overhaul and the whole site must have had a faintly melancholy air about it. Some repairs and restorations were undertaken but much of the castle was apparently uninhabited, although the Mill Tower was used for a while as a prison and the chapel was used as a court house. In 1926, after some two centuries of neglect, the castle was placed in the care of H.M. Office of Works and since then much clearing and restoration has been undertaken.

The long, roughly "L"-shaped outer bailey was known until the 15th Century as the barbican, and during the reign of King John, when it was first mentioned, it had a ditch and a bank with pointed stakes on top. Built across the old, original ditch is Rosamund's Tower; it is not clear why it is so named for there is no apparent connection between Fair Rosamund, who was the mistress of Henry II, and this castle. In the base of this tower is a small postern gate and this is protected by a small drawbridge. To the south of Rosamund's Tower is Diate Hill Tower; the origin of this name is also unclear but it may have something to do with a *diet* meaning a day's work, referring to the feudal obligation to work for the lord. Certain features suggest that the tower was added after the wall had been built. Against the inside of the curtain wall were the stables which in various surveys are described as being stone-roofed with two storeys, with three rooms above and two below. They were some 240 feet long by eighteen feet wide and eighteen feet high. At the south-west corner is the Mill Tower, and the Mill itself is referred to as early as the reign of Henry III (1216–1272). The tower is square and solid and the arrangements of the doors suggest that it may have been designed as a prison. The entry into the outer bailey is a comparatively poor piece of military architecture, and it has probably been considerably rebuilt. The original drawbridge which stood here does not appear to pre-date 1326. The entrance to the inner ward is now over a modern bridge crossing the original bailey ditch. A drawbridge was built in 1323 and beyond this bridge stood a pair of wooden gates over which was a chamber measuring 21 feet by nine feet with a lead roof, which probably housed the mechanism. It was not in use in 1537 and in that survey it is

referred to as His Grace's Chamber. On the right hand side of the entry is Coleman Tower, part of which has collapsed; but in 1323 it was called the King's Prison. The lower part probably dates from the 13th Century and was intended to give some protection to the gate as well as serving as a prison. It is square, and can only be entered from the first floor on the east side. Entering the inner bailey the keep is on the right at the top of the mount, and steps lead up to it. Near the foot of the motte on the left is the castle well; during the reign of Edward II a cord some 75 feet long was purchased for this well.

The motte probably dates from the reign of William the Conqueror when it would have had a wooden wall around the top which has long since been replaced by a stone, shell keep. There were buildings around the inside of the keep which was known, usually, as the King's Tower, but by the 16th Century they were in ruins and only the foundations now remain. The inner ward contained many of the larger buildings and on the western wall are the remains of the new hall built, in about 1314, for the wife of Earl Thomas of Lancaster, at a cost of over £340. It had a stone roof surmounting two storeys and the upper chamber, used by the countess, was plastered and had a decorated fireplace. Over 400 cart loads of stone were used in the building, although it had a timber frame. The main doorway was at the south-east corner and it was spanned by a very fine arch. Two steps lead down to the hall whilst on the left doorways led off to the buttery, kitchens and other domestic offices. The north-west corner has a small door which leads to the Old Hall and a small passageway turning to the right gave private access to the chapel. The Old Hall stood clear of the wall but when the curtain wall was rebuilt in the second half of the 12th Century the hall was enlarged and taken right up to the wall. The chapel which abuts the new hall is first mentioned in 1227 so it probably dates from that period. In the eastern corner of the inner bailey are the buildings usually known as the Constable's Lodgings. They were originally half-timbered and in 1537 consisted of a hall ten yards long and seven yards wide with a buttery, pantry, cellar and kitchen as well as sundry other odd buildings.

Open to the public:

	Weekdays	*Sundays*
March–April	*9.30 a.m.–5.30 p.m.*	*2–5.30 p.m.*

May–Sept.	*9.30 a.m.–7 p.m.*	*2–7 p.m.*
Oct.	*9.30 a.m.–5.30 p.m.*	*2–5.30 p.m.*
Nov.–Feb.	*9.30 a.m.–4 p.m.*	*2–4 p.m.*

Piel Castle. *On an island south of Barrow, Lancashire. Ferry from Roa Island.*

A licence to crenellate was granted in 1327 and there are still extensive remains. The keep is plain with a spiral staircase in the north-west corner. There are three other towers and some ruins of the chapel.

Pirton Castle, *Pirton, Hertfordshire. Three-quarters of a mile north of High Down, south-west of the church.*

The motte, known as Toot Hill, is 25 feet high with traces of several wards and ditches, and there are still some foundations visible.

Pleshey Castle, *near Chelmsford, Essex.*

In 1180 William de Mandeville was married at Pleshey in Essex, and to this same man Henry II (1154–1189) granted a licence to build a castle. The castle later came into the possession of the family of Bohun, Earls of Hereford. In 1397 the castle belonged to Thomas of Woodstock, Duke of Gloucester who was tricked by his nephew, King Richard II and taken to Calais where he was killed upon the king's orders. His body was brought back to Pleshey for burial. The contents of the castle were seized by the king and an inventory of all the items was made. To judge by some of the items—"a great bed of gold"—it would appear to have been well furnished.

Later the castle was to witness more violence, for in 1400 the Duke of Exeter, who had been involved in the capture and death of Richard, was beheaded by a mob outside the castle walls. In 1420 Henry V took over the castle and it formed part of the king's Duchy of Lancaster. Between 1450 and 1460 Margaret of Anjou, Queen of Henry VI, occupied the castle and some building, in the then-new material of brick, was carried out. By the reign of Elizabeth I (1558–1603) the castle had largely become a ruin, and is said to have been overrun by rabbits. In 1629 Robert Clarke pulled down most of the remains to build a house named The Lodge.

The area of the castle is quite considerable, more than eleven acres; it also incorporates part of a dwelling area which was also encompassed by a large ditch. The town lies to the north of the castle and the motte, which is over 60 feet in height, is surrounded by a deep ditch which is still full of water. The bailey rampart stands some eighteen feet above ground level; it is roughly kidney-shaped, and situated to the south of the motte. The bailey was entered by way of a two-span wooden bridge on the north-east side. In order to reach the motte the bailey had to be crossed and the strong point was at the top of the motte and could only be reached by a causeway. In the 15th Century the causeway was replaced by a brick bridge of which substantial remains can still be seen. Remains of the hall house were found on the top of the motte during excavations which were carried out in 1907.

The ditch which surrounded the dwelling area can still be seen and the roughly oval-shaped enclosure is well over a quarter of a mile across at its widest point.

Open to the public at any time, admission free.

Plympton Castle, *Plympton, Devonshire.*

Little remains of this castle, which originally had a large, rectangular bailey. The motte, some 70 feet high and 200 feet in circumference, is surmounted by some fragments of the circular keep wall, still standing some ten to eighteen feet high.

Podington Castle, *Podington, Bedfordshire. Behind Manor Farm.*

A very large, outer enclosure of a small motte and bailey castle.

Pontefract Castle, *Pontefract, West Riding, Yorkshire. West of All Saint's Church.*

Probably built by Ilbert de Lacy in the late 11th Century, the castle passed through the hands of various owners until the murder there of Richard II

Opposite, Porchester Castle, another Roman fort on the south coast improved by Norman masons; it has been used to house prisoners of many wars. Illustrated is Assheton's Tower

in 1400, when it became Crown property. It saw many stirring events during the Wars of the Roses, and later during the Civil Wars it was held for the king. In 1644 it was besieged by Fairfax but, despite several successful breachings of the defences, the Royalists held out until relieved by a force from Oxford. Parliament's troops returned and took it after another siege of three months, but in 1648 it was recaptured by the Royalists and then suffered yet another siege of six months before surrendering. Orders were then given for it to be slighted.

The castle as it stands comprises the inner bailey and the outer bailey extended down the hill. The walls are mostly 12th Century. There is a postern gate in the Paper Tower, and the chapel was in the middle of the south-west wall. The keep, known as the Round Tower, is a mid-13th Century shell keep, 60 feet in diameter, and is at the south-west corner; it is roughly trefoil-shaped and served as a prison. To the east is an inner and outer barbican, by two semi-circular towers. There are remains of some domestic offices, ovens, kitchens, etc., and on the south-east wall are the remains of Swillington Tower. At the centre of the bailey are some chambers excavated from the solid rock. During the late 19th Century the castle grounds housed a liquorice factory.

Open to the public daily 2 p.m.–dusk.

Porchester Castle, *Porchester, Hampshire.*

The site for the original Roman fort was chosen with care, and is at the tip of a long spit of land; it dates, probably, from the late 3rd Century A.D. when a stone fort was built here as part of the defences of the Saxon Shore. The fort followed the traditional pattern, being rectangular with slightly rounded corners; the walls were of flint and limestone and were surrounded by ditches. These walls still stand, being over eighteen feet high and ten feet thick, and they are complete on all four sides, although modifications were made during the medieval period.

When the Normans arrived they did the same as at Pevensey (qv) and cut off one corner of the Roman fort with a wooden palisade. During the rebellion led by his brother Robert, troops of Henry I's army were stationed at the Roman fort and, as a result of this struggle, Henry decided to strengthen the simple fortress. He began by building a large keep with walls twelve feet thick. The entrance was on the first floor and, originally, the keep was only one storey high, but later in the 12th Century two further floors were added. The interior is divided by a cross wall and the entrance was guarded by a pit crossed by either a temporary bridge or a drawbridge. As with most of these keeps the roof was quite sharply angled and the marks of this original roof can still be seen in the masonry. The keep is in the south-west corner of the castle; this corner of the bailey was cut off by a series of stone buildings, the domestic offices, and these, in turn, were protected by a moat. The keep was used by Henry II as both a treasure-house and a prison. In addition to the keep Henry I also had the curtain wall and a corner tower built. The gatehouse, known as Assheton's Tower, and the angle tower are three storeys high and extremely well built. Next to the gatehouse were the kitchens. In the opposite corner of the castle is a church and yard and, as at other castles, this was an established priory founded in this castle. The church was built during the first quarter of the 12th Century. During its lifetime the castle saw the embarkation of many troops for France and it also served as a prison for many of England's enemies including Dutch prisoners in the 17th century and Napoleonic Frenchmen. In the late 18th Century a series of timber huts were erected in the outer enclosure to house some 5,000 prisoners.

There are two gates directly opposite one another across the outer bailey, the water gate which faces the shore and a land gate on the opposite side. Both occupy the positions of gates used by the Romans. They were originally built by the Normans and heightened and modified by Edward II; Richard II had some further changes made to both gates. During the first half of the 14th Century it seems that a further earthwork was added, and traces of this can still be seen. The curtain wall is fitted with a number of projecting towers, including some "D"-shaped ones spaced around each of the walls. The gates are flanked by towers and although the keep constitutes one angle tower

there are three others, and each length of wall is set with projecting towers.

Open to the public:

	Weekdays	Sundays
March–April	9.30 a.m.–5.30 p.m.	2–5.30 p.m.
May–Sept.	9.30 a.m.–7 p.m.	9.30 a.m.–7 p.m.
Oct.	9.30 a.m.–5.30 p.m.	2–5.30 p.m.
Nov.–Feb.	10 a.m.–4.30 p.m.	2–4.30 p.m.

Portland Castle, *Portland, Dorset. Northern shore of the Isle of Portland.*

This is another of the castles built by Henry VIII to defend the coast of Britain. The exact date of construction is not known but a document of 1540 refers to a " bulwark of Portland ". During the 16th Century it saw no action although during the Civil War its fortunes fluctuated. It was seized by the Royalists in 1642, changed hands twice in that year and finally surrendered to Parliament in 1646. On one occasion it was captured by the Royalists by means of a trick. Groups of horse approached the castle, those in front bearing Parliamentary colours, the second apparently riding in hot pursuit. The first group was admitted to the castle by the unsuspecting Parliamentarians, but they immediately turned on the garrison and captured the castle. In about 1870 the government decided to utilise the castle and it has since been used for various military purposes including accommodation for the Royal Naval Air Service; but it is now under the care of the Ministry of Public Buildings and Works.

In shape it is like a segment of a circle, the curved side facing the sea, while at the rear is the tower. Internally it is octagonal but externally curved and with the side walls uniting with the sides of the segment. The tower and the wing walls were used as living accommodation by officers and the governor, while the troops were housed in barracks within the courtyard, which was originally roofed over. There are embrasures for five pieces of ordnance on the ground floor and nine on the top and there is room for another line of guns above the keep. In 1623 the number of guns within the castle is listed as thirteen. A moat runs round the outside and holes for the drawbridge chain are still visible above the entrance. There was an outer defence of a moat and a rampart but this has now disappeared. The great hall retains some of the original timber ceiling but the windows have been much altered. Other chambers leading off from the great hall are numerous including pantry, cellars, gun room and store rooms. To the south-east of the castle there is another open battery.

Open to the public:

	Weekdays	Sundays
April	9.30 a.m.–5.30 p.m.	2–5.30 p.m.
May–Sept.	9.30 a.m.–7 p.m.	2–7 p.m.

Powderham Castle, *Powderham, Devonshire. Eight miles south-west of Exeter on A379 to Dawlish.*

The land was originally granted to William, Count of Eu but he very soon lost his lands for rebelling against William I. It then passed, as did so many other estates, to the Courtenay family who made this their main castle. During its long history it has suffered many changes, but it was at one time an extremely powerful castle. In 1752 it was described as having six towers, but it has been greatly modified now and only two towers survive, on the east and west sides. The forecourt was designed by the architect Fowler during the 1840/45 period. It was remodelled, the chapel being made into a dining room, and one central brick porch and a brick wing were added to give the traditional Elizabethan "E"-style. Further modifications have been carried out until the whole thing is a considerable mixture of architectural styles. During the English Civil War it did see some action, being held against Fairfax, the Parliamentary general, but its resistance was short-lived.

Open to the public May 27th to September 7th; Sundays, Tuesdays, Wednesdays and Thursdays until July 13th; July 15th to September 7th Sundays to Fridays. Open Bank Holidays 2–5.30 p.m. Admission 40p, Children and OAPs 20p. Private rooms on view on Thursdays.

Prestonbury Castle, *Drew Steignton, Devonshire.*

On the opposite bank of the river Teign to Cranbrook Castle (qv), this too is an early Iron Age fort. There are incomplete earthworks with a moat, earth parapet, an inner ditch and another, stone-faced rampart.

Princes Risborough Castle, *Princes Risborough, Buckinghamshire. To the south-west of the church.*

A few remains of walls and ditches, of indeterminate origin.

Prudhoe Castle, *Prudhoe, Northumberland.*

High above the Tyne river, on the south bank, this castle dates from the 12th Century and was owned by the d'Umfraville and Percy families. Quite early it is recorded as having twice been under siege. In the bailey is a keep some 41 feet by 44 feet, and on the east face is a forebuilding containing a staircase. On the north-west corner of the inner bailey is a 13th Century circular tower, and against the well-preserved curtain wall stood the hall. There is a particularly fine gatehouse with good Norman arches on the lower floor although the upper floor was added, probably in the 13th Century. On the first floor was the chapel with a very early example of a curved, projecting, oriel window. In the 14th Century the defences were augmented by the addition of a barbican with long side walls and outer gatehouse. Around the castle was a double moat which also enclosed a pele-tower and a flat open space.
On private land.

Pulford Castle, *Pulford, Cheshire. On the border of Cheshire and Denbighshire by the road from Chester to Wrexham and behind the church.*

A strong earthworks, facing north-east, with a motte by the side of a stream. It is largely obscure although it knew a brief moment of glory during the rebellion of Owain Glyndwr during the reign of Henry IV.

Quatford Castle, *Quatford, Shropshire.*

Earl Roger de Montgomery built a small castle here in the 11th Century, but it was thought to be poorly sited and at the end of the 11th Century it was decided to abandon and demolish the building, concentrating on the castle at Bridgnorth (qv).

Queenborough Castle, *Queenborough, Kent.*

This is also known as the Castle of Sheppey. Although little or nothing remains of it, it is interesting for being the only Royal castle newly built during the latter Middle Ages, and it was also of a rather unusual design. It was demolished in 1650 by orders of Parliament and is described in a survey as being "circular built, of stone, with six towers and certain other offices, the roof thereon being covered with lead within which circumference is one small paved court". It was begun in 1361 but was not finished until 1375.

Raby Castle, *Staindrop, County Durham. One mile north of Staindrop on the Barnard Castle–Bishop Auckland Road (A688).*

Tradition has it that a hearth-fire has burned in this castle, the largest in the country, since the time of Edward the Confessor. In 1378 Sir John Nevill was granted his licence and it remained the family stronghold until 1569, when the 6th Earl of Northumberland was deposed. During the reign of James I it passed to Sir Henry Vane, and in 1645 his son lost the castle to a surprise attack by

Royalist troops from Bolton. His second son, Sir George Vane, rapidly assembled an army of 300 and retook the castle, but in 1648 it was again under siege by the king's men. A wide moat, originally wet, guarded the walls. On the west side is the entrance, Nevill Tower, built in 1378. To the right of it is Joan's Tower, named after Lady Joan of Beaufort. To the south are some later additons, including an octagonal tower which occupies the site of much earlier buildings demolished to make room for the new ones. On the east is the Chapel Tower, with chapel, priest's room and guard room. In front of the Chapel gateway, with its five turrets and machicolations, stood the barbican, destroyed in the 18th Century. On the north-east corner is Mount Raskelf, a solid tower; the curtain wall is modern, and connects with the Kitchen tower of *circa* 1370. An underground passage, now blocked off, led from the cellars through to Staindrop Abbey. Clifford's Tower, the largest, stands at the north-west and has numerous arrow slits and ten-foot-thick walls. The fine entrance hall, facing the gateway across the bailey, was built by Lord Darlington. Originally another great curtain wall, with its own gatehouse, encircled the entire castle.

Open to the public Easter Saturday, Sunday and Monday then Sundays to end of May and Spring Bank Holiday weekend. Wednesdays, Saturdays and Sundays June and July. Daily except Fridays during August, then Wednesdays, Saturdays and Sundays to end of September 2 p.m.–5 p.m. Admission 25p, Children 10p.

Ragged Castle, *Great Badmington, Gloucestershire.*

Built *circa* 1750, it has a square shape with one large, circular tower and great battlements, but its sole function was to improve the landscape.

Ravensworth Castle, *Gateshead, County Durham. Four miles south of Gateshead.*

Built in 1808 for the Lidell family by Nash, this stands on the site of an earlier castle of which fragments still survive.

On private land.

Reculver Castle, *Reculver, Kent. Three miles east of Herne Bay.*

Like Richborough (qv) Reculver is one of the Roman forts of the Saxon Shore. There is also some evidence, although less firm than in the case of Richborough, to suggest that it may well have served as a base for the Claudian invasion of England, A.D. 43. The present fort was probably built around 210 A.D. and is known to have been garrisoned at one time by a cohort of Baetasian troops who came originally from Belgium. The Roman fort is square with rounded corners, but there are no projecting towers or turrets on the walls which are ten feet thick and protected by wide, inner banks and outside ditches. The northern wall and north and western gates have all been undermined and demolished by the action of the tide. Over the ages much of the material has been removed and used for other purposes, to such an extent that the south-west corner and part of the other walls have disappeared. Some details of the method of construction of the gates can be seen from the outside where excavations have been carried out, but they are still covered by the banks at the back.

The fort was bisected by the main road running from east to west and to the south were the headquarters, the *principia*, and the officers quarters, while to the north was a bathhouse. Most of the buildings can be dated to the 3rd Century but the fort was garrisoned through most of this century, certainly during the rule of the break-away Emperors Carausius and Allectus between A.D. 286 and 296. The fort was apparently then abandoned but re-occupied again about A.D. 340–370, during the period when Saxon raids were especially bad; later it was again left to fall into ruin.

In 669 Egbert, King of Kent, granted Reculver for the foundation of a Minster or Monastery, and the remains of this church are still present.

Open to the public at all times: admission free.

Redcastle Castle, *Wem, Shropshire. Four miles east of Wem in Hawkstone Park.*

This Norman castle was in ruins by the 16th Century although licence was granted in 1232. Some repairs were presumably made, for it was

later ransacked by Parliament. Part of a tower survives as does a 200-foot-deep well.
On private land.

Reigate Castle, *Reigate, Surrey.*

To the north of the High Street is an 11th Century motte with a fine gatehouse, which is a complete sham, having been erected in 1777.

Restormel Castle, *Lostwithiel, Cornwall. One and a half miles north of Lostwithiel, Cornwall, on A390.*

This castle is of particular interest for the fine state of preservation of its exterior wall. Most early Norman castles comprise a motte surmounted by a tower within a bailey, but at Restormel there is no separate bailey. The motte, 125 feet in diameter, is big enough to be self-contained and there are no signs that the castle ever had a bailey. The keep on top of the motte was originally a simple, wooden palisade which was gradually replaced by stone walls; this process probably began at the turn of the 11th Century, on the south-west side, when a square gatehouse was erected. The wooden wall had been completely replaced with a stone wall early in the 13th Century and this has survived complete with its battlements. Inside the circle of the wall were the various timber buildings, the whole forming a fine shell keep. Towards the end of the 13th Century these simple buildings were replaced with some very fine apartments which extended all round the inside of the wall. Much of the work was probably undertaken by Edmund, Earl of Cornwall, between 1272 and 1299. A square tower was built on the eastern side which contained a chapel with an undercroft in which, no doubt, the priest lived. The gateway tower was extended by a barbican and on either side broad, straight stairs led to the first floor rooms and then to the wall walks. From the gateway, anti-clockwise, the first building was the kitchen, from which a passage and staircase probably led up to the hall. On ground level were cellars and above them were the great hall and private rooms leading one to another. Beyond the small, private withdrawing room is a blank wall and on the other side is a second hall which can

only be entered from the other end; the purpose of this room is not clear. It has been suggested that it was used for guests but it has been pointed out that it has neither fireplace nor windows on the outside. An alternative suggestion which seems far more reasonable is that it was a guardroom, with sleeping accommodation for the duty men in the loft above. Beneath this room were the stables large enough to hold six horses and these are listed in a survey of 1337. The same survey also mentions other buildings outside the wall, as well as a lead pipe taking in the domestic water supply. This survey indicates that the whole castle was in need of extensive repair. At the centre of the courtyard is a pit in which is situated that most important feature of castle life, the well, this one being some 50 feet deep. By the 16th Century the castle was seriously dilapidated, and it was neglected by the Tudors. The original castle was started by Baldwin FitzTurstin, and during the Barons' War was held for Simon de Montfort. It later passed into the possession of Richard, Earl of Cornwall, brother of Henry III. It was visited by the Black Prince in 1354 and 1362, but from then on its importance gradually waned. During the English Civil War it was held against the king but after a brief attack it surrendered to Sir Richard Grenville, a Royalist commander of brutal reputation. A Parliamentary report of 1649 describes it as being utterly in ruins and not worth the trouble of demolishing. In 1925 the Duchy of Cornwall handed over the castle to the care of the Commissioners of H.M. Office of Works.
Open to the public:

	Weekdays	Sundays
March–April	*9.30 a.m.–5.30 p.m.*	*2–5.30 p.m.*
May–Sept.	*9.30 a.m.–7 p.m.*	*9.30 a.m.–*
		7 p.m.
Oct.	*9.30 a.m.–5.30 p.m.*	*2–5.30 p.m.*
Nov.–Sept.	*10 a.m.–4.30 p.m.*	*2–4.30 p.m.*

Richards Castle, *Richards Castle, Herefordshire. To the west of St. Bartholomew's Church.*

This castle may well have been known as Auretone Castle, which is listed in the Domesday survey. The motte, 200 feet in diameter and some 40 feet high, has a bailey to the south-east, and there are substantial remains of the wall and an extensive outer bailey.

Richborough Castle, *Richborough, Kent. One and a half miles north of Sandwich, off the A256.*

Although still known as the Isle of Thanet, this piece of land is no longer separated from the mainland. In Roman times it was indeed an island and Richborough lay on the east side of a small peninsula jutting out into the channel of the river Wantsum which, at that time, separated the two pieces of land. Julius Caesar made two brief visits to the shores of this island in 55 and 54 B.C., but it was not until A.D.43 that the main Roman invasion was mounted by the Emperor Claudius. It is thought very likely that the main Roman army, of four legions with their auxiliaries, landed at Richborough and there are certainly traces of a defensive Roman ditch of this period. After the initial campaign Richborough became a supply centre and some buildings were erected on the north side, as well as granaries. About A.D. 85 there was a major reconstruction of the fort and most of the earlier wooden buildings were demolished. Probably to celebrate the final victory gained by General Agricola and to honour the Emperor Domitian (A.D. 81–96) a large building, cased in marble, was erected. Although the temple has gone the foundations remain at the centre of the fort. Remains of houses of wattle and daub, probably built for the workmen, have been excavated. During the 2nd Century A.D. it seems that part of the castle was given over to civilian occupation, for the remains of two stone houses and a cemetery have also been excavated. With the outbreak of Saxon raiding during the second half of the 3rd Century there was a fresh military occupation. A typical wooden fort, surrounded by three ditches, was built and this structure enclosed the site of the temple. As the danger increased the castle had to be strengthened and shortly after this the present walls were built, and at the same time the earlier earthworks were filled in. The castle of Richborough, called by the Romans Rutupiae, was occupied right up until the end of the Roman military presence in Britain.

Today the castle is surrounded by a double ditch; all the walls stand except for that on the east and half the southern wall. They pay tribute to the Roman builders, for they stand 25 to 30 feet high. At the centre of the northern wall was a small postern gate protected by a wall and there is every likelihood that a similar one existed in the vanished northern section. At each of the four corners was a rounded bastion built separately and bonded on to the walls which are fitted at intervals with square turrets. The walls are made with inner and outer faces of squared stone and the space between filled with layers of flint set in mortar, the whole bonded together making a very durable material. It is of interest to note in certain parts of the wall pieces of marble from the commemorative temple were used as fillings. The foundations of the wall are between twelve and thirteen feet wide and the walls were built in sections and bonded together as the ends met. The joins may be noted by kinks where lines of tiling do not quite match; the best example is to be seen in the north-west corner. When originally designed the fort was square but before it was finished it was evidently decided to move the eastern wall further towards the shore. The main gate was at the west and through this passed Watling Street, the Roman road from Canterbury, crossing the outer ditch by a causeway; the inner one was crossed by a bridge, parts of which can still be seen. The gatehouse had guard chambers, built of large stones taken from the ruins of the temple, on each side. Set into the outer face of the second tower on the north wall (the one on the left when entering through the main gate) is a large stone known, for many years, as Queen Bertha's head. It has been found that it is, in fact, the worn head and mane of a lion, the rest of which is imbedded in the wall.

In the north-east corner the wall of the castle actually passes over the remains of a large house, which was built in A.D. 85 and then rebuilt, on a more elaborate scale in the 2nd Century A.D. The various remains have been marked in brown for the earlier ones and white for the later ones. When the ditches were being dug during the 3rd Century the outer ditches stopped short of the wall, but the house itself was knocked down when the stone fort was built. A little to the south of the house may be seen the remains of the chapel of St. Augustine which lies just inside the line of the three ditches from the earliest fort. Tradition has it that St. Augustine landed here in 597 when on his way to visit King Ethelbert of Kent and tradition likewise has it that a stone preserved on the site bore the imprint of the saint's foot. Near the very centre of the fort stands the Great Foundation which is a platform, cruciform in shape and surrounded by some part of a wall. It was constructed about

A.D. 85 to support a monument, probably of bronze statues. The platform is over 30 feet thick and measures 126 feet by 82 feet. In the 3rd Century the monument was stripped of its ornaments and appears to have served as a lookout or signalling station. Just to the west of the Great Foundation are the remains of a 4th Century temple, although to which god it was dedicated is not known. It may possibly have been Mithras, for it is known that this god was worshipped by many of the Roman legionaries. Just to the rear of the tower of the north-west gate are the remains of a wine cellar in which was a flight of steps leading down to two rooms. In one were found the conical holes, into which the ends of the wine jars stood, cut into the floor. The museum houses a number of exhibits associated with the history of Richborough; a large number of objects have been excavated including the grave of a late Roman soldier buried with his shield, sword and spear. Over 50,000 coins were found; these cover in period the whole of the Roman occupation of Britain, and there were one or two of later Saxon period.

Open to the public:

	Weekdays	Sundays
March–April	*9.30 a.m.–5.30 p.m.*	*2–5.30 p.m.*
May–Sept.	*9.30 a.m.–7 p.m.*	*9.30 a.m.–7 p.m.*
Oct.	*9.30 a.m.–5.30 p.m.*	*2–5.30 p.m.*
Nov.–Feb.	*10 a.m.–4.30 p.m.*	*2–4.30 p.m.*

Richmond Castle, *Richmond, Yorkshire. South-west edge of town off B6274.*

Situated on the top of a hill overlooking the town, the castle is largely in ruins but is still of considerable interest, for it retains an unusually large quantity of 11th Century masonry. The Great Hall is one of the two oldest in the country.

The land on which it stands was given by William the Conqueror (1066–1089) to Alan the Red, a son of the Count of Penthièrre, who began building the castle in 1071. The great curtain wall dates from the 11th Century and forms two sides of a triangular defence, the third side being protected by the river Swale. Originally the entrance was through a gatehouse at the northern end of the apex of the triangle. The great square keep, over 100 feet high, was built over this gatehouse, so blocking the original entrance. A new gateway, with a portcullis, was cut through the wall roughly on the site of the present entrance. There are a few interesting examples of graffiti still surviving on the walls of the eastern chamber on the second floor of the keep. A staircase leads from this floor directly on to the battlements of the wall which originally included three towers, only two of which survive. The first, the Robin Hood Tower, has some claims to fame, for it held, for a while, a royal prisoner. In 1174 William the Lion, King of Scotland, was captured near Alnwick during one of the frequent Scottish raids. He was detained for a while in Richmond Castle until his subsequent removal to Normandy. The upper part of the tower is of 14th Century construction.

Not, perhaps, the most romantically appealing part of the ruins is the Gold Hole Tower, but it is interesting, for it is a fine example of medieval latrines; the lower pits date from the 11th Century, with 14th Century repairs and rebuilding to the upper storey.

Projecting from the east wall is another courtyard known as The Cockpit, which was originally protected by a curtain wall which has now largely disappeared.

At the southern tip of the eastern wall is Scolland's Hall, a two storey building of the 11th Century, with the ground floor designed as storage cellars. To the west of the wall stood the buttery, pantry and kitchens, and it is interesting to record that at an early date there was a serious fire which probably gutted the building, for there are still scorch marks on the masonry and some rebuilding was carried out in the 13th Century.

The castle formed part of the Honour of Richmond, but it is situated rather far away from the main lines of travel and seems to have been built here primarily because the site was so naturally strong. Its position preserved it from any serious action and it saw little, if any, fighting.

The Honour of Richmond and the castle had a varied ownership over the ages, and its owners have included John of Gaunt, the Duke of Clarence and Richard III. The title of Duke of Richmond was given by Henry VIII to his illegitimate son, Henry Fitzroy, but when he died the title lapsed. It was revived once in 1641 and again in 1675 when Charles II gave the Dukedom to his illegitimate son Charles Lennox, whose descendants still hold it.

A survey carried out in 1538 already described the castle as being in a very decayed condition, and repair and rebuilding were recommended, but little was done. In 1732 some minor repairs and restorations were carried out. Some more was done in 1761 but the castle was again left to decay and in the 19th Century a large barrack was built along the west wall and much of the area was adapted for other purposes, all to its detriment.

In 1910 the Commissioners of H.M. Works took it over and extensive restoration has since been carried out.

Open to the public daily, May to September; weekdays and Sunday afternoons, October to April. Admission free.

Ripley Castle, *Ripley, West Riding, Yorkshire.*

This belonged to the Ingilby family; most of it dates from the 16th Century, although the gatehouse may be 15th Century. Much of the original fabric was removed when extensive rebuilding took place in 1780.

Open to the public May to September, Sundays 2–6 p.m.; Spring and Late Summer Bank Holiday Mondays 2–6 p.m. Gardens open Saturdays and Bank Holiday Mondays 2–6 p.m. Admission: House and Gardens 25p, Children 15p; Parties 20p, Children 10p. Gardens only 10p, Children 5p.

Risinghoe Castle, *Goldrington, Bedfordshire. Two miles east of the village.*

A motte and bailey castle with 20-foot-high mound.

Road Castle, *Winsford, Somerset.*

Standing on the high ground in Lyncombe Wood by the river are a few ramparts of a castle.

Rochester Castle, *Rochester, Kent. On the east bank of the Medway, just south of Rochester Bridge.*

Kent is well-endowed with castles, but as an example of the large square Norman keep, Rochester is unbeatable. It owes its position to the Romans, who knew it as Durobrives; it was at this point that Watling Street, which ran from Dover to London, crossed the river Medway. In view of its strategic position it is not surprising that it was at Rochester that one of the first Norman castles in Britain was erected. It would have been one of the motte and bailey type and was probably erected on the hill known at present as Boley Hill, a name usually taken to be a corruption of the word bailey. The castle was one of several under the command of William the Conqueror's half-brother, Bishop Odo, who was dissatisfied with the arrangements made upon the death of William I and led many of the barons in a rebellion against the new king, William II "Rufus" (1089–1100). During the subsequent campaign Odo was captured by William but later released by the garrison of Rochester, and was then besieged within the castle. The defenders were finally forced into surrender— although they were allowed to leave riding their horses and carrying their arms—and Odo was banished to Normandy.

It is not certain whether it was the first castle that was involved in this siege or the one which stands today, but it is known with certainty that the present castle was begun between 1087 and 1089. The builder was a churchman, Gundulf, Bishop of Rochester and the total cost was £60. This castle was probably little more than a curtain wall surrounded by a ditch, the remains of which can be seen on the south-eastern corner between the present surviving curtain wall and the cathedral. The keep was built during the reign of Henry I; he gave the constableship to Archbishop William de Corbeil, who was ordered to make a "fortification or tower" within the castle. Under the charter of Henry II the custody of the castle was vested in the Archbishop of Canterbury, but during the reign of John (1199–1216) there was a deal of controversy over this. In 1215 when the barons revolted against King John, Rochester Castle saw its first big siege. The castle was seized by the rebels, who held it with 100 to 140 knights as well as other troops. John gathered together a mercenary army, and on 13th October 1215 he reached Rochester. The bridge over the river was breached to prevent supplies reaching the castle from London, and for the next two months the castle was surrounded by royalist troops commanded by the king himself. John pressed the siege vigorously, ordering the construction of at least five large catapults which, according to the chroniclers, maintained a ceaseless bombardment against the walls and keep. In addition to the artillery bombardment there was a constant volley of arrows and crossbow bolts. There is some dispute amongst the chroniclers as to how effective this bombardment was, but there is no argument as to the effectiveness of the mining undertaken by the king. The outer wall was breached and the royalist forces penetrated into the outer bailey. Still they were faced with the keep, of tremendous strength. Having seen the success of his previous mine, the king set to work against the keep. The usual method was to dig a tunnel beneath the building, removing the foundations bit by bit and replacing them with timber props. The props were surrounded by bundles of straw and inflammables such as bacon fat or pitch, and when all was ready the inflammable mixture was fired. As the props burned through the unsupported weight of the tower or wall literally dragged the stones free, and the buildings collapsed. It was usual to dig under the weakest point, and in the case of a Norman tower this was invariably the corner. So determined were the defenders of the castle that even when the south-east tower collapsed as a result of this mining they maintained their defiance. They continued fighting within the keep until eventual starvation forced them to surrender. Despite the traditional view of King John he was, on this occasion, merciful, and seems to have hanged only one of the rebels. Ironically, the royalist occupation of the castle was brief, for in 1216 the castle was in the hands of Prince Louis of France. On the death of the king, however, he withdrew his troops and returned home.

Over the next twenty or so years considerable amounts of money were spent on restoring and strengthening the castle. The mined south-east tower was rebuilt but this time it was made round, a shape which is architecturally much stronger, there being no weak corners. Among the improvements made was the erection of a number of towers along the wall as well as a dividing wall, long since gone, which split the bailey into an inner and outer section. The chapel was decorated and later rebuilt, new stables were built, and it is apparent that Rochester had become one of the strongest, best-built major castles in the country. It was not long left in peace, for in 1264 the Barons' War broke out, and Rochester Castle was held for the king by Roger de Leybourne. In view of its importance it is not surprising that it was soon under siege.

After some heavy fighting the rebels broke into the town, taking it on Good Friday, and on the Saturday the bailey was in their hands although the keep was still held by the king's men. As on other occasions the keep proved difficult to capture. Despite continuous bombardment the barons were unable to take it, and on Saturday 26th April they lifted the siege and withdrew.

The considerable damage caused during the siege was left unrepaired and dilapidation and the theft of materials soon demolished the greater part of the outer defences. By the mid-14th Century the castle was said to have had only the keep and the first and second gates standing, and even these were described as "ruined". Edward III took vigorous action, and between 1367 and 1370 well over £2,000 was spent on restoring the castle. Parts of the curtain wall were rebuilt, some towers were reconstructed and there are references to the erection of a drawbridge. In 1381, when the peasants of Kent rebelled and produced that isolated phenomena, the Peasants' Revolt, they captured Rochester Castle and seem to have inflicted some damage. From the end of the 14th Century onwards the story is the familiar one of the castle gradually falling into disrepair through neglect. By the 16th Century it seems to have been in a state of decay, and later James I gave it over to Sir Anthony Weldon, whose family owned it until the late 19th Century. In 1870 the Corporation of Rochester bought the lease of the castle grounds and turned them into a pleasure garden. During this period a certain amount of demolition and reconstruction was carried out, and in 1965 the Corporation of Rochester placed the castle in the hands of the Ministry of Public Buildings and Works.

Today much of the curtain wall, together with some of the bastions and towers, survive while on the south-west and south-east sides traces of the original ditch can still be seen. The drawbridge and main gate were on the eastern side; the present entrance was cut through the ruins of a 14th Century bastion. The impressive looking Norman arch is actually modern, and both this and the entrance were erected in 1872. The surviving curtain wall is largely of 11th Century origin; although the foundations are earlier, going back to Roman times, later reconstruction and modification can be seen. Some of the original battlements still exist; it seems that the original west wall

Opposite: Rochester Castle has the tallest keep in the country, on a site recognised for its strategic importance for nearly two thousand years

stood some 22 feet in height, was over four feet thick at the base, and tapered to two feet thick at the top. The surviving wall to the south of the castle dates from the time of Henry III, whilst that portion of the curtain wall running from the round tower of Henry III at the south-west corner, and that running up to the present main entrance, date from the time of Edward III.

It is the keep which dominates the site, for it is 70 feet square and rises 113 feet to the top of the parapet; four turrets rise a further twelve feet above this, giving a total of 125 feet—making it the highest keep in the country. On the east side of the keep, and on the south-east corner tower, the holes which accommodated the wooden supports for the shuttering can still be seen. The walls are built mostly of Kentish ragstone faced with square-hewn ashlar which was transported all the way from Caen. The walls taper very slightly from some twelve feet at the base to ten feet at the top, and their thickness enabled the builder to incorporate a number of rooms into the walls. The interior of the castle was divided from top to bottom by an internal cross-wall. On the lower section of the keep the windows are, naturally, quite small, whilst those at the top are round-topped and much larger, allowing some light and air to filter to the interior. As with many Norman castles the entrance, on the first floor, was protected by a fore-building on the north side, and this extends from the ground floor right to the third floor. The fore-building also contained a portcullis. The centre dividing wall of the keep is pierced from top to bottom by the well shaft, while the main walls contain numerous small chambers designed as garderobes. The second floor has a gallery running around it level with the windows. At some period or other the entire centre of the castle, as at Hedingham (qv), was gutted by fire and there is a rosy pink finish to the walls caused by the flames, as well as a spattering of lead from the roof. The second floor contained the state apartments and on the third floor was a fine chapel in addition to a smaller one housed in the forebuilding. The turrets and top of the keep were fitted with battlements with merlons connected by a wall walk.

Open to the public:

	Weekdays	Sundays
March–April	9.30 a.m.–5.30 p.m.	2–5.30 p.m.
May–Sept.	9.30 a.m.–7 p.m.	2–7 p.m.
Oct.	9.30 a.m.–5.30 p.m.	2–5.30 p.m.
Nov.–Feb.	10 a.m.–4.30 p.m.	2–4.30 p.m.

Rockingham Castle, *Rockingham, Northampton-shire. North of Rockingham Park by the river Welland.*

There is a motte some 100 feet in diameter at the top and 30 feet high, with a moat around it; to the north was the bailey with a gatehouse on the north-east corner. The curtain wall had a series of circular towers and numerous buttresses. It had various owners, mostly royal, until the 16th Century when it was leased to Edward Watson, who set about converting and restoring the then-dilapidated castle. In 1643 Lord Grey of Groby took possession for Parliament and there were considerable modifications to the fortifications, but it did not see any action. The gatehouse, *circa* 1200, stands, as does the hall of Edward I which was modified by Watson; most of the other buildings date from the same period, *circa* 1580.
Open to the public Easter to September 30th. Sundays, Thursdays and Bank Holidays (Mondays) 2–6 p.m. Admission 30p, Children 20p.

Romden Castle, *Smarden, Kent.*

Built in the 18th Century and modified *circa* 1866. *On private land.*

Roper Castle, *Signal Station, Bowes, North Riding, Yorkshire. North of the A66.*

A rampart and ditch 10 feet wide mark off a rectangle 55 feet by 60 feet with an entrance on the south side. There is a centre platform 27 feet by 20 feet. The site is of Roman origin.

Roper Castle, *Brough, Westmorland. One-and-a-half miles south-west of Maiden Castle.*

This was probably the site of a Roman signal station; the earthworks measure 60 feet by 46 feet and there is an entrance on the south side.

Ros Castle, *Chillingham, Northumberland.*

A hilltop fort with double ramparts, over 1,000 feet above sea level.

Rose Castle, *Rose Castle, Cumberland. Seven miles south of Carlisle by Caldew River.*

There was some form of fortified building here in the 13th Century, and in 1300 it was the home of Edward I after one of his campaigns. It suffered at the hands of Robert Bruce in 1322 and again a little later.
The castle was quadrangular, with the hall on the east side while on the west was a Council chamber. The building was enclosed with a moat which, in turn, was within another moated and walled enclosure. In the 15th Century Bishop Strickland restored the old tower and it still bears his name. Another tower was added later and a third was added to the west side in the 16th Century. During the Civil War it was captured by Parliament in 1645, being retaken by the Royalists in 1648, and by 1680 it was in ruins. Bishop Percy restored the Palace, and between 1829/31 the work was under the direction of Thomas Rickman.
On church land—not open to the public.

Rougemont Castle, *Exeter, Devonshire. In the town gardens.*

Little remains beyond the moat, some of the walls, Athelstone's tower and one of the finest of early Norman gateways, although this has been much restored.
Open all year round.

Round Castle, *Bladon, Oxfordshire. In the woods on Bladon Heath.*
The minor traces of a hill-top fort consisting of two earth defences.

Rowton Castle, *Rowton, Shropshire. Two-and-a-quarter miles south-west of Ford.*

The existing building is a 19th Century reconstruction of a castle which was razed in 1482.

Ruyton Castle, *Ruyton - of - the - Eleven - Towns, Shropshire. West of the church.*

The remains of a castle built by Edmund, Earl of Arundel, early in the 14th Century. Only three walls of a small keep still stand.

Saffron Walden Castle, *Saffron Walden, Essex. To the north of the town.*

Considerable masonry fragments of the 12th Century keep indicate the site of this castle, which had a shell keep. The newer tower was erected in 1834 by Lord Howard de Warden.
On private land.

St. Briavels Castle, *St. Briavels, Gloucestershire.*

Dating from the 13th Century; much has survived including walls and a fine gatehouse which was exceptionally well defended. It has the usual two flanking towers forming a passageway to the entrance; there were no less than three portcullises. It is three storeys high, and strong, with a pit beneath one of the side rooms which may well have been a prison. The 13th Century hall range, now used as a Youth Hostel, has been greatly modified, and there are the masonry fragments of a tower which was demolished in the 18th Century.
Another earthwork near Stowe Grange, over a mile to the north, was probably the site of the first castle.

St. Mawes Castle, *St. Mawes, Cornwall. Two miles east of Falmouth across the Estuary.*

In 1538 developments on the continent of Europe

made it seem highly likely that France would invade England and Henry VIII took urgent steps to improve the country's defences. A large number of castles were built along the coast between Hull and Milford Haven; St. Mawes Castle was one, begun in 1540 and finished in 1543. Although the French never came the castle was maintained in a state of readiness for some considerable time. In 1595 the Spanish raided Penzance but did not come near the castle. Since St. Mawes was designed primarily to guard against invasion little thought was given to the defence of the landward side and consequently in 1646 when Lord Fairfax, the Parliamentary general, arrived before St. Mawes the commander negotiated a surrender apparently without a single shot being fired. During the First World War the castle did play some small part in the coastal defence of the country, and in 1920 it was handed over to the Commissioners of H.M. Works. Like Pevensey (qv) it saw another brief spell of military activity in 1939 but was reopened to the public in 1946.

In shape the castle consists of four overlapping circles; in the centre is the strong tower which can be considered as the keep. Spaced equidistant around three sides are the three circular bastions which were intended as gun platforms. The main entrance is on the north-eastern landward side and is guarded by a hexagonal guard house. There was a stone bridge, originally a drawbridge (the slots through which the chains passed can be seen over the archway) and on either side are slits

allowing gunners to defend the entrance. Above the entrance are the royal arms and around the keep are a series of Latin inscriptions. The entrance leads directly to the first floor, and on the left hand side is a staircase which leads to the other floors and to the rampart walks of the bastion. On the right hand side, behind a very fine oak door, is a square shaft terminating in a shallow alcove. Over the doorway of the first two rooms are some 16th Century carvings including the Tudor rose and Fleur de Lys, both badges of Henry VIII. At the end of the corridor an arch leads to the southern bastion and this is battlemented with slots cut for the use of muskets; the square recesses cut into the wall were for storing the cannon balls. Again on the wall of this keep are some carved shields and some laudatory mottoes to Henry VIII. The doorway has two arches leading to the other bastions each of which has five embrasures and sockets for light guns. Grooves cut at the top of the battlements were for the mantlets or wooden shutters. The wall walk leads round to the main staircase of the keep which goes up to the second floor, which was referred to in the old surveys as the Gun Room. On the stone platform inside the door was the winch for raising the drawbridge. Eight recesses spaced round the room held ammunition cupboards. The staircase led straight up to the roof, a modern replacement, where there was a small

153

St. Mawes Castle, the important Tudor artillery fort built in the new "clover-leaf" style: the bridge and entrance gateway

watch tower. From the first floor the main staircase goes down to the ground floor which was probably used as a mess room for the garrison. There is a fine fireplace as well as a smaller Tudor fireplace, which has a recess on the right hand side known as the "salt box": for here salt, notoriously prone to dampness, could be kept dry. In the basement was the kitchen, the ceiling of which is supported on granite pillars. Near the entrance is a pedestal which possibly supported some sort of metal basin. Access from the ground floor is made to the court yard and the walls are pierced with eleven casements capable of taking quite large cannon. The central court was originally roofed and corbels for the beams can still be seen under the wooden gallery and at the angles of the masonry. Again on the exterior walls of the bastions are a number of Latin mottoes and sentiments. Below the castle are a magazine and gun emplacements of the 19th Century as well as a small Tudor blockhouse large enough for four guns. The garrison varied in size from a mere handful up to a hundred or so men, depending upon the state of readiness, and in 1609 a survey of armament lists quite a large number of guns. In 1623 there is mention of a gun on a wooden carriage on the roof and the same survey mentions two earthworks built outside the east and west curtain walls.

Open to the public:

	Weekdays	Sundays
March–April	9.30 a.m.–5.30 p.m.	2–5.30 p.m.
May–Sept.	9.30 a.m.–7 p.m.	9.30 a.m.–7 p.m.
Oct.	9.30 a.m.–5.30 p.m.	2–5.30 p.m.
Nov.–Feb.	10 a.m.–4.30 p.m.	2–4.30 p.m.

St. Michael's Mount Castle, *Mounts Bay, Cornwall. East of Penzance.*

A pyramid of rock, 195 feet high and five furlongs in circumference, traditionally separated from the land in 1099 and now connected only by a causeway. The original buildings were set up by Edward the Confessor as a Priory for Benedictine Monks. During the time that Richard I was away from England on the Third Crusade Henry de Pomeroy seized the Mount in support of John. On his return Richard took back the mount and put a small force in residence to prevent a recurrence of the event. It was seized again in 1471 by John, 13th Earl of Oxford, who resisted attack by the king's forces but later surrendered the place. Perkin Warbeck, the pretender for the crown of Henry VII, landed there; and it later saw action in the reign of Edward VI during a Cornish rebellion. During the Civil War it stood for the king but was taken by Parliament after a siege. The path leading to the top is defended half way up by a battery and there is another at the top. The castellated house retains much of the fabric of the old monastery.

Open to the public all the year Wednesdays and Fridays, also Mondays June to September. Parties leave at set times between 10.30 a.m. and 4.30 p.m. (other months 10.30 a.m.–3.30 p.m.). Additional rooms on show Mondays June to September. Closed Good Friday. Admission Wednesdays and Fridays 15p, Children 5p. Mondays 25p, Children 10p.

St. Ruan Castle, *Lanihorne, Cornwall. Three miles from Tregony at the head of a creek, near the church.*

The remains of a castle which was the home of the "Erchdeckne" or "Archdekne". It is described by contemporary accounts as having eight towers, but in 1718 the last remaining ruins were pulled down.

Salcombe Castle, *Salcombe, Devonshire. North of Northsands.*

This castle is also known as Fort Charles. It was one of the numerous castles built by Henry VIII to offer some coastal protection during the mid-16th Century. It was known during the Civil War as the Old Bulwark. It saw a little action in the Civil War but quickly surrendered.

Saltmarsh Castle, *Saltmarsh, Herefordshire.*

Only the lodge was left standing when the rest of this castle, built by Edwin Loach, was demolished in 1955.

F.K.MASON '73

Saltwood Castle, *Saltwood, Kent.*

This was the chief residence of Archbishop Courtenay in the late 14th Century. It had a barbican with a triangular outer bailey and an oval inner bailey. The gatehouse was extended and was fitted with flanking towers. There was a drawbridge, and the towers contained guard rooms and turrets which were restored late in the 19th Century. The wall of the inner bailey is fairly complete. There are three towers on the north, east and west walls which are set flush with the outside face of the wall. There have been two halls at the east end, the present one dating from 1930.
Open to the public May 28th to September 16th, Wednesdays, Sundays and Bank Holidays (closed July 29th to September 2nd) 2.30–6 p.m. Admission 20p, Children 5p.

Sandal Castle, *Sandal Magna, West Riding, Yorkshire.*

Little remains beyond the earthworks, some fragments of masonry and a circular moat. The castle was built in about 1320, and was of the shell-keep type. There were at least two other towers, one semi-circular and one polygonal.

Sandgate Castle, *Sandgate, Kent.*

This was originally one of the blockhouses built by Henry VIII, in the shape of an "ace of clubs". In 1806 the Prime Minister, William Pitt, had part of it converted into a Martello Tower. Little survives.

Sandown Castle, *Sandown, Kent.*

This was the largest of the coastal forts of Henry VIII, but it fell into such a sadly ruinous state that in 1894 it was blown up by the Royal Engineers and little survives.

Sandsfoot Castle, *Weymouth, Dorset. One mile from town.*

The remains of one of Henry VIII's forts. It was a

two-storeyed building with a tower at the north end and a gatehouse, but much has been destroyed by the sea.

Sauvey Castle, *Launde, Leicestershire. One mile north-west of village.*

Fine example of a motte and bailey castle site, probably dating from the reign of Stephen. It is guarded by steep valleys on the north and south and on the east by streams; the west is protected by a ditch 30 feet deep and 70 feet high to the bailey.

Scaleby Castle, *Scaleby, Cumberland. Six miles north-east of Carlisle.*

Given by Edward I to Richard de Tilliol; in 1307 a licence was granted to Robert de Tylliol to crenellate. It stood for the king in the Civil War in 1644; it was captured in 1645 and then retaken for the king, but soon surrendered again, and was fired by Parliament's troops. It was long neglected but subsequently restored. It has two moats and substantial remains.
On private land.

Scarborough Castle, *Scarborough, North Riding, Yorkshire.*

As with so many other castles, the site chosen for this one was a naturally good defensible position, being situated on a headland which rises some 300 feet above sea level. The castle is built so that it is defended on the seaward side by the cliffs. The natural advantages of the position were very apparent, for there are traces of habitation going back to the Bronze Age. When the Romans arrived they set up a signal station to give warning, by means of beacons, should Saxon invaders be sighted. It was a fortified post and the beacon itself consisted of a large ironwork basket on top of a square stone tower, at the centre of a walled enclosure and encircled by a ditch. Excavations on this site have uncovered the skeletons of men, women and children, many of which bear unmistakable signs of a violent death; it must be presumed that at some point of its history the station was overrun by the Saxon raiders. Much later, during the medieval period, a group of chapels appear to have been erected on this site, but as much of the cliff has fallen here it is difficult to be precise. In 1066 the town was sacked by the Norsemen—the very name of Scarborough is derived from a Viking who had a hare-lip.

The castle at Scarborough, which was begun about 1135, has seen more than its fair share of violence. The first recorded major action was an attack by the discontented barons, led by the Earl of Lancaster, at a time when the castle was held by the hated Piers Gaveston, the favourite of Edward II (1307–1327). Piers held out despite determined attacks until starvation among the garrison forced him to surrender. He was promised a safe conduct and a fair trial, but the Earl of Warwick disregarded these solemn promises and had him beheaded on Blacklow Hill. In 1318 the Scots, led by Douglas, descended upon Scarborough and put it to the flames, but failed to capture the castle. In 1377 it was the prison of a notorious Scottish pirate named Mercer, and in an attempt to rescue him his son sailed into Scarborough harbour with a fleet of ships. Thanks to one of the Aldermen of London, a fleet was gathered to send after Mercer and returned triumphant with the ships as well as some captured treasure. In 1536 Scarborough was again the scene of battle when the Northern Pilgrimage of Grace—a popular revolt against the policy of Henry VIII on closing the monasteries, and essentially a religious crusade—attacked the castle. It was successfully defended by Sir Ralph Evers despite serious damage to the defences from the cannon of the attackers. Some 40 years later, in April 1557, the castle was captured with hardly a drop of blood spilt, when Thomas Stafford decided to take direct action in protest against the marriage of Queen Mary I to King Philip of Spain. Together with some 30 companions, all disguised as peasants, he overpowered the sentries and took the castle. He then proclaimed himself the leader of the country and preached a campaign to throw off the Spanish connection, but the castle was very soon recaptured by the Earl of Westmorland with surprisingly little effort. Stafford was sent to London to be tried and there executed for treason on Tower Hill.

Unlike most of eastern England Scarborough declared for the king during the English Civil Wars (1642–48). It was besieged by Parliament from February 1644 to July 1645, but ably resisted under the leadership of Sir Hugh Cholmley. Parliamentary leader Sir John Meldrum was killed during one of the attempts to take the castle and Sir Matthew Boynton was appointed in his place. Batteries of heavy artillery were set up on the North Cliff to destroy the castle defences but once again, as with Piers Gaveston, it was disease and hunger that drove the Royalists to surrender. So gallant was their defence that they were accorded the full honours of war and were allowed to march out with drums beating and banners flying. So important was the capture considered that 19th August 1645 was appointed by Parliament as a day of Thanksgiving. By one of those ironic twists of fate Sir Matthew Boynton, who had captured the castle, was made governor and was succeeded by a colonel of the same name, who in 1648 turned his coat, abandoned Parliament and declared for the king. The castle was then once again besieged, from the 4th August, but the defenders were sorely troubled and on the 15th December the castle was surrendered to a Colonel Bethel. Boynton was later killed fighting for the king.

For the next century the castle was left to rest undisturbed. In 1746 the great panic caused by the landing of Bonnie Prince Charlie and his invasion of England stimulated the authorities into building extra barracks for troops to be accommodated in the castle, and these buildings on the curtain wall are easily recognised by their red brick and iron work. Bonnie Prince Charlie was defeated at Culloden in 1746 and once again Scarborough sank back into comfortable anonymity. Scarborough has the distinction of being one of the very few English castles to have suffered shelling by the Germans, for on 16th December 1914 the town of Scarborough was bombarded by two German cruisers. Many of the five hundred shells fell on the castle, the barracks were destroyed, and there were many casualties within the town. Amongst the buildings wrecked was a coast guard station which had, unbeknown to the designers, been erected on almost exactly the same site as the old Roman one.

Entrance to the castle is still by way of the barbican, with its very large and impressive half-round towers completed in 1343. Around the top of the barbican towers are the usual machicolations. The walls of the barbican are close enough to form what is almost a passageway; they are further defended by two smaller towers and eventually reach a ditch with a stone bridge of two arches. This was the site of the original drawbridge, which was not demolished until 1818. The drawbridge was operated from, and defended by, two small round towers. On the right hand tower was a small doorway allowing messengers from inside the castle to slip out during a siege. Further towers are spaced along the barbican walls. From the barbican, on the right and left hand, may be seen the remains of the long curtain wall which was begun during the reign of Henry I, probably by William le Gros, Earl of Albermarle and Holderness, and which carries a number of the characteristic Norman pilasters. The original line of le Gros's wall runs through the present site of the keep. The keep was built by Henry II, who took over the castle as crown property between 1158–1164. It is square, measuring 55 feet a side, and is very similar to those at Rochester (qv) and Hedingham (qv). It had three storeys and was originally over 100 feet high although, at present, it reaches to only 85 feet. Most of the west wall has collapsed but enough of the other walls remain to give an idea of its impressive solidity. The missing wall was demolished by cannon fire during the siege of 1645, and as the walls are between eleven and fifteen feet thick some idea of the power of this early artillery may be gained. Like similar examples the entrance was actually on the first floor and was approached up a flight of stone stairs. Again, in common with other castles, the door was protected by a fore-building which was some 40 feet high, twenty feet wide and 30 feet long. In the basement of the castle was a dungeon and a cess pit, whilst the first floor seems to have been a chapel. The spiral staircase which led to all floors is not set into one of the corner towers, the normal usage, but is built into the wall. The great hall was on the first floor and was some 32 feet square, with the ceiling and the floor above, like those at Hedingham, supported on a single arch which spanned the roof from north to south. On the second floor the arch supported a wall which divided the whole of the floor into two smaller chambers.

The keep stands inside its own curtain wall within the inner bailey, which is fairly small, measuring only some 330 feet from north to south and 220 feet east to west. Access to the rest of the castle was through a small gate set in the wall. The inner bailey also houses the well, seven feet in diameter, which is exceptionally deep, certainly in excess of 150 feet, with the first 68 feet carefully stone-faced on the inside. The curtain wall to the south-west of the keep is strengthened by the addition of two round towers which were erected during the reign of King John (1199–1216). He also had erected another tower known as the Queen's Tower, which has now disappeared. The open space on the headland between the inner bailey wall and the edge of the cliff was used for sporting purposes, and a record of 1275 states that Edward I held court at Scarborough and celebrated the occasion with tilting on this open space. On the eastern side of the inner bailey wall are the foundations of a 12th Century building but the purpose of this and its history are unknown. Other foundations of a much larger building can be seen against the inner face of the curtain wall. These belonged to the Mosdale Hall, a large dwelling place which was probably erected during the reign of King John but which takes its name from the John Mosdale who was governor about the year 1400. There was a further tower along the curtain wall known as the Cockhill Tower, and this was used primarily as a prison for important people, but unfortunately it was lost when part of the cliff face fell. Over against the cliff edge on the eastern side of the keep are the remains of the Roman signal station and some medieval chapels. The first one appears to date from the year 1000; this was destroyed in 1066, and when William le Gros was building the wall he erected a larger chapel which was later replaced with yet a third to which a priest's dwelling house was attached. Also in this same area is the Well of Our Lady; the water from this well was for long believed to have magical or curative powers. However, little is known of the early history. In 1920 the Ministry of Public Buildings and Works took over the care of Scarborough Castle.

Open to the public:

	Weekdays	Sundays
March–April	*9.30 a.m.–5.30 p.m.*	*2–5.30 p.m.*
May–Sept.	*9.30 a.m.–7 p.m.*	*9.30 a.m.– 7 p.m.*
Oct.	*9.30 a.m.–5.30 p.m.*	*2–5.30 p.m.*
Nov.–Feb.	*9.30 a.m.–4 p.m.*	*2–4 p.m.*

Scotney Castle, *Lamberhurst, Kent. One mile south-east of Lamberhurst (A21).*

A house, built about 1840 for Edward Hussey,

faces the remains of a moated castle licensed in the late 14th Century to Roger Ashburnam. It had a curtain wall with four circular towers, of which the southern one remains, complete with its machicolations. Part of the curtain wall remains and has a gatehouse in the centre and a stone bridge which replaced the original drawbridge. There are some 17th Century features indicating modification to the structure.

Open to the public: Gardens only April to October— Wednesdays, Thursdays, Fridays, Saturdays, Sundays (including Bank Holidays, but closed Good Friday) 2 p.m.–6 p.m. Admission 25p, Children 10p.

Seaton Castle, *Seaton, Cumberland. Near Workington on the west coast.*

This was the seat of the Curwen family as early as the 12th Century, but little remains beyond some masonry known as Barrow Walls which were, in the 19th Century, used as shooting butts for the local Volunteers.

Sebergham Castle, *Sebergham, Cumberland.*

A late 18th Century castellated folly.

Seckington Castle, *Seckington, Warwickshire. North-west of the church.*

A bailey with a 30-foot-high motte, 150 feet in diameter, the whole site covering more than two acres.

Sedgwick Castle, *Horsham, Kent. Two and a half miles east of Horsham.*

The only traces are some walls and the line of a moat.

Sewingshields Castle, *north-east of Peel Crag, Northumberland.*

Mounds and ditches only mark the site of a tower which was here in the late 16th Century.

Shaftesbury Castle, *Shaftesbury, Dorset.*

In the Parish of St. Mary at the west of the town are Castle Hill and Castle Green—there are traces of the earthworks of a castle.

Sham Castle, *Bath, Somerset. On Bathwick Hill.*

By the side of the river Avon, a pile built about the middle of the 18th Century with a central, pointed arch and two circular towers.

Sham Castle, *Leyburn, North Riding, Yorkshire.*

This is in the grounds of Thornburgh Hall.

Shank Castle, *Stapleton, Cumberland. Two-and-a-quarter miles south-west of Stapleton.*

The ruins of a pele-tower with some later modifications.

Sheffield Castle, *Sheffield, West Riding, Yorkshire.*

There are virtually no traces of this castle, once the home of the Earls of Shrewsbury, and the site is covered by the Castle Hill Market. The entrance was on the south side by way of a drawbridge and moat and it may well have been the site of an Anglo-Saxon earthworks. It was held for the king during the Civil War but surrendered after a short siege and bombardment and was then slighted.

Sherborne Castle, *Sherborne, Dorset. To the east of the town.*

On a rocky hill and covering an area of four acres, defended on the north and west by the slope of the ground and on the south and east by a wet moat. It was octagonal, with corner towers and a keep in the centre. There was a three-storeyed gatehouse with drawbridge and portcullis. The land was given by the Conqueror to Osmund, a Norman, who later became Bishop of Sarum. In 1102 it was acquired by Roger Niger, who built the castle, but

following Stephen's victory it became a royal castle as the owner had supported Maud. In 1338 a licence to crenellate was granted to the Bishop of Sarum, and another was granted in 1377. There was some dispute over its ownership during the reign of Edward III, and the then-Bishop of Sarum donned armour ready to fight Montacute, Earl of Salisbury, to settle the matter; however, it did not come to blows and the bishop was confirmed in ownership. Later the land was owned for a while by Sir Walter Raleigh, who built part of the present house. In 1642 it was held for the king and saw two sieges, the last being very severe with heavy fighting, before its eventual capture by Parliament. It was slighted and heavily damaged but continued to serve as a residence.
Open to the public Easter to September, Wednesdays, Thursdays, Sundays, and Bank Holiday afternoons.

Sheriff Hutton Castle, *Sheriff Hutton, North Riding, Yorkshire. South of the church.*

The land belonged to Bertram de Bulmer in *circa* 1140, but the present ruins date from 1382 when John, Lord Neville of Raby was granted his licence. There were two baileys; there are four large towers, each approximately 35 feet by 55 feet, in the four corners, with connecting walls, leaving an inner courtyard 120 feet by 100 feet. The towers are tall, with four storeys, and the north-west one five storeys. The south-west tower is best preserved with fireplaces and garderobes. The gatehouse is 15th Century and there are smaller towers spaced along the walls. It is described as being in decay by 1618.

Shilbottle Castle, *Shilbottle, Northumberland.*

Parts of a castle mentioned in the 15th Century are incorporated into the vicarage.

Shirburn Castle, *Shirburn, Oxfordshire. Near Watlington.*

A castle, probably by Sir Robert d'Oyley, stood here and in 1141 passed into the possession of Maud. It then changed hands several times until

in 1377 Warine de L'Isle was given a licence to crenellate. Eventually in the 18th Century it was owned by the Earl of Macclesfield. During the English Civil War it was nominally for the king but did so little that when it was surrendered to Lord Fairfax in 1646 no slighting action was taken. It is rectangular with corner towers and a west moat, and no less than three drawbridges protected the entrance as well as a portcullis.

Shocklack Castle, *Shocklack, Cheshire. Near the church on the west side of the road to Chester.*

A twenty-foot-high motte supported the Norman keep and was protected by a deep ditch, with the building situated to the west. On the other (east) side of the road is a kite-shaped mound.

Shoreham Castle, *Shoreham, Kent. One mile north of Shoreham.*

A farmhouse with some fragmentary remains. *On private land.*

Shrewsbury Castle, *Shrewsbury, Shropshire.*

Roger de Montgomery received much of Shropshire from William I and *circa* 1080 began his castle, removing fifty houses to make room for it. Robert de Beleme followed, and extended the fortifications, but he was forced to surrender it to Henry II. It saw many royal visits but declined in importance after the union of England and Wales and by the 16th Century was already falling into decay. It was held for the king in the Civil War but was captured with no difficulty or fighting. A Mr. Goswell acquired it *circa* 1730 and converted it into a home, and later Sir William Pulteney restored it somewhat. The keep is square with circular corner turrets and a good proportion of the walls and inner bailey still survive, as well as a Norman gateway.
Open to the public weekdays 9–12 a.m. and 2–5 p.m. Sundays 2–5 p.m. (March to end of October only).

Shurland Castle, *near Minster, Kent.*

The castle, which was started during the reign of Henry III, lay to the east of Minster, and only part of the gatehouse survives.

Charming marriage of a 19th Century house with the ruins of Roger Ashburnam's 14th Century castle at Scotney, near Lamberhurst in Kent

Sissinghurst Castle, *Sissinghurst, Kent.*

This is a brick castle built in the 16th Century by Sir John Baker, who was both Chancellor and an ambassador. It had square courtyards and two towers facing centre. It lay uninhabited until the 18th Century when it was taken over by the government to house 3,000 prisoners. It was extensively restored by Sir Harold and Lady Nicolson.
Open to the public: Good Friday to October 15th daily Mondays to Fridays 12–6.30 p.m.; Saturdays, Sundays and Bank Holiday Mondays 10 a.m.–6.30 p.m. Admission 20p. No dogs.

Sizergh Castle, *Helsington, Westmorland. Three miles south of Kendal.*

For long the home of the Strickland family, certainly from the 13th Century. The tower is quadrangular, measuring 60 feet by 40 feet and dates from *circa* 1340; it has two tall turrets on the west side. On the south side is an 18th Century window. Next to the tower are some buildings of

the 14th and 15th Centuries. Katherine Parr lived here for a while before her marriage to Henry VIII, and one room is still known as the Queen's Room. The house has some fine Tudor woodwork and fireplaces.
Open to the public April to September Wednesdays 2–5.45 p.m. Gardens only Tuesdays and Thursdays 2–5.45 p.m. Admission 30p, Children 15p, Gardens only 12p.

Skelton Castle, *Guisborough, North Riding, Yorkshire. Approximately three miles north-east of the town.*

Originally this was a 12th Century moat and remains of a chapel but there is now a house of *circa* 1800.
On private land.

Skipton Castle, *Skipton, West Riding, Yorkshire.*

Owned originally by Robert de Remille, who built

it, the castle passed to the Clifford family in 1310, later being held for the king in the Civil War. Fully roofed, it stands on high ground overlooking a ravine on the north side. The 14th Century gatehouse is protected by massive drum towers and walls. Other features include a Norman porch, 16th Century Great Hall, remains of a 13th Century Chapel, and a 17th Century Grotto.
Open to the public weekdays 10 a.m.–6 p.m.; Sundays 2–6 p.m. or earlier sunset. Closed Good Friday and Christmas Day. Admission 20p, Children 5p.

Sleaford Castle, *Sleaford, Lincolnshire. North-west of the Station.*

A few mounds and bits of stone mark the site of a 12th Century castle belonging to Bishop Alexander.

Slingsby Castle, *Slingsby, North Riding, Yorkshire.*

Built in the 1620s for Sir Charles Cavendish with four corner, tower-like extensions, complete with turrets—now in ruins.
On private land.

Snape Castle, *Snape, North Riding, Yorkshire.*

Similar in design to Bolton Castle (qv) with four corner towers, now in ruins. Some work was carried out in the 16th Century by Thomas Cecil. The south range is still lived in and the chapel to the north of the south-east corner is in good condition.
On private land.

Sneaton Castle, *Sneaton, North Riding, Yorkshire. One-and-a-half miles west of Whitby.*

This was built in the early 19th Century for James Wilson. It has two corner towers with turrets and a curtain wall.

Snodhill Castle, *Dorstone, Herefordshire. One mile south-east of Dorstone.*

This was, at one time, part of the holdings of the Chandos family. There are fragments of masonry as well as part of the gatehouse still standing. It was large, some ten acres, and there is a steep motte which was surrounded by a polygonal keep of the early 13th Century. The gateway was on the west side, flanked by round towers. Most of the remains in the bailey date from the 14th Century. The castle was slighted by Parliament.

Somerton Castle, *Somerton, Oxfordshire. North-west of the village on the east side of the Cherwell.*

The town was Bishop Odo's and presumably his tenant, Rainald Wadard, built the castle. It was deserted by the 18th Century and has now largely disappeared.

Somerton Castle, *Somerton Castle, Lincolnshire.*

A licence was granted in 1281 to Anthony Bek, Bishop of Durham. It was quadrangular, 330 feet by 180 feet, with circular corner turrets, of which parts of three survived into this century. The one on the north-east was interesting architecturally for it dispensed with the usual central pier so common in towers of this period. The south-east tower had some 16th Century additions. There were one or two unexplained buildings and the arrangement of the moats was unusual. King John of France was held prisoner here for a while in 1359/60.
The site has now been built over.

South Kyme Castle, *South Kyme, Lincolnshire. North-east of Sleaford.*

Owned for a long time by the Kyme family, this castle passed to the Umfravilles in the 14th Century. Anne Askew, burnt at Winchester by Henry VIII, was the wife of an owner of this castle. After several changes of ownership it came to the Dymokes. This family was responsible for supplying a King's Champion who, at the Coronation, would challenge all who might query the king's right to the throne. Most of the castle built by the Umfravilles was demolished in 1735 but one tower survives in very good condition. This keep stands

77 feet high and is square, with a turret containing a staircase on the south-east corner. The windows show grooves which once held glass as well as the hooks used to secure the wooden shutters. On the first floor is the room known as the Chequered Chamber. The moat is still traceable.
On private land.

Southsea Castle, *Southsea, Hampshire.*

This was one of the coastal defence forts built by Henry VIII in about 1540. In 1642 it was captured by Parliament and for a very short time it served as a prison under Charles II. In 1760 an accidental explosion of gunpowder stored there destroyed much of it, and in 1814 it was converted to a modern fort.
On Government land.

Stainborough Castle, *Wentworth, West Riding, Yorkshire.*

A folly with four towers and a gatehouse, standing in the grounds of Wentworth Castle and built prior to 1739.
On private land.

Stamford Castle, *Stamford, Lincolnshire. South-west corner of the town, junction of Castle Street and Castle Dyke.*

A few fragmentary remains of a castle, largely removed to accommodate a car park.

Stamford Castle, *Stamford, Northamptonshire. North-west of the town.*

Some stronghold was here in the 10th Century and saw considerable action at various periods, but it was demolished during the reign of Richard III and the remains were used to build a Carmelite Friary. The mount and some fragments survive.

Stanhope Castle, *Stanhope, County Durham. On the west side of the town square.*

Late 18th Century castellated house.

Stapleton Castle, *Stapleton, Herefordshire.*

This may well have been an outpost of Richard's Castle (qv) and there are traces of an outer bailey to the north. The main building is of 17th Century origin.

Star Castle, *Hugh Town, Isle of St. Mary, Scilly Isles.*

Situated on a hill near the town is a Tudor star-shaped fort built by Francis Godolphin during the reign of Elizabeth. This was one of the places in which Prince Charles stayed during his period of escape after the Battle of Worcester (1651). It is now in the grounds of a hotel.

Sterborough or Starborough Castle, *Sterborough, Surrey. One-and-a-half miles to the east of Lingfield.*

Reginald de Cobham was given his licence to crenellate in 1341; his castle had four towers and a gate, but today there are only traces of the structure along the side of the moat. The summer house in Gothic style dates from 1754.
On private land.

Stock Castle, *Lynton, Devonshire. South-east of Lynton, on the west slopes of the ridge by Lyncombe Woods (cf Roborough Castle).*

Slight traces of a square, earthen enclosure, probably of Roman origin.
On private land.

Stockport Castle, *Stockport, Cheshire. North of the church.*

There are some fragmentary remains on the same site as some Roman ruins.

Stockton on Tees Castle, *Stockton on Tees, County Durham. At the end of High Street.*

Only the trace of a tower survived after this castle's

capture and slighting by Parliament in 1652.

Stogursey Castle, *Stogursey, Somerset. South of the village.*

Some fragmentary remains of the walls and towers are all that remain of a castle held by a Norman, Falk de Brent, who terrorised the surrounding countryside so much that a complaint was sent to the court of Henry III, who ordered the Sheriff to dismantle the castle. Falk was exiled. The castle was burned by William, Lord Bonville, during the Wars of the Roses and it has been in ruins since then.

Stokesay Castle, *Stokesay, Shropshire. Three-quarters of a mile south of Craven Arms on the Shrewsbury–Ludlow road, A49.*

This is essentially a 13th Century manor which was later fortified. It was held from the 11th Century by the De Lacys of Ludlow and from the late 13th Century by the Ludlow family, who gained a licence in 1291. They probably built the great south tower. During the Civil War it was surrendered to Parliament, who contented themselves with removing the battlements on top of the north tower. The courtyard is roughly oblong with a curtain wall encircling it and the whole is surrounded by a moat 20 feet wide and six feet deep. In the north-west corner is an outwork projecting into the moat—probably the oldest part of the castle. The gateway lies in the east wall and is a Tudor timber-framed building which replaced an earlier drawbridge house. The 13th Century hall is especially fine, 51 feet by 31 feet, and there are four early English windows on the west wall and three on the east overlooking the courtyard. Heating was by means of a brazier in the centre of the floor. To the south-east of the hall lies the great tower, which is rather like a combination of two octagonal towers. It is 66 feet high—three storeys—and with walls six feet thick.

Open to the public all the year, daily except Tuesdays. Summer 9 a.m.–6 p.m. (last admission 5.30), winter 10 a.m.–4.30 p.m. Admission 15p, Children 5p.

Stone Castle, *Stone, Kent. Half a mile from village.*

Near the church is a medieval house much altered in the 19th Century. The original structure probably dated from the late 12th Century.
On private land.

Stourton Castle, *Stourton, Staffordshire. On the road from Bridgnorth to Stourbridge.*

Its history is uncertain except that it was surrendered to the king's forces in 1644. There are some remains incorporated into the 19th Century house.
On private land.

Streatam Castle, *Streatam Castle, County Durham. Two miles north-east of Barnard's Castle.*

The present building dates from the 18th Century and incorporates the traces of a castle built, probably, by the Baliol family which, in turn, had replaced one demolished by Sir William Bowes in the 16th Century.

Studley Castle, *Studley, Warwickshire.*

In 1834 the place was given a very full "face lift" with a conglomeration of styles, and it includes traces of the original castle. It is now an Agricultural College.

Studley Old Castle, *Studley, Warwickshire. North of the church.*

Early 16th Century house on the site of an earlier castle.

Sudeley Castle, *Sudely, Gloucestershire.*

The surviving buildings date from the late 14th Century when the castle was owned by Ralph Boteler, although it did not long remain in this family. The castle passed through many owners until the English Civil War when, like so many others, it was slighted. Restoration began early in the 19th Century and was completed *circa*

1930/6. A gateway to the north and some of the west side of the inner court date from the early 15th Century, although there has been some "Victorianisation". Two towers, Portmane at the west and Garderobe at the east, are also from this early period. In the 15th Century the inner court was rebuilt and standards of accommodation greatly raised. Part of the kitchens has been built into the modern house and the Dungeon tower was also altered. To the east of the court were the living rooms and one, Queen Katherine Parr's Room, has its own cloister leading to the church. Some of the windows in this block are particularly fine. During the last quarter of the 16th Century the outer court was largely rebuilt.

Open to the public March 24th to May 26th, week-days except Mondays, 2–5.30 p.m.; Sundays 12–5.30 p.m. May 29th to September 23rd, daily except Mondays 12–5.30 p.m. Bank Holidays 11 a.m.–5.30 p.m. Admission 40p, Children 20p.

Sundorne Castle, *Sundorne, Shropshire. Half a mile west of Haughmond Abbey.*

A brick mansion of the early 19th Century.

Sutton Valence Castle, *Sutton Valence, Kent. Half-a mile east of village.*

Near the church are some scanty remains, including a fragment of the keep wall, which probably dates from the time of Henry II.

Swerford Castle, *Swerford, Oxfordshire. Seven miles south-west of Banbury, north side of the church.*

Earthworks and masonry remains mark the site of a castle with an eighteen-foot-high motte.

Swinburne Castle, *Swinburne Castle, Northumberland.*

Only fragments of a basement survive from the old castle; the house was built in the 17th Century and has 18th Century stables.

Swineshead Castle, *Swineshead, Lincolnshire. Half a mile north-east of the church at Bayford.*

A motte and bailey castle recorded during the reign of John and of unusual design, both motte and bailey being very low.

Tamworth Castle, *Tamworth, Staffordshire. Fifteen miles north-east of Birmingham.*

When Alfred the Great died in 901 his daughter Ethelfleda continued his work of resisting the Danes. She was known as the Lady of Mercia, which was one of the so-called "seven kingdoms" or Heptarchy, and of which Tamworth was the capital. At Tamworth she built a palisaded borough intended either as a place of safety when attacked or as a forward base for attacking the Danes. The connection of the town with this courageous lady is commemorated by a statue at the foot of the motte. After 1066 the town was given by William the Conqueror to Robert de Marmion, whose family was subsequently to supply the King's Champion, whose duty it was to ride out and challenge any who disputed the king's right to the crown. Whether the Marmions simply used the Saxon motte as it stood or altered or modified it is not clear, but it now stands some 50 feet high with a base diameter of about 100 feet. By the end of the 11th Century the top of the motte carried a polygonal curtain wall of red sandstone rubble whilst a secondary wall came down the slope to connect with the walls of the borough which seems to have served as a bailey. The wing wall shows very clearly the herring-bone style of building used by the Normans around the turn of the 11th Century. During the 12th Century a square tower was fitted into the curtain wall so that part of it projected clear of the wall to enable archers to give enfilading fire. As it was used as a dwelling place for many years the internal buildings were naturally greatly modified and the present structures are mostly of much later periods, with those of the 17th and 18th Century predominating. Some are of stone and some of brick, and the gradual encroachment of these buildings into the courtyard has reduced its size considerably. There is a very good Tudor banqueting hall with a fine roof and an interesting little collection of armour. The doorways, chimney pieces and heraldic friezes are well worth a closer look. Although occupied at various times by both Cavaliers and Roundheads, Tamworth Castle escaped any serious damage during the English Civil War.

Open to the public March to October, weekdays 10 a.m.–8 p.m. or one hour before sunset; Sundays 2–8 p.m. or one hour before sunset. November to February, weekdays except Fridays 10 a.m.–4 p.m.; Sundays 2–4 p.m. Closed Christmas Day. Admission 10p, accompanied child free, unaccompanied child 2p. Parties of 20 or over, 5p.

Tanfield Castle, *Tanfield, Yorkshire.*

A gatehouse is about all that remains of this castle, licensed in 1323 to Robert Marmion and known as The Hermitage.
On private land.

Tarset Castle, *north-west of Bellingham, Northumberland.*

There are indications that there was a castle here, licensed in 1267, which was oblong with four turrets. It was destroyed early in the 16th Century and used as a source of supply for building materials by the local people. Traces of the ditch remain indicating a rectangular site.

Tattershall Castle, *Tattershall, Lincolnshire. Twelve miles north-east of Sleaford on the A153.*

Tattershall Castle stands on the site of a 13th Century castle built by Robert Tattershall, but the present castle was erected by Ralph, Lord Cromwell. He had fought in the Hundred Years War and returned from the Agincourt campaign a rich man and was, for a while, treasurer for the King's

Exchequer. The castle later passed to Henry VIII who gave it to the Duke of Suffolk on his marriage to the king's sister; later it passed to the Earls of Lincoln and descended to the Fortescue family. In 1911 the tower was bought by an American group who planned to dismantle it and take it to the United States. Lord Curzon of Kedleston was determined to prevent this happening and so acquired the castle, restored the fireplaces which had already been removed prior to shipment, and presented the building to the National Trust.

In 1434/36 Lord Cromwell added a second moat around the original 13th Century castle and dammed off part to create fish ponds. He removed or reconstructed some of the earlier buildings and turned them into a great hall with a parlour, an upper chamber and a chapel. To the west of these buildings, but connected to them by corridors, Lord Cromwell added his own private dwelling in the form of a remarkable tower house which still stands. In the outer wards were various buildings including a wool house and a large stable, for Cromwell kept something like 100 people in his household. The walls of the tower are built of red bricks which were made locally, and the other work is of green or red Salmondby sandstone and limestone from Ancaster. The bricks were made in Cromwell's own kilns, some at Boston but most at Edlington Moor, a little to the north of the present tower. The clay was dug from pits; there are records of over a million bricks being paid for and this is probably not the final figure.

There are octagonal turrets at the corners of the tower which have crenellated parapets. The main building is four storeys high with a basement below ground level, and has a very heavy overhanging machicolated parapet. On the first floor is a very large hall which is completely separate from the upper floors and was probably used as a general meeting hall or a court of justice. Above this is the Lord's hall, the Camera, and the Solar which are reached by long corridors built into the east wall. The fireplaces, replaced by Lord Curzon, are magnificent heraldic pieces. The tower stands over 100 feet high or, to the top of the turrets, 112 feet, and the walls are fourteen feet thick at their widest point. The large windows reduce the defensive qualities of the tower considerably but the double moat would have compensated for this to some degree. On the second floor of the castle there is a gallery nearly 40 feet in length with a

parapet walk above it and outside the Great Chamber on the second floor are dove cotes. Altogether the tower has some 48 separate rooms.
Open to the public all the year. Weekdays 9.30 a.m.– 7 p.m., Sundays 1–7 p.m. (or dusk if earlier). October to March closed 1–2 p.m. Admission 20p, Children 10p.

Taunton Castle, *Taunton, Somerset. In St. James Street.*

This castle is on the site of an early British earthworks; it was a stronghold of the Norman Bishops of Winchester. Taunton Castle was built by Henry of Blois but it has been much altered over the centuries. The gateway is basically 13th Century whilst the parts to the north-west are mainly 12th Century. The inner moat and keep site are now taken over by the garden of the Castle Hotel, and the undercroft is part of a 12th Century hall which was larger than that which stands now. Much of the present buildings were added or altered in the 18th Century. There are a mixture of masonry styles ranging from 12th Century— the Parlour—to 18th Century on the north side. It now houses a fine library and museum.
Open to the public daily except Sundays, 10 a.m.– 4 p.m.

The Castle, Elloughton, *Elloughton, East Riding, Yorkshire.*

Built in 1886, complete with turrets and battlements.
On private land.

The Castle, *Stroud, Gloucestershire.*

Late 18th Century or early 19th Century. It has a fake curtain wall and towers.
On private land.

The Castles, *Barrow-on-Humber, Lincolnshire. Three-quarters of a mile north-west, at Barrow Haven.*

A large motte with two baileys with moats.

Thetford Castle, *Thetford, Norfolk.*

A very high motte—45 feet—with some traces of outer earthworks and bailey on the north-east. The castle was demolished in the late 12th Century.

Thirlwall Castle, *Greenhead, Northumberland. One mile north of the village.*

Although built with Roman materials, the tower dates only from the 16th Century. Half has collapsed on the south side.

Thirsk Castle, *Thirsk, North Riding, Yorkshire.*

Destroyed by Henry II in 1175, only the moat of Roger de Mowbray's castle survives.

Thornbury Castle, *Thornbury, Gloucester. East of Alveston on B4461.*

This castle, never completed, is of particular interest since it has a strong claim to being the last genuinely defensive castle to be built in England. It is a mixture of military and domestic planning and building. In general pattern it is much the same as the castle of Tattershall (qv) a square main structure with towers at the corners, leaving a central courtyard for the lord's dwellings while the numerous retainers were housed in an outer bailey. In this castle, intended to house almost a small army, these retainers' quarters were extensive. The outer bailey is defended by a gatehouse of conventional design with towers front and back and a portcullis. A similar but much more impressive gatehouse defends the inner bailey on the west side; it has a portcullis and two very strong towers, although one is incomplete, lacking the upper machicolations and parapet. There are numerous gun-ports and arrow slits let into the wall. On the southern side are the rooms intended for the living quarters of the Duke of Buckingham and these are on a lavish scale, with far less consideration for defence needs than for comfort. It would appear that the south-western tower was intended as a strong defence point should it be needed, and there is a strong wall enclosing the

entire area, but the final design is uncertain since the owner did not live long enough to complete the building. In 1824 some restoration was carried out by the Stafford Howard family.
On private land.

Thorpe Waterville Castle, *Thorpe Waterville, Northamptonshire.*

A licence was given to Bishop Langton in 1301 but only masonry fragments exist, although moat and foundations can be traced. The castle saw action during the Wars of the Roses.

Thurgaton Castle, *Thurgaton, Nottinghamshire. Two miles west of the village.*

A small hill fortress with a motte.

Thurland Castle, *Tunstall, Lancashire.*

In 1402 Sir Thomas Tunstal received his licence to crenellate, but today there are very few remains of this castle. In 1876 a fire did considerable damage and between 1879–85 much restoration, adaptation and alteration was undertaken. There is a gravel mound 40 feet high with surrounding moat 30 feet wide and six feet deep.

Thurleigh Castle, *Thurleigh, Bedfordshire. On Bury Hill, east of the church.*

A motte survives, and there are substantial traces of the moat and another enclosure which encircles the village.

Thurnham Castle, *Thurnham, Kent. Half a mile north-east of village.*

Near the top of the hill above the village are the remains of a building sometimes known as Goddard's Castle. It was probably built on the site of a Roman camp. Only fragments of a shell keep and curtain wall survive, so overgrown as to be almost obscured; the castle is known to have been in ruins by the early 16th Century.
On private land.

Tickhill Castle, *Tickhill, West Riding, Yorkshire. Junction of A60 and A631.*

William the Conqueror created the Honour of Blyth extending from Yorkshire into Derbyshire, Lincolnshire, Nottinghamshire and Leicestershire. The Honour was given to Roger de Buisli, and he made his chief castle at Tickhill. In 1102 the owner, Robert of Belleme, rebelled against Henry I and as a result his lands were confiscated. The castle remained Crown property during the reign of Henry II whose wife, Eleanor of Aquitaine, founded within the castle a chapel devoted to St. Nicholas. She gave sufficient money to maintain a warden and four chaplains. The castle has seen a certain amount of action, for while King Richard I (1189–1199) was absent on the Third Crusade (1189–1192) the castle was taken by his brother Prince John. It was besieged and recaptured by Hugh Pudsey, the Bishop of Durham. When he became king John had the castle repaired and later gave it to the Count of Eu. In 1244 the castle was again in royal hands, and in 1254 Henry III (1216–1272) granted the castle to his son Edward. Tickhill saw action again in 1322 when it was attacked by the king's cousin, Thomas of Lancaster. The castle was attacked with catapults and other siege engines, but Edward II was victorious, leading the relief column himself. Edward III, in 1372, gave the castle to John of Gaunt, and for centuries it knew peace. During the Civil War (1642–48) it was held for the king but, like so many strongholds, surrendered after the battle of Marston Moor in 1644. In keeping with Parliamentary practice it was subsequently demolished.

The castle itself is typically Norman, with a large motte, and it is likely that by the end of the 11th century the wooden superstructures were being replaced by stone. The motte is over 70 feet high and 80 feet across at the top; the lower third is a natural mound and is partly of red sandstone. The motte is circled by a very deep ditch and a broad counterscarp. The oval bailey is also surrounded by a wet ditch, which is still partially filled with water to this day. The gatehouse is the oldest surviving stonework and dates from the very early 12th Century, whilst the curtain wall was built in about 1130. The shell keep is attributed to Henry II, who had it built about 1178–80. During Tudor times part of the gatehouse was rebuilt using red sandstone. The curtain wall shows

characteristic stonework of many periods, parts being covered with ashlar whilst other parts are rubble. The original tower on the mount has completely disappeared except for the foundations, which indicate that it was decagonal, with buttresses at the corners. Only a 17th Century doorway built into the garden wall of the modern house survives from the buildings of the bailey.
On private land.

Tintagel Castle, *Cornwall. Five miles north-west of Camelford, Cornwall.*

One of the great folk heroes of the Middle Ages, whose stories were enjoyed by people throughout the whole of Western Europe, was King Arthur. Around him was built up a great legend involving knights in shining armour, maidens in distress, dragons, magic, and the Round Table. At a very early date, certainly by the 12th Century, the castle at Tintagel was associated with Arthur. The story says that, with the aid of Merlin's magic, King Uther Pendragon entered the castle and made love to Eygraine, the wife of the Duke of Cornwall; and that from this magical seduction came Arthur. Although this connection with King Arthur is of very long standing, modern research has, alas, established that King Arthur, if indeed such a person ever existed, must be dated to around the 5th Century, some six centuries before Tintagel was built.

Although history may demolish the legend Tintagel is ideally situated for such a connection, It stands on the stout, rocky cliffs of Cornwall amidst rugged scenery, bounded on one side by the Atlantic Ocean, from which thick mists can roll in to add to the air of mystery. Ironically it is to the mythical association with Arthur that the castle probably owes its survival. It was the great upsurge of interest in the Arthurian legend, generated by the poetry of Alfred Lord Tennyson, which created a public demand for repairs and restoration to the castle. (The pathway up to the island also dates from this period.) For the incurable romantic who refuses to be deterred by cold, hard facts, hope for a Arthurian connection can be sustained by the fact that there are remains on the site of a Celtic monastery which seems to have existed from about the middle of the 4th Century up to the middle of the 9th Century.

The geography of Cornwall has always rather set it apart from the rest of the country. The Roman occupation seems to have left the county largely untouched, and it was the last part of England to submit to the Saxon invader, which it did only in the 9th Century. The county was not so successful against the Norman invasion, for by the time of the Domesday survey, in 1086, the vast majority of the county, probably some eighty per cent, was under the rule of Robert of Mortain. In common with most of the Norman lords Count Robert built himself a small wooden and earth castle, situated at Bossinnet, half a mile west of the village, and this sufficed for some considerable time. When Robert died the land and the castle passed to his son William, who was ill-judged enough to support Robert of Normandy in his struggles against his brother, Henry I of England. Henry triumphed at the Battle of Tinchebrai in 1106, and William lost all his lands. In 1140 the illegitimate son of King Henry, Reginald, married the daughter of one of the most important Cornish lords and was later created Earl of Cornwall. Reginald died in 1173 leaving no son, and the land was granted by Henry II to his youngest son John, but he did not, in fact, give him the title of Earl of Cornwall. When John was crowned in 1199 he retained these lands but, as was common practice, granted part to a sub-tenant; and Tintagel went to one Gervase de Hornicote. When Gervase died in 1218 Robert of Tintagel took over the land, but it reverted to the Crown in 1220.

Owing to a variety of circumstances in 1299 Tintagel once again became Crown property, and during this period the castle received scant attention. Piers Gaveston, the favourite of Edward II (1307–1327) was at one time owner, and later it belonged to the Black Prince who was also Duke of Cornwall, but again there is little evidence to suggest that he placed much value upon the castle. From this period onwards Tintagel formed part of the Duchy of Cornwall and so was traditionally part of the lands of the eldest son of the ruling monarch.

When viewing the castle today it must be remembered that it was built originally not upon an island, but on a small headland jutting out from the main coast. In the 12th Century the castle is described by Geoffrey of Monmouth as being surrounded by sea but with a very narrow entrance through the rock small enough to be defended by a handful of men. By the 14th Century the headland had been noticeably eroded and there are also mentions of a bridge connecting the two parts of the castle; obviously the sea had broken through, completely isolating the inner ward on a separate island. With the advent of the 16th Century all interest in the castle seems to have evaporated and it was allowed to fall into ruins. Some restoration was carried out during the middle of the 19th Century, and in 1930 the Duchy of Cornwall gave the castle into the care of the then Commissioners of His Majesty's Works.

The castle today has the lower and upper ward, complete with the main gate, on the mainland and the inner ward, the great hall and other buildings situated on the island. To approach the castle one must take the road leading to the beach and turn off on the left taking a small path roughly half way down the hill. The entrance to the castle is situated at the base of a tall cliff, from which projects a protective wall. Passing through the main gate and on the right can be seen a hole into which slotted the bar used for bolting the door. The lower ward, roughly rectangular, is surrounded by a wall at least five feet thick and around which were battlements and a walk, and the remains of a staircase which led up to these can be seen on the longer side. Nearly all this part of the castle was probably built during the time of Earl Richard, around the middle of the 13th Century. During the 14th Century the gate was strengthened by building buttresses at the back and on the lower side. Two small towers, intended to give extra covering positions for archers, were also built on the north-east curtain wall and the remains of these can still be seen. In the corner, between the gate and the south-east wall, is a small room which probably dates from about the 15th Century, and around the doorspace can be seen the slot which held the wooden door frame. To reach the upper ward, which overlooks the approach to the path and main gate, one must climb a flight of steps cut into the rock. The east side of the ward is enclosed by a curtain wall which is of the same date as that of the lower ward and runs straight to the edge of the cliff, which falls sheer on the western side. Opposite the gate are the remains of a number of small rooms dating from the late 14th or early 15th Century and which were almost certainly the quarters of the soldiers forming the castle guard. Originally the lower ward and inner wards were joined, but when the

sea separated them a bridge was built which stood until the 16th Century. Now the only way to reach the inner ward is by steps down the cliff or by a path leading from the gate to the road. From the seaward side a path leads to some steep steps which rise to a door set in a modern wall; the date 1852 cut into the stone commemorates the opening of the castle to the public. This door leads into the inner ward, on the right of which is the Great Hall. This was originally very large, for the surviving wall is 88 feet long and a further length has fallen over the cliff. This hall dates from the 12th Century, but it became ruinous in 1337 when the roof was taken off and between then and 1345 a smaller hall, incorporating some of the earlier walls, was built. This was only 30 feet wide (compared with the 36 feet of the original hall) and some 36 feet long, with the buttery and various rooms at the southern end. A door cut through the outer wall gives access to a garderobe. Apparently so little care was given to the building that after the middle of the century even this smaller hall had become dilapidated and a third building, a small house, was erected in the central part. Again some of the earlier walls were incorporated into the later building. On the ground floor of this house were two small rooms, one of which was obviously a living room, for there is a large fireplace in its south wall. A spiral staircase leads to a bedchamber which is situated above the other room. Remains of the fireplace can still be seen in the bedroom. The purpose of this small house is uncertain but as it is known that during the latter part of the 14th Century the castle was used as a prison, it may well have served as the quarters for important prisoners. Between the northern end of the hall and the northern gate there are three small buildings erected during the 14th Century, and these too were probably used by officers and prison guards. Of some interest is the covered drain running along the side of the hall which takes the rainwater from the courtyard out through the curtain wall near the northern gate.

To the west and separate from the hall and its cluster of buildings are some further chambers, the lower section of which have been cut from the rock, which has been shaped to serve as a bench. It is likely that these small buildings were used by one of the minor officials, perhaps the chaplain of the castle. At the foot of the cliff, to the north of the great hall, is a cove whose sheltered position made it ideal for the landing of small boats, and to guard against sudden attack it is protected by a curtain wall. The gateway was previously closed by an iron gate, the name by which it is still known. The wall was probably built around the middle of the 14th Century although, at a later date, it was further extended and strengthened. Well to the west on the plateau of the island is a walled garden some 75 feet by 50 feet. Stone slabs marked the paths, two feet wide, from each wall and it is fairly certain that this area would have been used for growing fresh vegetables for the castle. The type of masonry indicates an early date, probably the 12th or 13th Century. Food supply was always a problem for castles but of even greater importance was the supply of fresh water. To the west of the chapel lies a 12th Century well, some 18 feet deep and four feet in diameter, this is supplied by a small spring which continues to flow even during dry periods. The small mounds near the well are thought to be part of an artificial warren to house a colony of rabbits which would have provided a convenient source of fresh meat for the occupants of the castle. More mysterious is a tunnel over on the western edge of the plateau; this has been cut through the solid rock and presumably leads down towards the sea. It is no more than five feet high and was certainly in existence as early as the 16th Century. Its purpose is unknown although it may well have been intended as an escape route should the castle fall to an enemy. To the north-west of the inner ward will be found the castle chapel, mostly built during the 12th Century but lengthened during the 13th Century. The other sites and excavations dotted around the plateau are connected with the early Celtic monastery.

Open to the public:

	Weekdays	Sundays
March–April	*9.30 a.m.–5.30 p.m.*	*2–5.30 p.m.*
May–Sept.	*9.30 a.m.–7 p.m.*	*9.30 a.m.–7 p.m.*
Oct.	*9.30 a.m.–5.30 p.m.*	*2–5.30 p.m.*
Nov.–Feb.	*10 a.m.–4.30 p.m.*	*2–4.30 p.m.*

Titchmarsh Castle, *Titchmarsh, Northamptonshire. South-west of the village.*

The moat of a small, rectangular castle licensed in 1304 but in ruins by 1363.

Tintagel Castle, romantically associated with the Arthurian legends, and dramatic enough in its own right

Titlington Castle, *Titlington, Northumberland. Three-and-a-half miles north-west of Alnwick.*

A motte and bailey castle stood here with the motte south of the hall and the bailey occupying the site of the present lawn, but nearly all trace was swept away in 1745.

Tiverton Castle, *Tiverton, Devonshire. Just north of the church.*

One of the castles of the Courtenay family, although originally it belonged to Richard Redvers and it passed later to the Carew family. It is of substantial size, covering an area of approximately one acre. The castle was quadrangular with four corner towers. The walls stand some 20/25 feet high, and on the south-east, north-east and north-west corners were round towers about 35 feet high. On the south-west corner there was a square tower with the gateway on the east side. It had two moats, on the north and south, and two gateways. There were modifications during the 16th Century, and some Tudor windows may still be seen in the masonry. During the English Civil War Tiverton declared for the king. Sir Thomas Fairfax attacked it, and it was bombarded before it finally surrendered.

Open to the public by previous written appointment June, July, August and October *(Saturdays excepted). Admission 75p, including Guide Book and V.A.T. (1973).*

Tonbridge Castle, *Tonbridge, Kent.*

Tonbridge Castle was certainly in existence by 1088, for it is then recorded as being captured by William Rufus. It is situated on the north bank of the river Medway, south of the town. It has a large, tall motte at the west end and a roughly oval shaped bailey extending eastwards down the stream. The original wooden walls were soon replaced and part of the wing wall, rising up the side of the motte, suggests Norman work, probably of the 12th Century. Early in the 13th Century a shell keep was built on top of the motte and, in 1531, this was described as having a lead roof. Later in the 13th Century, the current lord left the shell keep where, presumably, he was cramped for space and moved down into the larger bailey where he had built a large, stately hall measuring 55 by 29 feet. The entrance to the bailey was probably on the north side away from the town, but by about the year 1300 it was replaced by a large, strong keep-gatehouse. It had two round drum towers and two small towers at the rear, which contained the spiral staircase. The entrance was defended by a drawbridge and there are front and rear portcullises to the passageway as well as two folding gates. The vaulted passageway is fitted with a number of murder holes at the top. On either side of the passage doors lead into the two towers, one of which was a guard room and the other a store room. Even these inner doors are each fitted with a small portcullis. Below the towers on each side there is an underground room. One was a cellar the other, presumably, a prison. The first floor of the gatehouse is divided into three compartments, the centre one being the portcullis room. Above this, on the second floor, is the lord's hall and above this a third storey was planned although it seems doubtful that this was ever built. Little survives apart from parts of the wall to a height of about three feet and part of the gatehouse. Apart from normal decay the castle suffered the common fate of slighting in the English Civil War.

On local authority land: not open to the public.

Tong Castle, *Tong, Shropshire.*

North of the village is a tower. The mansion, with grounds planned by "Capability" Brown in 1765, was pulled down in 1954.

Tonge Castle, *Tonge, Kent. A quarter of a mile to the south, near Teynham.*

The earthworks of a motte and bailey probably dating from 12th/14th Century, but traditionally associated with Hengist and Horsa, Saxon invaders of the 5th Century.

Torksey Castle, *Torksey, Lincolnshire.*

Remains of a Tudor mansion which belonged to Sir Robert Hermyn.

Totnes Castle, *Totnes, Devonshire.*

Totnes was the site of a mint during the reign of King Edwig (died 959). Although some other towns in the county resisted the Normans, Totnes surrendered. A castle was soon erected by a Breton named Judhael or Juhellus, son of Alured. During the rebellion against William II Judhael supported the losing side and, consequently, lost all his lands and was exiled. Totnes was given to Roger de Nonant, but when Henry I came to the throne in 1100 Judhael was restored to favour and given Barnstaple in place of Totnes. His family were unfortunate in again supporting the losing side during another rebellion, and lost their lands in 1136. After some dispute over the ownership Totnes eventually went to Henry, son of Earl Reginald of Cornwall, the illegitimate son of Henry I, but this ownership did not last for long and in 1219 Henry III granted it to Reginald de Braose, who rebuilt the castle. He seems to have erected a fairly ramshackle shell keep, slate roofed, with a lean-to on the south-west. The uncertainty of ownership did not encourage care of the castle and by 1273 the whole thing was described as weak and ruinous. Throughout the latter part of the Middle Ages the legal position of the castle seems to have been insecure and beyond forming a seat of local government, in which the manorial courts were held, it played little or no part in the life of the kingdom. For the greater part of its life since the mid-16th Century it has been owned by the Dukes of Somerset, but its history is very sketchily recorded; the then-Duke of Somerset placed it under the control of the Ministry of Works in 1947.

Totnes is a very good example of a motte and bailey castle and stands on a hill commanding the main part of the river Dart where three valleys meet. It stands on a salient which projected into the town and was, therefore, in a good position to command it. The motte is one of the largest in England, with its base chiselled out of the rock but most of it made of pounded earth and rock covered with a layer of puddled clay. There was originally a ditch right round the motte, which is now occupied by the town gardens. The original entrance to the bailey was probably by way of the path which followed the curtain wall on the right. On top of the motte stood a roughly square tower about fifteen feet across, which was on a stone foundation extending at least eleven feet down into the motte. Since it is only two-and-a-half feet thick it was probably used as a base for a timber foundation. The roughly circular shell keep has a diameter of about 70 feet and the walls, six feet thick, are of hard limestone rubble with a sloping foot. There never was another inside wall, but part of the curtain wall did support a lean-to on the inside. This keep was probably built in the early 13th Century, but at some time during the first quarter of the 14th Century it was rebuilt and the red sandstone dressings belong to this period. The wall walk was approached by means of a staircase built inside the wall. A garderobe chamber was added and this stood out beyond the line of the original wall, but it later collapsed and was rebuilt. The parapet dates from the 14th Century restoration and is unusually complete, with 33 merlons or crenellations. Some of the merlons are pierced with arrow slits. The bailey is a very large one and is enclosed by a deep moat, originally wet, contained by a strong outer bank and for part of the circuit there was a second ditch. There are traces of an earthen bank around the inner wall of the moat where stood the palisades which were later replaced by a stone wall. No traces of the domestic buildings remain but the foundations can still be seen. The hall was probably near the west wall and the chapel at the north end. There are some signs

of another fortification bank or ditch in the fields and these may well have guarded the cattle of the castle.

Open to the public:

	Weekdays	Sundays
March–April	9.30 a.m.–5.30 p.m.	2–5.30 p.m.
May–Sept.	9.30 a.m.–7 p.m.	2–7 p.m.
Oct.	9.30 a.m.–5.30 p.m.	2–5.30 p.m.
Nov.–Feb.	10 a.m.–4.30 p.m.	2–4.30 p.m.

Totternhoe Castle, *Totternhoe, Bedfordshire.*

A motte and bailey castle with several baileys. It is high on a hill, and the earthworks probably date back to the Bronze Age.

Tower of London, *London. Near Tower Hill Underground Station.*

Roman London was enclosed by a wall, and it was in the south-east corner of this that William I decided to site one of his castles intended both to protect and to overawe London. In 1078 Gundulf, Bishop of Rochester, was placed in charge of the building of the White Tower, but it was not finished until the time of William II (1087–1100); since Gundulf lived to be 83 it is possible that he saw the tower completed. From this tower Ralph Flambard escaped after first making the guards drunk. A curtain wall was added to the White Tower, and it seems likely that Richard I carried out further extensions. In 1215 the castle was besieged by the barons but successfully resisted until given by John as a token of good faith. There were further extensions during the reign of Henry III. In 1244 Griffin, son of Llewellyn, Prince of Wales, died as a result of a fall whilst trying to escape. In 1254 a new building was erected—an elephant house, to accommodate a gift of the King of France! In 1381 the fortress was taken by a mob during the Peasants' Revolt, and Sir Thomas Hales and Archbishop Sudbury were promptly executed by them. Extra towers and defences were being added throughout this period; the building served as a prison, a mint, a zoo, a palace and an arsenal and, naturally, it has undergone extensive alteration and restoration.

The present entrance to the Tower is by way of the stone causeway over the moat which was built by Edward I in 1278; by it stood the Lion Tower which for years held the royal menagerie. The moat, now dry, became so offensive that in 1843 it was cleaned and drained, and apart from a flood in 1928 has remained dry ever since. The path next leads through the Middle or St. Martin's Tower, again of Edward I's reign although largely rebuilt in the 18th Century, and from here a causeway crosses the inner moat to the Byward Tower which was the main gatehouse for the inner ward. Near this tower is a small postern gate set in the wall. The corner tower of the inner curtain wall is known as the Bell Tower, and probably dates from the reign of Richard I. Next to this tower can be seen a large window which is set in a room of the Lieutenant's Lodgings where Guy Fawkes was questioned after his arrest. The bell from which the tower takes its name was a general warning bell indicating time for prisoners to return to cells.

On the other side of the roadway is St. Thomas' Tower which is above the famous Traitor's Gate, originally opening directly on to the river and therefore convenient for the delivery of prisoners by boat. Almost directly opposite are the Bloody and Wakefield Towers, which guarded the Gate-house of Henry III. Traditionally the Princes in the Tower were murdered in the Bloody Tower, but on whose orders they were killed remains a matter of controversy; its earlier title of Garden Tower was abandoned in the 16th Century. The Bloody Tower still has its portcullis and its machinery. The Wakefield dates from Henry III's time; the Great Hall stood next to it, and this tower was therefore known at one time as the Hall Tower. It has two storeys, and was the scene of the murder of Henry VI.

The wall running south-west has an entrance which leads into the inner ward and thus to the oldest part of the castle, the White Tower. It is 90 feet high and approximately square with four turrets, three square and the north-east one circular. It derives its name from the fact that it was normally coated with whitewash. Originally the tower was entered on the first floor on the south side, the narrow doorway passing through walls which vary in thickness between eleven and fifteen feet. Internally it is divided by a thick wall running from north to south, and on the east wall there is one apse which forms part of the chapel of St. John. In the latter part of the 17th Century Christopher Wren was commissioned to carry out some

modernisation and he had the windows altered and enlarged. In the basement is the well, some 40 feet deep and dating from the 12th Century, and there is also the cell known as 'Little Ease', which now serves as a passage way between the two sections of the basement. The present entrance leads on to the Gun Floor which was an arms store-room until 1916 but now houses some unique exhibits. A staircase leads up to the Chapel of St. John, a beautiful example of a very early church in superb condition, and the rest of this floor houses a fine display of arms and armour. The roof is almost flat; in Tudor times it was modified to hold cannon, and the circular turret was, at one time, equipped to serve as an observatory.

To the north of the White Tower lies the Waterloo Barracks built in 1845 following a fire which destroyed the great store which stood here. To the east of the White Tower are the New Armouries erected in the 17th Century. To the north-west of the tower is the Royal Chapel of St. Peter ad Vincula (St. Peter in Chains) which was probably consecrated in the reign of Henry I; it was rebuilt in the 13th Century and again in the 16th Century. Within its walls were buried many of the illustrious victims of the executioner, and it is therefore appropriate that it faces, on the south, Tower Green where stood the block on which at least seven people were executed. Dotted around the curtain walls are numerous towers including the Beauchamp, probably named after a member of that family imprisoned here in the 14th Century, whose walls are well covered with carving and graffiti by various past prisoners. The Salt Tower, at one time known as Julius Caesar's Tower, also has some inscriptions on the walls. The Martin Tower dates from the reign of Henry III and held the Crown Jewels when Colonel Blood made his attempt to steal them in 1671, but these are now housed in specially constructed premises.

Open to the public mid-March to April (including Easter Eve and Monday) 10 a.m. to 4.30 p.m. May to September 10 a.m. to 5.30 p.m. October to mid-March 10 a.m. to 4 p.m. Sundays in British Summer Time only 2 p.m. to 5 p.m. Closed on Good Friday.

Treago Castle, *St. Weonards, Herefordshire.*

A 14th Century castle with corner towers and walls around an inner courtyard. A castle was here in

the 13th Century, and from early in the 14th Century it belonged to the Mynors family. It was greatly altered during the 17th and 18th Centuries. On the north side is an entrance while the main tower stands on the south-east and held the kitchens.
On private land.

Treen Dinas Castle, *Porthcurno, Cornwall.*

This is a cliff castle of about the 1st Century A.D. It is situated on the cliffs above the village, and was given to the National Trust by Sir Courtenay Vyan.

Tregony Castle, *Tregony, Cornwall.*

Situated on the east side of the Fal river and of Castle Hill, just below the hospital at the lower end of the town, are some minor remains of a castle built by Henry de Pomeroy at the time of Richard I (late 12th Century). There are also some traces of a Roman fort.

Trematon Castle, *St. Stephen-by-Saltash, Cornwall.*

The remains of this castle are situated on a rocky hill; there are traces of a very early earthwork, but the masonry remains are those of a Norman keep. The land was granted after the Conquest to the Earl of Mortain and Cornwall, but became Crown property for part of the time. Later the castle was in the hands of private individuals but finally finished up as part of the Duchy of Cornwall. There is an oval curtain wall standing some 30 feet high and six feet thick, the entire area covering about three-quarters of an acre. There is a high motte on top of which are the remains of a Norman shell keep. The walls of the keep are some 30 feet high and ten feet thick, and the keep itself measures about 72 feet by 50 feet and is embattled. There is a ditch around it. The entrance was on the south-west with a square gatehouse with arched gateway which still retains its original portcullis groove. There is a postern at the north, and the entire castle is surrounded by a ditch. There are no remains of any outbuildings. In 1594 the castle was besieged during one of the local Cornish rebellions when Sir Richard Grenville and his wife defended the castle, but he was lured out and captured and the castle was seized.

Triermain Castle, *Gilsland, Cumberland. Two-and-a-quarter miles south-west of Gilsland.*

This castle was licensed in 1340, and only one tower remains. It was known as Tradermayne in the 16th Century, and was held for many years by the de Vaux family. The original tower was built largely of stone from the Roman quarry and was in ruins by Tudor times. In 1832 most of the ruins collapsed. The castle was rectangular with turrets and a moat.

Tutbury Castle, *Tutbury, Staffordshire. Near Needwood Forest on a sandstone rock cliff 100 feet high above Little Dove River.*

There are traces of an outer wall enclosing an area of approximately three acres. The castle was at one time royal and belonged to John of Gaunt who restored its somewhat decaying walls. Mary, Queen of Scots was imprisoned here for a while. In 1646 it was badly battered by Parliament. The keep has gone and there is now a sham ruin, but the gatehouse at the north-east corner is of late 14th Century with late 17th Century buttresses. On the east wall is a large mural tower and only the outer wall of the great hall remains although some other 15th Century buildings are in a reasonable state.
Open to the public summer 10 a.m.–dusk, winter 10 a.m.–4 p.m.

Twizell Castle, *Twizell, Northumberland.*

There are ruins of a 15th Century castle incorporated into the ruins of a mansion which was built by George Wyatt for Sir Francis Blake; it was never completed and is now very overgrown.

Tytherington Castle, *Tytherington, Gloucestershire.*

A quarter of a mile west of the church is an Iron Age hill fort with ten-foot-high ramparts.

Uffington Castle, *Uffington, Berkshire.*

On Whitehorse Hill is a large earthworks area of some eight acres, standing near the White Horse of Uffington. The entrance is on the north-west side.

Ullersford Castle, *Bollin, Cheshire. To the north of Bollin.*

Castle Mill shows traces of earthworks which may have been simply an outwork of Dunham Castle.

Upnor Castle, *Upnor, Kent. Nearly two miles north of Strood.*

The river Medway was of great importance to the Tudor navy since its slow-moving water and difficult channels (to those unused to the river) made it an ideal anchorage for ships undergoing repair, out of commission or being provisioned. However, moored ships are very much at the mercy of fast-moving attackers and consequently those in the Medway were at grave risk. During Elizabeth's reign it was decided that all such ships needed some form of protection from the shore. In 1559 a small committee examined the position and chose the present site on which to build a castle. The work was undertaken using as many local materials as possible, including some rubble from Rochester Castle, and apparently by 1567 construction was complete.

At the end of the 16th Century additions and repairs were made and some additional buildings were added to the fort. A timber palisade was erected in front of the bastions and a great platform with a parapet was raised, complete with loopholes for some heavy guns. By May 1600 the palisade had been completed and a ditch had been dug which was 18 feet deep and over 30 feet wide, covered by flanking towers built at each end. The ditch was turfed, and timber platforms by the tower were replaced and given a covering of lead. However, by 1623 the castle was already in some disrepair, for the reports stated that the drawbridge mechanism was broken, the platforms needed renewing and that some of the wall had collapsed. In 1642 Upnor Castle and two secondary forts were garrisoned by Parliament; in 1648 a local Royalist uprising in Kent seized the castle, but the small-scale rebellion was soon suppressed. In 1667 the Dutch fleet mounted a very serious raid on the Medway, breaking through a guard chain and destroying or capturing several British ships. As a result of this nasty shock plans were made to increase the defences and a battery of eight guns was set up near Upnor Castle. Some further plans for extended defences along the banks of the river were undertaken. The function of the castle was changed to that of a magazine, and it so remained until 1827. From then on its uses were varied and finally, in 1961, it was taken over by the Ministry of Works.

The main part of the present building dates from the second half of the 16th Century, at which time the moat was dug, which was crossed by a drawbridge. The greater part of the courtyard is 17th Century in origin but the two towers facing the water are of late 16th or early 17th Century date. The main building dates from 1559–67.

Open to the public:

	Weekdays	*Sundays*
March–April	9.30 a.m.–5.30 p.m.	2–5.30 p.m.
May–Sept.	9.30 a.m.–7 p.m.	2–7 p.m.
Oct.	9.30 a.m.–5.30 p.m.	2–5.30 p.m.
Nov.–Feb.	10 a.m.–4.30 p.m.	2–4.30 p.m.

Verdley Castle, *Cowdray, Sussex. Four miles from the town.*

This was probably more of a hunting lodge, built by the Bohuns, rather than a full castle, but there are virtually no traces left.

Wadhurst Castle, *Wadhurst, Sussex. Three-eighths of a mile to the north-west of Wadhurst.*

A house with four octagonal towers built in 1842. *On private land.*

Walkern Castle, *Walkern, Hertfordshire. One mile east of Walkern.*

A motte and bailey castle with ditches; it is now partly covered with buildings, but in some places the ditches still hold water.

Wallingford Castle, *Wallingford, Berkshire.*

The castle is situated in the north-east corner of the town. It has two ditches and at the south end of the bailey there are fragments of masonry. The castle was probably built on the site of a pre-Conquest motte which stands by the church of St. Nicholas near the north gate of the town. The motte is at the south end of the bailey. *On private land.*

Wallington Castle, *Wallington, Northumberland.*

Only some cellars of the old castle remain; the present square house was built in 1688 by Sir William Blackett.

Walls Castle, *Ravenglass, Cumberland.*

Remains of a probable Roman fort with some masonry.

Walmer Castle, *Walmer, Kent. South of Walmer.*

This castle is closely associated with Deal, and with the other castle at Sandwich formed a group of three to protect the coast. It was built by Henry VIII in 1539/40. The castle has a central, circular keep and around this four semi-circular lunettes or large towers, separated from it by a narrow courtyard. It is essentially an artillery fort designed to have cannon on the bastions and on the roof of the keep. The buildings have seen a certain amount of modification including a gatehouse which, in 1874, was castellated and modified to give more living space. A drawbridge led over the moat into the entrance passage. The castle became the official residence of the Lord Warden of the Cinque Ports, a group of towns originally responsible for the defence of the Channel—Hastings, Romney, Hythe, Dover and Sandwich. Here lived William Pitt, often visited by Nelson and, probably the best-known resident of all, the Duke of Wellington, who died here on 14th September 1852. The interior has been modified to accommodate the various notables who lived in or visited the castle, and it now houses a fine collection of items associated with the Duke and other Lord Wardens.
Open to the public:

	Weekdays	Sundays
March–April	*9.30 a.m.–5.30 p.m.*	*2–5.30 p.m.*
May–Sept.	*9.30 a.m.–7 p.m.*	**9.30 a.m.– 7 p.m.*
Oct.	*9.30 a.m.–5.30 p.m.*	*2–5.30 p.m.*

Nov.–Feb.   10 a.m.–4.30 p.m.   2–4.30 p.m.
When the Lord Warden is not in residence.

Walworth Castle, *Walworth Castle, County Durham.*

Dating from the very early 17th Century, this three-storey, semi-circular angle tower has had the windows altered at a later date. There is a very fine porch and some good decoration in the interior of the house.
On private land.

Warblington Castle, *Warblington, Hampshire. North of the church.*

The octagonal gatehouse and part of the walls remain of this castle belonging to Margaret Pole, Countess of Salisbury 1514–26. It was largely ruined during the Civil Wars.

Wardour Castle, *Wardour Park, Wiltshire. One-and-a-half miles south-west of Tisbury.*

The largest Georgian house in Wiltshire, built in 1769–1776 for Lord Arundell.
Open to the public July 23rd to September 1st, Mondays, Wednesdays, Fridays and Saturdays, 2.30 to 6 p.m. Admission 15p, Children under 14 7½p.

Wareham Castle, *Wareham, Dorsetshire. Between the rivers Frome and Piddel.*

Traces of earthworks indicate a Roman fort. In the south-west corner is a 50-foot-high mound with a surrounding moat 60 feet wide, and on this was built a Norman castle. Although little is known about the castle it has seen considerable military activity culminating in the Civil War, when it was slighted.

Wark-on-Tweed Castle, *Wark-on-Tweed, Northumberland.*

This castle was used by the Bishops of Durham, and was in existence in the 12th Century. It was captured by the Scots in 1126 and, in consequence, was strengthened in 1153/6 by Henry II. It was destroyed by fire in 1216 and again rebuilt, with a four-storey keep which was an irregular polygon 255 feet by 165 feet. There were special architectural features in the keep for the use of heavy artillery within the walls. There was a high lookout tower on the roof. There were two baileys separated by a high curtain wall, and entrance to the first was by iron gates in a passageway. Only fragments and the motte and bailey can still be seen.

Warkworth Castle, *Warkworth, Northumberland. On the river Coquet. Seven-and-a-half miles south-east of Alnwick.*

Castle builders were not slow to take advantage of any natural feature which would increase the effectiveness of their defences. At Warkworth it can clearly be seen that the site is well chosen, for the castle and the town nestle on a spit of land which is surrounded on three sides by a large loop of the river Coquet. The steep banks render attack from the river very hazardous, and the site is an ideal defensive position. The castle is on the highest ground which is at the "open" end of the loop. The early history of the castle has not been clearly established prior to the 12th Century. Unlike many other English castles Warkworth was continually in action, for its position near the Scottish border made it a base for attack and defence during the almost incessant border warfare. Warkworth was held by the Clavering family until 1332, when Edward III (1327–1377) gave the castle to the Percy family; the head of this very powerful clan was the Earl of Northumberland, and the castle is still the property of the Duke of Northumberland. The castle was given as part of the payment made to offset the expenses incurred by Sir Henry Percy in defending the North of England against the raids of the warlike Scots.
As was usual, the first castle built on this site—during the 12th Century—was of the motte and bailey type. Surprisingly in view of its importance, the upkeep of the castle seems to have been lax for in 1173 it was captured by the Scots and its defences were then described as being "feeble". During the period that it belonged to the Claverings there is little doubt that the original wooden fences

were gradually replaced with walls of stone, and soon a curtain wall faced with ashlar had been erected with flanking towers added. During the course of the replacement with stone the bailey was, in fact, reduced in size, for the evidence shows that the wood and earth fortifications were actually 70 feet longer than the curtain on the eastern side. Late in the 12th or early in the 13th Century the two great towers were built. The Grey Mare's Tail Tower has one particular feature which distinguishes it from all others. The loop holes cut in the walls are excessively large; some are actually over seventeen feet long, far bigger than normal. Through these loopholes the archers could maintain a steady discharge of arrows against the enemy. Of about the same date is the tower on the southernmost corner, the Carrickfergus Tower. Along the inside of the curtain wall were erected a variety of domestic buildings including the chapel, hall and sundry rooms.

The gatehouse is ingeniously planned, for the front entrance leads to a vaulted passageway with guard chambers on both sides, so that any attacker who had forced his way through the gate then had to pass along the passage during which time he was open to attack by defenders. There was also a drawbridge; although it has disappeared, the recess for it can still be seen at the entrance. Above the gate a number of square holes are cut into the fabric and these were designed to hold the wooden beams which held the bratticing. This was a wooden structure which was fitted to the top of the tower and projected far enough forward from the walls to enable the defender to rain down missiles on an attacker. After forcing the drawbridge the attacker was still faced with a gate, a portcullis, and then the long passageway.

When the castle passed into the hands of the Percys the new owners felt the need to improve their defences and they replaced the previous structure on the motte with an enormous and unique form of keep. Heraldic devices carved on the wall of the new building indicate that it was not built prior to 1390 and it may be assumed that the keep was the work of the first Earl of Northumberland, the father of "Harry Hotspur". The keep is square, each side 65 feet long, but at the centre of each of the four walls a smaller, square building projects to give a cruciform appearance to the keep. The entrance was fitted with a portcullis, and trap doors set just inside gave a drop to a sixteen-foot-deep

pit. In the middle an open space ten feet by eight feet extends from top to bottom of the keep and so allows some extra natural lighting as well as providing a means of collecting rainwater, for it leads down to a large stone tank in the basement. From this tank conduits take the water off to flush the latrine shafts.

Warkworth Castle is remarkable in having that vital ingredient of all medieval romances, an underground dungeon. Despite the frequency with which they appear in stories they are, in fact, quite rare. This one has eight chambers, all of them vaulted. On the first floor of the keep were the kitchen, hall, chapel and the great chamber; they all rise through two storeys, and on the third storey was a parlour. The roof is flat and surrounded by battlements and there is a tall watch tower. On one of the walls, carved in high relief, is the lion rampant, forming part of the coat of arms of the Percy family. At about the same time as the tower was being built plans were made to found a collegiate church as at Windsor. A start was made on a cruciform-shaped church but it seems never to have been completed.

The fortunes of the castle varied over the centuries: it was captured by the Scots in 1173, but in 1327 it successfully withstood two sieges. In 1405 when the Percy family rebelled against King Henry IV the attackers had to bring in artillery to batter down the immensely strong walls. In 1644 it again fell into the hands of the Scots when the Army of the Covenant attacked it. As with so many castles it had fallen into some degree of disrepair but today certain parts of the keep are still inhabitable, and are used by the Duke of Northumberland when he visits Warkworth.

Open to the public:

	Weekdays	Sundays
March–April	*9.30 a.m.–5.30 p.m.*	*2–5.30 p.m.*
May–Sept.	*9.30 a.m.–7 p.m.*	*9.30 a.m.– 7 p.m.*
Oct.	*9.30 a.m.–5.30 p.m.*	*2–5.30 p.m.*
Nov.–Feb.	*9.30 a.m.–4 p.m.*	*2–4 p.m.*

Warwick Castle, *Warwick, Warwickshire.*

The castle at Warwick is one of the few that still serves as a home and retains the greater part of its original masonry. Standing as it does by the river Avon the town of Warwick was a good defensive position, and it seems that the Saxon princess Ethelfleda built some sort of mound to hold off the Danes. Probably because of its defensive value Warwick became part of the Crown lands; it is so recorded at the time of the Domesday survey (1086), and some extension to the original fortifications were made. In 1068 the castle and the borough were given by William the Conqueror to Henry de Newburgh, who had a large motte raised, and later a shell keep was erected. Much of this castle was destroyed during the barons' revolt in 1264 when troops led by Simon de Montfort are reported to have demolished the castle. During this period the owner, the Earl of Warwick, was captured and taken as prisoner to Kenilworth Castle (qv). When he died in 1265 he left no sons and the title passed, through the daughter, to the Beauchamp family. It was Thomas Beauchamp who built most of the masonry which survives today; he died in 1369, probably as a result of illness caused by his service in France during the Hundred Years War. In 1356 the castle had been used as a prison for a number of Frenchmen taken at the Battle of Poitiers.

The powerful Earls of Warwick were often involved in political issues of the time and many met their death as a result of this involvement. In 1388 Earl Thomas de Beauchamp supported a revolt against Richard II, but the revolt failed and he retired from public life. He rather foolishly accepted an invitation to a banquet at which he was arrested, and imprisoned in the Tower of London (qv), in the building which has ever since borne his name, the Beauchamp Tower. He was banished and his lands were then forfeit. He served yet another spell in the Tower in 1398, but was released when Henry IV became king in 1399.

Possibly the best-known of all the Earls of Warwick was Richard Neville, known because of his power and importance as "the King Maker". Warwick met a violent death at the Battle of Barnet in 1471 and the castle then passed, via his daughter Isabel, to George, Duke of Clarence—who in his turn met an unpleasant death in a butt of wine in the Tower of London but was immortalised by Shakespeare. In 1499 the then Earl of Warwick was executed because of his alleged complicity in the plot to place Perkin Warbeck on the throne. Warbeck claimed to be the son of Edward IV, but he too was executed by Henry VII. For some 60 years the title was in abeyance but was given by Henry VIII to

John Dudley, Viscount Lisle, who was made Warwick in 1547. Dudley was involved in the attempt to make Lady Jane Grey queen of England and was subsequently executed in 1554. His son Ambrose inherited the title but in 1589 it again reverted, for lack of an heir, to the throne. The title was revived in 1618 by James I and granted to Robert Rich; in the 18th Century Francis Greville, Baron Brooke of Beauchamps Court became the Earl of Warwick, and the title has remained in the family ever since.

The majority of the present castle dates from the 14th Century and the walls, towers and hall are all of this period. The castle faces towards the northeast and has a most impressive and very strongly defended gatehouse. Not only is the gatehouse itself almost impregnable but there is an extra tower situated in front and known as a barbican. Even more impressive are the towers at either end of the long wall; the one on the left, known as Caesar's Tower, is most unusual in its shape, for in section it is rather like a clover leaf. It rises for six storeys to a height of 133 feet and at the top is crowned with a double parapet. The lower parapet has the characteristic feature known as a machicolation, which appeared first during the late 13th Century. A parapet, originally of wood but later of stone, projected from the top of the tower and a series of holes cut into the floor permitted the defenders to pour down arrows, stones, hot liquids or any other unpleasant missiles on an enemy who had gained the base of the wall. The double parapet such as that on this tower is a characteristically French feature of castle building. At the other end of the wall is Guy's Tower which is not quite as tall, only 128 feet. This, unlike Caesar's tower, is polygonal in section and has only five storeys; it has a single machicolated parapet. A large, square tower with rounded corners which projects out from the curtain wall on the north-east front dates from the 15th Century. It was designed to give defenders a field of fire which would cover the base of the main walls and its shape suggests that it was intended to house some form of artillery.

The living quarters of the castle face to the south-east and the section of wall is pierced by a large number of very fine Gothic windows. The Great Hall is somewhat smaller than one would expect for a castle of this size and measures only some 62 by 42 feet. The interior has been largely restored after a serious fire in 1871 badly damaged the building. In fact much of the interior of Warwick Castle dates from the 17th Century, for in the reign of James I Sir Fulk Greville was granted the castle and spent an enormous amount of money on repairs and extensions. He did not long live to enjoy his new home, for in 1628 he was murdered by one of his servants. During the 18th Century the work started by Greville was extended and a collection of superb *objets d'art* was built up by various owners. Today the armoury houses one of the best private collections in the country, and in the state apartments are some superb art treasures including portraits by Holbein, Rubens and other famous artists. During the 18th Century the grounds were also laid out by the master landscape gardener, "Capability" Brown.

For a castle of such importance Warwick has seen surprisingly little action; in fact it was only during the Civil War that it really heard shots fired in anger. It was held for Parliament by Robert, Lord Brooke and was under siege by the Royalists for only three days. The commander of the garrison refused to surrender and the Royalists withdrew. *Open to the public Good Friday to September daily 10 a.m.–5.30 p.m. Shorter hours out of season; closed November to February. Admission (1972) Ground, Gardens, Castle Armoury and Guy's Tower 30p, Children 15p; State Rooms 10p. Reduction for prepaid parties.*

Watermouth Castle, *Berrynarbor, Devonshire. One mile north of the village.*

A mansion of the early Victorian period with

Warkworth: the heraldic lion of the Percy family can be traced on a wall of this important border castle

battlements, built in 1825. There are one or two traces of earlier work.
On private land.

Wattlesborough Castle, *Wattlesborough, Shropshire. Near Rowton Castle, west of Shrewsbury.*

It has a small, conventional square keep in which the windows have been modified at later dates. It is three storeys high, although it may well have had a fourth once. A small building abuts it on the north side and there are foundations of other buildings as well as an earthwork 70 feet square, although this may predate the castle.

Waytemore Castle, *Bishops Stortford, Hertfordshire. Between the town and the village of Hockerill.*

A mound with some fragmentary masonry remains of a castle which may have been destroyed by King John.

Weeting Castle, *Weeting, Norfolk.*

Unexcavated traces of a late 12th Century castle.

Welbourn Castle, *Welbourn, Lincolnshire. South of the church.*

Remains of earthworks, although masonry defences were mentioned in the 12th Century.

Wentworth Castle, *Wentworth, West Riding, Yorkshire.*

A three-storeyed, seven bay house built *circa* 1670.
On private land.

Weobley Castle, *Weobley, Herefordshire. Quarter of a mile south of the church, to the west of Hereford Street.*

This belonged to the Lacy family and parts date from the 13th Century. The earthworks have a double ditch. In the 17th Century it still stood, with circular corner towers, a semi-circular bastion on the east and west curtain wall. The entrance was on the north side with two square towers and a keep at the south end.

Weoley Castle, *Birmingham, Warwickshire. Four miles south-west of the centre of the city.*

In 1264 Roger de Somery was given his licence to crenellate. The castle had six towers and was surrounded by a moat.
Open to the public Saturdays 10 a.m.–5 p.m., Thursdays, Fridays, Sundays, 2–5 p.m. Admission $2\frac{1}{2}p$.

Westernhanger Castle, *Stanford, Kent. Near the station of the Parish of Stanford, two-and-a-half miles from Hythe.*

This castle was quadrangular in shape, with a strong curtain wall of nine towers; the four corner ones were round and the centre wall towers were square. Of these three survive in reasonable condition and the others can be traced. One of the towers is known as Fair Rosamond's, because tradition has it that Rosamond Clifford lived here before going to Woodstock. The castle was sold in 1701—for £1,000—and much of it was then demolished.
On private land.

Whitchurch Castle, *Whitchurch, Shropshire.*

On Castle Hill there were some remains of a castle which belonged to William, Earl Warren.

Whitley Castle, *Alston, Northumberland. Two miles north-west near Whitley Castle Farm, off the road to Hallbankgate.*

A Roman fort; little is visible apart from a six-ditch defence on one side.
Permission to view must be obtained from Whitley Castle Farm.

Whitstable Castle, *Whitstable, Kent.*

On Tower Hill stands a mansion with ocatagonal towers of flint and red brick complete with battlements, which was built about 1827.
On private land.

Whittington Castle, *Whittington, Shropshire.*

The castle of Fulke FitzWarren, licensed *circa* 1221, has largely disappeared apart from one round tower. There was a keep on the 30-foot-high motte, and a gatehouse with two circular protecting towers.

Whitwick Castle, *Whitwick, Leicestershire.*

The castle was, apparently, first built in 1150 and a licence to crenellate was granted in 1321, but hardly anything remains.

Whorlton Castle, *Whorlton-in-Cleveland, North Riding, Yorkshire.*

A two-and-a-half acre motte and bailey site with a 60-foot ditch. The motte, cellars and an oblong gatehouse still survive.
On private land.

Wigmore Castle, *Wigmore, Herefordshire. Quarter of a mile west of the church.*

This castle was built in the 11th Century by William FitzOsbern and later belonged to the Mortimer family. It is now overgrown, but earthworks indicate the outer bailey on the south-east whilst the inner bailey was protected by walls and towers of 13th and 14th Century construction. There are remains of the gatehouse and the south tower, and at the north-west corner is the mound with remains of a shell keep on top, mostly 14th Century work although the castle was largely in ruins by the 16th Century.

Willersley Castle, *Cromford, Derbyshire.*

Built in 1782/8 in classical style with some semi-circular and circular turrets.
On private land.

Willimontswick Castle, *Willimontswick, Northumberland. Two miles west of the village.*

Two tall towers survive by the side of a modern house, with some other fragments.

Wilton Castle, *Bridstow, Herefordshire. Quarter mile to the south-east of Bridstow.*

The original castle dates from *circa* 1300 and is rectangular with corner towers of which that on the south-west corner has an aspidal projection and may have been the gatehouse. The north-west tower was polygonal and in the east wall garderobes were fitted. There are some Tudor additions, especially in the south-west.

Witton-le-Wear Castle, *Witton-le-Wear, County Durham. South of the river near Bishop Auckland.*

Licensed in 1410; the castle was burnt down in late 18th Century and the living quarters were rebuilt in 1790/95. During the Civil War it was held for the king and was captured but, surprisingly, was not slighted. It was rectangular in shape with strong angle towers, three circular and one square, and there was a strong keep with an entrance at the centre of the north wall.

Winchester Castle, *Winchester, Hampshire.*

Started by a FitzOsborne, it was strengthened by Stephen. It was apparently quadrangular with a very large keep, about 100 feet square, set at the north-east corner of the bailey, defended with the usual drawbridge and square towers. During the Civil War it was held by the king. In 1645 it surrendered after the Roundheads had opened a bombardment on it; and, in keeping with policy, it was slighted by Parliament. Now only the great hall remains; this dates from about 1235 and is in early English style. It was the scene of a number of important trials and is still used as a court house. On the wall hangs a representation of the mythical Round Table of King Arthur.

Windsor Castle, *Windsor, Berkshire.*

There was a Saxon palace at Old Windsor; Edward the Confessor held court here, and later William I used the old palace—it probably stood to the west of the church. William decided to build a new castle two miles to the north-west on top of a hill overlooking the river; he is known to have visited the area in 1070 and by 1086 the castle is listed in the Domesday survey. In 1095 Robert de Mowbray, Earl of Northumberland, was imprisoned there, and the castle was to serve as a prison until the 18th Century. It was from here that John made his way to Runnymede for the meeting with the barons in 1215. Following the breakdown of negotiations the barons called upon the French for help, and on May 30th 1216 the Dauphin landed and later besieged Windsor without success. Henry III carried out some extensive building here including some fine apartments for his own use. In 1278 Edward I held a great tournament here. Edward III made this castle his main residence and he built the Round Tower on the 135-foot-diameter motte in 1348, as well as remodelling many other parts, the work being supervised by William of Wykeham, later to be Bishop of Winchester. David Bruce, King of Scotland was held prisoner here in the 14th Century, as was John, King of France, captured at Poitiers in 1356. In 1344 Edward III ordered the holding of tournaments here, and in 1348 he instituted the Order of the Garter, limited to twenty-six knights. During the Civil War Windsor was in the hands of Parliament, who took many of its treasures and had them melted down or sold, including the mail coat of Edward IV. Charles I was sent here after his surrender and remained a prisoner for a while before leaving for London, and later returning as a corpse for burial. Following the Restoration a great deal of modification took place, including the filling in of the outer ditch, and subsequent monarchs all had thoughts or plans for modifying the castle. George IV did much to return it to something like its earlier simplicity. Windsor has more than one bailey, with the motte at the centre, and it was on this that Henry II's shell keep was erected with its chapel, hall and probably chambers as well. His masons also enclosed the upper bailey as well as erecting other stone buildings. Edward III (1327–1377) was born at Windsor in November 1312 and, possibly

for this reason, seems to have treated the castle with particular affection and care. He brought in workmen from all over England when he began work in *circa* 1350 on the old chapel of Henry III; in 1355 the emphasis was on the residential section, including bath houses, mews for the royal birds and the queen's dancing chamber. A new hall was built and the earlier one converted into living quarters and new kitchens were added. Enormous quantities of materials were used; one account alone mentions the felling of 2,000 oaks.

Open to the public: Castle Precincts—Daily 10 a.m. to sunset all the year. State Apartments—weekdays (subject to the requirements of the court) November to February 11 a.m.–3 p.m. March to April 11 a.m.– 4 p.m. May to September 11 a.m.–5 p.m. October 11 a.m.–4 p.m. Also on Sundays (April to October) from 1.30 p.m. Admission 15p, Children 5p. St. George's Chapel—weekdays 11 a.m.–3.45 p.m. (Fridays 1–3.45 p.m.) Closed in January. Open Sundays 2.30–4 p.m. Admission 15p, Children 5p. Queen Mary's Dolls' House and Exhibition of Dolls, Old Master Drawings—Daily all the year except Sundays, November to April, Christmas Day or Good Friday. Hours as for State Apartments. Admission 5p each. (State Apartments usually closed approximately 6 weeks for Easter, 3 weeks for Ascot Visit and 3 weeks around Christmas.)

Wingfield Castle, *Wingfield, Suffolk. Quarter of a mile south-west of the church.*

A castle is mentioned in the reign of Edward I but the licence was not granted until 1384, when Michael de la Pole owned the property. The gatehouse has survived well, with a good gateway and portcullis grooves; two flanking towers are octagonal and three storeys high. Some of the curtain wall remains, although on the western side there is a farmhouse, and the other towers have been restored.

Wisbech Castle, *Wisbech, Cambridgeshire.*

This castle was founded by the Conqueror at the mouth of the river Ouse but was apparently overwhelmed by storm and flood in 1236. It was replaced by the Bishop of Ely and served for a while as a prison. The site has been laid out as a garden but the foundations are still visible.

Wiverton Castle, *Wiverton, Nottinghamshire.*

Probably built by Sir Thomas Chaworth, who had a licence in 1446, the castle was demolished after the Civil War, although part of the gatehouse survived.

Wolsty Castle, *Wolsty, Cumberland. Two miles from Silloth.*

The licence for this was granted in 1349 and it was used as a treasure house by the Abbots of Holme Cultram. Only a ditch now remains.

Wolvesey Castle, *Winchester, Hampshire.*

The wall of the keep and the curtain wall are still to be seen east of Winchester Cathedral, but no substantial remains survive of this former residence of the Bishops of Winchester. The keep dates from about 1130–40, and a large gatehouse was probably erected at about the same date. A Great Hall was built some 30 years later. Wolvesey saw action during the civil wars of Stephen's reign; in 1141 there was a confused siege and counter-siege of the town and certain isolated strongholds within it, including Wolvesey.

Woodcroft Castle, *Elton, Huntingdonshire. One-and-a-half miles south of Elton.*

The earliest fragment appears to be of 13th Century origin with a strong, two-tower gatehouse leading to a courtyard. There are some Tudor additions.

Woodsford Castle, *between Wareham and Dorchester, Dorsetshire. On the river Frome.*

The castle was built by Guy de Brian during the reign of Edward III (1327–1377); it was quadrangular, with square corner towers and the principal entrance on the west. The remaining tower is known as Beacon Tower and was restored by Lord Ilchester during the 19th Century.

Wooler Castle, *Wooler, Northumberland.*

Owned by the Muschamp family, a Norman motte and bailey castle stood here, but nearly all traces of this castle have gone. In the 16th Century there are mentions of a new castle. It seems to have fallen rapidly into disrepair, until only fragments survived on top of the motte.

Wooston Castle, *Drew Steignton, Devonshire. Two miles south-east of village.*

An early Iron Age earthwork site, very similar to those at Prestonbury and Cranbrook (qqv).

Worcester Castle, *Worcester, Worcestershire.*

A terraced garden by the side of the river, and backing on to King's School, is virtually all that remains of the great motte and castle which once stood here.

Worksop Castle, *Worksop, Nottinghamshire. On Castle Hill, north-west side of the town.*

The castle was built by William de Lovetot early in the 11th Century but most traces had disappeared by the 17th Century.

Wormegay Castle, *Oxburgh, Norfolk. South side of the village, seven-and-a-half miles from Downham Market.*

A castle owned first by the Warrennes and then by the Bardolphs stood here, on the surviving mound.

Wraysholme Castle, *Allithwaite, Lancashire. South of the village.*

Only a large tower remains. The site belonged to the Harrington family and is traditionally the site of the killing of the last English wolf.

Wressle Castle, *Wressle, East Riding, Yorkshire.*

This castle was founded by Sir Thomas Percy, brother of the 1st Earl of Northumberland, *circa* 1380; it later passed to the Crown for a while and was then restored to the Percy family in 1496. It was occupied by Parliament during the Civil War in 1642 and 1648, and was slighted in 1648. Today two of the original four towers are standing, together with part of the south wall, and it is encircled by a moat. The front range contains a basement and a hall, with a very fine fireplace. The square towers have newel staircases to the roof ending in an octagonal turret; the west tower had the dining room, and in the east tower was the chapel. Until 1796 it served as a farmhouse, when fire destroyed much of the interior.
On private land.

Yarmouth Castle, *Yarmouth, Isle of Wight.*

Henry VIII did not originally plan to build a castle here when he was creating his coastal defence system, which included Calshott Castle and Hurst Castle (qqv) as well as towers near Cowes. At that time the only defence near Yarmouth was a tower built a mile to the west at Sharpnode Point by Sir James Worsley. In 1545 the French mounted an audacious raid, sailing into the Solent and landing troops on the Isle of Wight, but these were repelled by the local militia. As a result a fort was started on Kingsland; by 1547 it was in service and contained three cannons and culverines and twelve smaller guns. To increase the defensive ability of the island each parish was ordered to supply a gun with a team to man it. Since Yarmouth Castle postdates the earlier forts it incorporated the latest thinking in military architecture in which the old, round, artillery bastions were replaced by arrow-pointed ones; one such bastion was fitted at Yarmouth and another at Sandown. This fort was

certainly completed by 1559, for it appears on a plan made about that date. Under the renewed threat of the Spanish Armada in 1587 some extensive repairs were carried out, and at the end of the 16th Century some extra fortifications were added. Further repairs were carried out early in the 17th Century, including a new length of sea wall, and other modifications were carried out at various periods; unlike so many of the other castles Yarmouth was still useful, serving as a centre of embarkation and disembarkation of troops and supplies. When civil war came in 1642 the area was strongly Royalist, and Captain Barnaby Burley was quite ready to defend the castle. He surrendered it on condition that he remained on guard but, in fact, the island was taken over by Parliament. Fearing the possible results of any plots by Charles II, Parliament's garrison was increased quite considerably and at times as many as 70 men were on duty. When the Restoration took place the garrison was considerably reduced and seems to have been abolished for a time. In 1669 Sir Robert Holmes was appointed Captain for the Island and undertook vigorous re-organisation. He demolished some of the earthworks, filled in the moat and built himself a house which is now the present George Hotel. The old entrance was blocked, a fresh one made on the south side and all the guns were moved to concentrate on the seaward side. The fort remained in use throughout the 18th Century with a garrison which was usually made up of a Captain, a master gunner and five gunners, and presumably the local militia supplied the bulk of the men required. The fort saw little military use after this period and the garrison was withdrawn in 1885, but it continued to be used by the coastguard as a signalling post until 1901. It was then transferred to the Commissioners of Woods and Forests who, in turn, passed it to H.M. Office of Works in 1913, but it did see some use by the military during the two World Wars.
The castle is essentially square with sides about 100 feet long, with a bastion which comes to a very sharp point. The north and west sides are protected by the sea and the south and east were originally protected by a 30 feet wide moat. The original entrance was from the east; when the moat was filled in, in the 17th Century, the gatehouse was blocked, although it has been recently uncovered. It leads into the garden of the hotel and is not in public use. From the late 17th Century the northern entrance

has been used. From the long sides of the bastion small pointed casements project in order that lateral fire might be directed along the walls should an opponent gain them. These were added in 1609.

Open to the public:

	Weekdays	Sundays
March–April	*9.30 a.m.–5.30 p.m.*	*2–5.30 p.m.*
May–Sept.	*9.30 a.m.–7 p.m.*	*2–7 p.m.*
Oct.	*9.30 a.m.–5.30 p.m.*	*2–5.30 p.m.*
Nov.–Feb.	*10 a.m.–4.30 p.m.*	*2–4.30 p.m.*

Yarmouth Castle, *Great Yarmouth, Norfolk. Opposite Newgate of the sea wall.*

A mound only marks the site of this largely unknown castle, which probably dated from the late 13th Century. It had four turrets, one of which served as a signal station, but it was all demolished in 1621.

Yarnbury Castle, *Winterbourne Stoke, Wiltshire. Two miles south-west of the town.*

An earthworks, probably of Iron Age date, with a ditch and banks with an inside flint kerbing which probably dates from Roman times. The site covers nearly 30 acres.

Yeldon Castle, *Yeldon, Bedfordshire. At Castlefield.*

Some earthworks which enclose a rectangular motte 130 feet by 90 feet, with two large baileys and other enclosures. There are a few fragmentary masonry remains.

York Castle, *York, East Riding, Yorkshire.*

The situation of York, in a valley by the side of a river, makes it a natural defensive site. It is not surprising that when the Romans were moving north in A.D. 71 and reached this spot, Eburacum, they set up a legionary fortress. Built and garrisoned by men of the IX Legion, it stood on roughly the area occupied by the present Minster and, no doubt, conformed to the standard Roman pattern, rectangular with rounded corners. At first the walls were of wood but were later replaced by masonry,

of which a small section still remains to the north of the Minster, although they are covered by the earth bank which supports the medieval walls. Part of the Roman Masonry can still be seen in the small tower in the grounds of the Yorkshire museum, which was on the south-west of the Roman fort, for the medieval builders erected their foundations on a lower Roman section. During the Dark Ages following the collapse of Roman rule the city of York changed hands on several occasions, and at one time was a very important Danish centre. Following the Battle of Hastings in 1066 most of the south of England succumbed fairly quickly, but in the north resistance continued. William I visited York in 1068 and built a motte and bailey castle, and raised yet another on his second visit in 1069. Neither of these was to last long, for in 1069 a Danish fleet sailed up the Humber and reached York. The local population rose against the hated Normans, the Norman garrisons were overwhelmed, and in September the castles were destroyed. William the Conqueror determined to make an example of the rebels, and sent a punitive expedition which ravaged much of Yorkshire. One of the castles of York was rebuilt. The one situated on the south bank of the river Ouse has disappeared, although near the end of Skeldergate Bridge the place known as Bailehill indicates the site of the old bailey, while traces of the motte can still be seen in the eastern corner. Bishopsgate Street and Prices Lane follow the line of the old ditch. The other motte is as prominent as ever, and excavations in 1903 showed that unlike most examples it was not simply a great heap of earth but had been carefully built up with layers of gravel, clay and stone. During the excavation the remains of the original timber platforms were found. There was an oval bailey, and traces of the early bank and ditch were found to the east of the mound. The defences were further strengthened by damming the river Fosse to create a reservoir, a water defence and a fish pond.

The Jews were always the target of suspicion and ignorant hatred amongst the medieval English, and in 1190 the Jews of York were attacked by a mob. Most of those in the city took refuge in the wooden tower but, fearing for their lives, they refused to let in the Sheriff and the mob besieged the castle. Many of the Jews killed themselves rather than risk the fury of the mob and, either deliberately or accidentally, the whole castle was burnt down. It was rebuilt, and there is evidence to suggest that the height of the motte was increased at the same time. Some replacement of the wooden defences by masonry was carried out during the reign of John (1199–1215) although the main building seems to have been of wood as late as 1228 when it was blown down by a gale.

War between England and Scotland was endemic during much of the medieval period and in 1244 Henry III (1216–1272) determined to strengthen the castle. He placed the work in the hands of two top craftsmen of the time—Royal Master Mason Henry of Reynes, who was also responsible for much of the 13th Century work in Westminster Abbey, and Master Simon, the carpenter of Northampton. Both men had also done work in Windsor Castle. It seems likely that Master Henry was familiar with the French style of building, for the tower which he erected on the motte is very similar to those built in France at this period. Work was begun in 1245 and over the next 30 years some £2,400 were spent. Basically the shape is that of four overlapping circles; there is only one other British castle, at Pontefract (qv), which is built to the same design although similar French keeps are not uncommon. Until the late 16th Century this tower was known as the King's Tower but then it became Clifford's Tower. The association of names would seem to date from 1322 when the body of Sir Robert Clifford, with those of other Lancastrian leaders, was hung in chains from the top of the tower. The connection is further enhanced by the coats of arms carved above the doorway, the top one being the Royal arms and the lower one those of the Clifford family. The base of the tower spreads out slightly and the outside is covered with ashlar masonry. Both storeys were used as living quarters. The top floor was supported on a central pillar and it may well have been intended to add a third storey.

The steps leading up the mound are modern, although they probably follow the same path as the original staircase. The doorway was protected by a gatehouse which was demolished during the 17th Century, and the present one was built following the Restoration (1660). The right hand side of the arch and the stone bench date from the 13th Century, and the holes for the bolts and bars and the portcullis can still be seen on the right hand side of the arch. The corbels, projecting stones which held the first floor timbers, still survive on the

walls. Two spiral staircases led to the upper floors and the battlements; the one on the left also led into the chapel which was over the entrance passage. This part has been much altered for originally there was another room above the chapel, which housed the portcullis. There were other spiral staircases from the upper floor leading up to the battlements and there were latrines on both levels as well as fireplaces on either side. Much of the original masonry was removed by Robert Redhead, the prison jailor in 1596, who increased his income by removing and selling the inner face and core of the wall leaving the outside intact! He was very successful in his ploy, removing the turret and battlements of Clifford's Tower as well as other parts of the bailey, and it required all the efforts of the Mayor and Corporation of the city to stop him. At the top of the walls, inside the Tower, traces of his demolition work can still be seen, while the reddening of the stonework was caused by a fire in 1684. Originally the junctions of the various curved, outer sections were protected by small turrets which were supported on corbels. The well is situated on the right of the entrance to the tower and is over 50 feet deep. In the 14th Century the castle was refurbished and repaired and owing to the war against the Scots extra buildings were erected for the large number of officials the king brought with him when he moved to the city to take command of the campaign. After his heavy defeat at the Battle of Bannockburn (1314), Edward II (1307–1327) spent a great deal of time at the castle.

One of the problems of erecting heavy stone buildings on the top of earth mounds is that the weight often causes subsidence. Cracks from top to bottom were reported in the walls of Clifford's Tower in 1360, and very expensive repairs were carried out. Like so many others the castle fell again into disrepair, and in 1614 it was sold.

By 1270 the castle seems to have acquired its final shape and it then had a curtain wall with at least five towers. The main gateway was on the south side of the bailey and a second one was on the north and led into the city by way of Castlegate. On the north-west side the wall was of wood and a wooden fence encircled the main tower. Inside the bailey were the chapel, kitchen, prison and a great hall. A water filled moat encircled the walls and the river water also drove some mills which belonged to the king. Some remains of the original curtain walls may be seen behind the Debtors' Prison where the original main gate stood.

During the English Civil Wars (1642–48) York supported the king, and was bombarded; much of the original gateway to Clifford's Tower was demolished, being rebuilt in 1660 when the coats of arms, mentioned above, were carved. The city surrendered to Parliament after Cromwell's great victory at Marston Moor in 1644.

In 1684 on St. George's day, 23rd April, the inside of Clifford's Tower was gutted by a fire. Mystery surrounds this event, for there was much ill-feeling between the soldiers and the citizens and it was said that there were grave suspicions about the fire—which started during the firing of a salute in honour of St. George. It was also noted that all the soldiers had removed their own personal belongings from the Tower before the cannonade started —but nothing was ever proved!

As was common practice York Castle was used as a Government headquarters, a court and a prison and between 1353–1546 there was also a mint inside the grounds. There is mention of a jail inside the castle as early as 1205. The prison became very dilapidated and by the 17th Century it was in complete disrepair. The Debtors' Prison was rebuilt in 1705 on the far side of the castle bailey, and an Assize Court was built in 1777. On the opposite side a prison for women was erected in 1780. It was at York that the greatly over-rated highwayman, Dick Turpin, was hanged in April 1739.

Open to the public:

	Weekdays	*Sundays*
March–April	*9.30 a.m.–5.30 p.m.*	*2–5.30 p.m.*
May–Sept.	*9.30 a.m.–7 p.m.*	*9.30 a.m.– 7 p.m.*
Oct.	*9.30 a.m.–5.30 p.m.*	*2–5.30 p.m.*
Nov.–Feb.	*9.30 a.m.–4 p.m.*	*2–4 p.m.*

Clifford's Tower at York: threatened by subsidence of the motte in the 14th Century, and by the dishonesty of the custodian in the 16th. He partly dismantled it and sold the materials for his own profit!

APPENDIX

THE following are among castles which are known to have existed but of which all physical traces have now disappeared:

Aldworth Castle, Aldworth, Berkshire
Ampthill Castle, Ampthill, Bedfordshire
Bampton Castle, Bampton, Devonshire
Baynards Castle, London[1]
Beckley Castle, Beckley, Oxfordshire
Bedale Castle, Bedale, Yorkshire
Beer Ferrers Castle, Beer Ferrers, Devonshire
Brightwell Castle, Brightwell, Berkshire
Bow and Arrow (or Rufus) Castle, Isle of Portland, Dorset
Calne Castle, Calne, Wiltshire
Castle Carr, Halifax, West Riding, Yorkshire
Castle Eaton (or Cricklade), Cricklade, Wiltshire
Chipping Warden Castle, Chipping Warden, Oxfordshire
Chumleigh Castle, Chumleigh, Devonshire
Coleshill Castle, Coleshill, Warwickshire
Connington Castle, Connington, Huntingdonshire
Cublington (or Cubbertson) Castle, Medley, Herefordshire
Darsley Castle, Darsley, Gloucestershire
Eridge Castle, Eridge, Sussex
Faringdon Castle, Faringdon, Berkshire
Gloucester Castle, Gloucester, Gloucestershire[2]
Gresley Castle, nr. Ashby-de-la-Zouch, Derbyshire
Helston Castle, Helston, Cornwall
Heton Castle, Near Norham, Northumberland
Horton Castle, Blyth, Northumberland
Hull Castle, Hull, Yorkshire
Ipswich Castle, Ipswich, Suffolk
King's Castle, Stafford, Staffordshire
Liverpool Castle, Liverpool, Lancashire[3]
Malton Castle, Malton, Yorkshire
Maxey Castle, Maxey, Huntingdonshire

Melton Mowbray Castle, Melton Mowbray, Leicestershire
Montifichet Castle, London[4]
Mountsorrel Castle, Mountsorrel, Leicestershire
Newbury Castle, Newbury, Berkshire
Newcastle-under-Lyme Castle, Newcastle-under-Lyme, Staffordshire
Newport Pagnell Castle, Newport Pagnell, Buckinghamshire
Reading Castle, Reading, Berkshire
Sandwich Castle, Sandwich, Kent
Scoulton Castle, Scoulton, Norfolk
Seaton Delaval Castle, Seaton Delaval, Northumberland
Seagrave Castle, Seagrave, Leicestershire
Segenhoe Castle, Segenhoe, Bedfordshire
Shipbrook Castle, Davenham, Cheshire
Shotwick Castle, Shotwick, Cheshire
Simonburn Castle, Simonburn, Northumberland[5]
Skipsea Brough Castle, Skipsea, North Riding, Yorkshire[6]
Somerton Castle, Somerton, Somerset
Southampton Castle, Southampton, Hampshire
Steephill Castle, Ventnor, Isle of Wight
Theodore's Castle, Hayle, Cornwall
Thorpe Arnold Castle, Thorpe Arnold, Leicestershire
Trejago Castle, Trejago, Cornwall
Truro Castle, Truro, Cornwall
Walton Castle, Walton, Suffolk
Widdrington Castle, Widdrington, Northumberland
Woodward Castle, Woodward, Hampshire

1. Last traces destroyed in Great Fire of 1666. Considerable foundations were traced and recorded in 1972 during excavation on the site before it was covered by a civil engineering project.
2. This had almost disappeared by the 17th Century, surviving buildings being used as a prison. It was demolished to make room for the new prison late in the 18th Century.
3. At the south end of Castle Street in Derby Square, this was pulled down in 1663 and the site was finally cleared in 1720. The church of St. George was built on the site.
4. Demolished as early as the 13th Century, this stood at the west end of the City Walls near Carron Wharf at the foot of Addle Hill beside the river Fleet.
5. A few fragments of 13th Century masonry were incorporated into a sham ruin or folly in the mid-18th Century.
6. Possible site of a Norman motte on an earlier earthwork. A fascinating local tradition has it that as late as 1890 four footprints were still visible in the turf on the west of the mound, which were always cleaned out and preserved by the villagers at Martinmas. They were supposed to have been made centuries before by two rivals who fought and killed each other over a woman.